FAVORITES
FROM THE
LITTLE
MUSHROOM

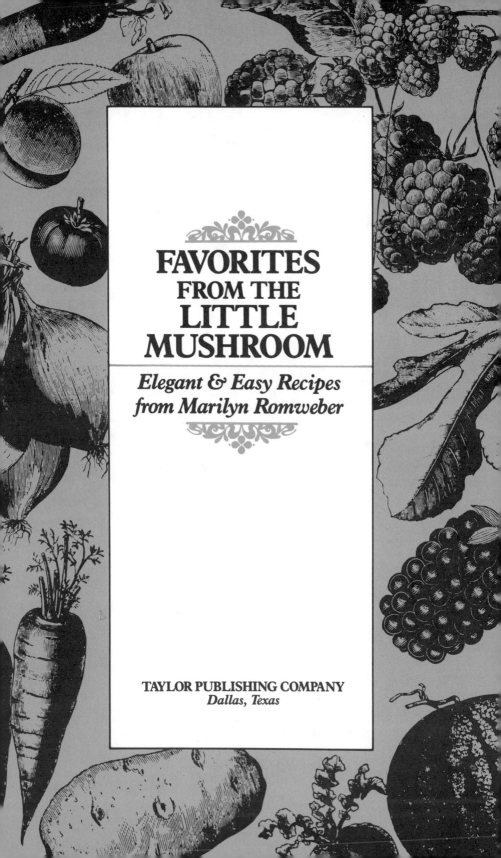

FAVORITES
FROM THE
LITTLE
MUSHROOM

Elegant & Easy Recipes
from Marilyn Romweber

TAYLOR PUBLISHING COMPANY
Dallas, Texas

Library of Congress Cataloging-in-Publication Data

Romweber, Marilyn.
  Favorites from the Little Mushroom.

  Includes index.
  1. Cookery—Texas. 2. Little Mushroom
(Restaurant: Dallas, Tex.) I. Little Mushroom
(Restaurant: Dallas, Tex.) II. Title.
TX715.R7613 1987   641.509764'281'2
87-21049
ISBN 0-87833-594-3

Printed in the United States of America

9 8 7 6 5 4

Contents

Foreword

A new restaurant in town usually provokes a flurry of interest and The Little Mushroom restaurant aroused more than the usual response when it opened in 1968. The food was fresh, unique and uncharacteristically homestyle.

After repeated requests for many of the recipes, I decided to put them into print. *Under the Mushroom* and *Another Mushroom* quickly became as popular as the recipes they contained!

Now, you'll find the favorites from both in this volume. And although The Little Mushroom restaurant no longer exists, you can continue to create the kinds of elegant and easy meals in your kitchen that helped usher in a new way of dining over two decades ago.

Marilyn Komueher

APPETIZERS

Artichoke Nibbles

2   6-ounce jars marinated artichoke hearts, drained and finely
    chopped (save ¹/₂ of the marinade)
1   onion, finely chopped
4   eggs, lightly beaten
¹/₄   cup Italian seasoned bread crumbs
¹/₄   teaspoon oregano
¹/₄   teaspoon basil
¹/₄   teaspoon Italian herb seasoning
    Dash Tabasco
2   cups grated Cheddar cheese

Preheat oven to 325°. In a skillet saute the onion in the artichoke marinade
until soft. Combine all the ingredients, including the onion mixture, and pour
into a greased 8″ square baking dish. Bake for 20 minutes or until firm. Cut
into small squares and serve hot or at room temperature.

Artsy Artichokes

6   ounce jar marinated artichoke hearts, drained
¹/₂   teaspoon lemon juice
1   cup mayonnaise
1   cup grated Parmesan cheese
4   green onions, tops and bottoms, chopped
1   package green onion dip mix or onion soup mix
2   7-ounce cans artichoke bottoms, drained (7 to 9 artichokes to
    each can)

Preheat oven to 450°. In a blender or food processor puree all the ingredients,
except the artichoke bottoms. Season with salt and pepper. Fill the artichoke
bottoms with the mixture and bake until bubbly.

GOURMET HELPER—To peel an avocado pull the skin off by hand
being careful not to break the inner green surface. This will prevent the
flesh from discoloring.

Easy Stuffed Artichoke Bottoms

7 ounce can artichoke bottoms (7 to 9 artichokes to the can)
1 package Stouffer's corn souffle, thawed
1/2 package Hidden Valley Ranch Party Dip (or substitute any packaged dip)
1/2 cup Pepperidge Farm herb seasoned croutons, crushed
1/2 cup grated Parmesan cheese
1/2 stick butter, melted

Preheat oven to 400°. Place artichokes side by side in a shallow baking dish. Gently fold the dip mix into the corn mixture and stuff in the artichoke bottoms. Top with the croutons and cheese and pour the butter over the top. Bake for 20 minutes or until puffed and browned.

Avocado Corn Quiche

10" partially baked pie shell*
4 ears fresh or frozen corn on the cob, scraped of kernels
3/4 cup grated Havarti cheese (or any white cheese)
4 green onions, tops only, chopped
1 1/2 ripe avocados, peeled and chopped
1/2 cup heavy cream
1/2 cup milk
3 eggs, lightly beaten
1/2 teaspoon salt
Dash Tabasco

*Using your favorite pie crust recipe fit the dough into a 10" false-bottom quiche pan. Line with foil and fill with rice. Bake 10 minutes in a preheated 400° oven. Remove foil and rice and bake 5 minutes longer or until lightly colored.

Preheat oven to 375°. Combine the first 4 ingredients and toss gently. Spread over prepared crust. Combine the remaining ingredients and pour into the crust. Set quiche on a baking sheet and bake 50 minutes or until knife inserted in the center comes out clean. Slice in wedges and serve hot or at room temperature.

In a Hurry Watercress Dip—In a blender puree 1 bunch watercress leaves, 3 ounces cream cheese, 1/4 cup heavy cream and 1/4 cup chives. Salt and pepper, to taste and serve on crackers.

Avocado Cream Cheese Dip

4   avocados, peeled and mashed (save the seeds)
3   8 ounce packages cream cheese, softened
2   tablespoons lemon juice
1   onion, grated with juice
1   teaspoon garlic salt
1   teaspoon Tabasco
    Seasoning salt, to taste

Beat cream cheese with an electric mixer until smooth. Add all other ingredients and continue to beat until the texture is smooth. Transfer to a serving bowl and place avocado seeds in the center of the dip until ready to serve. (This will prevent the dip from turning brown.) Chill. Serve with corn chips.

Avocado Green Chili Dip

2   avocados, peeled and sliced (save the seeds)
8   ounce package cream cheese, softened
4   ounce can green chilies
4   ounce can taco sauce
1   tablespoon Worcestershire sauce
    Juice of 1 lemon
    Salt and pepper, to taste
    Dash Tabasco

Combine all ingredients and purée in an electric blender. Transfer to a serving bowl and place avocado seeds in the center of the dip until ready to serve. (This will prevent the dip from turning brown.) Chill. Serve with corn chips.

GOURMET HELPER—To ripen an avocado place in a brown paper bag and store in a warm place.

Avocado Curried Dip

4   avocados, peeled and mashed (save the seeds)
1/4   cup lemon juice
2   tablespoons Worcestershire sauce
1   teaspoon curry powder
1   teaspoon garlic sat
1/4   teaspoon cayenne pepper
1/4   teaspoon sugar
1/4   cup slivered almonds
2   tablespoons butter
8   slices bacon, fried and crumbled

Brown the almonds in butter. Add to all the other ingredients and mix well. Transfer to a serving bowl and place the avocado seeds in the center of the dip until ready to serve. (This will prevent the dip from turning brown.) Chill. Serve with corn chips.

Avocado Logs

1   cup mashed avocados
1½   cups toasted cashew nuts, finely chopped
8   ounces cream cheese, softened
1/2   cup sharp Cheddar cheese, grated
2   teaspoons lime juice
1   garlic clove, crushed
1/2   teaspoon Worcestershire sauce
1/2   teaspoon salt
  Dash Tabasco
  Spanish paprika

Combine all ingredients, except the paprika, and mix well. Cover the mixture and refrigerate for 30 minutes. Divide the mixture in half and shape each half into a 1½″ thick cylinder. Roll in paprika and chill them, wrapped in foil, for 2 hours. Slice and serve with crackers.

In a Hurry Sesame Soy Spread—Marinate large package of cream cheese in soy sauce for several hours. Sprinkle heavily with sesame seeds. Add more soy sauce. Serve with wheat thins.

Banana Chutney Chunks

12   bacon slices, cut in half
6   bananas, cut into 1½" chunks
½   cup smooth peanut butter
¼   cup chopped chutney
1   tablespoon curry powder

Preheat oven to 350°. Blanch bacon in boiling water for 10 minutes. Drain on paper toweling. Roll the banana chunks in the peanut butter, then in the chutney and then in the curry powder. Wrap a bacon strip around each chunk and bake for 10 minutes or until the bacon is crisp.

Bacon and Leek Quiche

9"   partially baked pie shell*
6   slices bacon, fried crisp, drained and crumbled
2   tablespoons bacon drippings
1   cup leeks, sliced (white part only)
4   eggs, lightly beaten
2   cups evaporated milk
1   tablespoon melted butter
1   tablespoon flour
½   teaspoon salt
½   teaspoon Dijon mustard
⅛   teaspoon cayenne pepper

*Line a pie pan with your favorite pie crust. Place a piece of foil over the crust and fill with rice. Bake for 10 minutes in a preheated 400° oven. Remove foil and rice and bake for 5 minutes longer or until lightly colored.

Preheat oven to 375°. In a skillet saute the leeks in the bacon drippings until tender. Remove and toss with the bacon. Spread over the bottom of the prepared pie shell. Place the remaining ingredients in a blender or food processor and blend for 1 minute. Pour over the bacon mixture and bake for 30 minutes or until set. Cool slightly and cut into wedges to serve.

In a Hurry Hot Sausage Puffs—Saute 1 pound hot sausage meat until browned. Add 1 pound Old English cheese, 1 teaspoon Worcestershire sauce, 1 teaspoon soy sauce, and ½ teaspoon garlic powder. Season with salt and pepper and spread on party rye. Bake at 350° for 15 minutes or until bubbly.

Beef Roll-Ups

1   pound lean ground beef
1   package onion soup mix
1   cup grated Monterey Jack cheese
3   8-ounce packages refrigerated Crescent rolls

Preheat oven to 375°. In a skillet saute the meat until browned. Drain off any excess liquid. Add the soup mix and cheese to the meat and let cool. Roll out dough. Cut each crescent in half, making 16 triangles from each package. Place a heaping teaspoon of meat mixture on each triangle and roll to enclose. Place on baking sheet and bake for 15 minutes.

Beer Cheese Stuffed Jalapeño Peppers

     Whole canned large jalapeño peppers
3   rolls Kraft Nippy Cheese Roll, softened
¼   ounce Roquefort cheese, softened
2   tablespoons butter, softened
½   cup green onions, tops and bottoms, chopped
2   garlic cloves, crushed
1   teaspoon Worcestershire sauce
½   teaspoon Tabasco
½   cup beer, heated and slightly cooled

Slice jalapeño peppers lengthwise and remove seeds. Soak in ice water for several hours. Drain and set aside. Mix the remaining ingredients, except the beer, with an electric mixer until the mixture is well blended. Gradually add the beer and mix until smooth. Fill the cavities of the peppers with the cheese mixture. Chill for at least 1 hour before serving. (If you do not like jalapeños serve the cheese spread with crackers or with chunks of French bread.)

Mini-Beef Wellington

PASTRY

1   stick butter, softened
3   ounce package cream cheese, softened
1   cup flour
     Dash salt

Beat together the butter and cream cheese until smooth. Cut in the flour until the dough holds together. Form into a ball, wrap in wax paper and chill for at least 12 hours. Roll out on a floured surface (⅓ at a time) and cut into 2½" circles.

FILLING

½	pound ground beef
1	small onion, chopped
1	tablespoon oil
½	package taco seasoning mix
4	ounce can diced green chilies, drained
¼	cup sour cream
½	teaspoon cumin
¼	teaspoon coriander
¼	teaspoon garlic powder
¼	teaspoon chili powder
½	cup grated Monterey Jack cheese

Preheat oven to 375°. In a large heavy skillet saute the beef and onion in the oil until the beef is browned. Add the remaining ingredients and remove from the heat. Place 1 tablespoon filling in the center of each round of dough. Fold dough over and pinch edges together to seal. Bake until pastry is golden brown.

Frosted Cheese Rolls

2	cups Cheddar cheese, grated
½	cup onion, minced
½	stick butter
¼	cup Hellmann's mayonnaise
1	pimento, chopped
¼	cup parsley, minced
	Dash Tabasco
12	slices white bread, de-crusted

Combine all ingredients, except bread, and mix until well blended. Spread mixture on one side of bread slice and roll each slice. Secure with a toothpick. Place side by side on a cookie sheet and frost top of each roll with the remaining cheese mixture. Cut in halves and bake at 375° until rolls are hot.

Cheese Puffs

1¹/₄ cup flour
    Dash salt
    Dash cayenne pepper
³/₄ stick butter, softened
1 cup Cheddar cheese, grated
3 tablespoons heavy cream
1 egg, lightly beaten
1 cup Swiss cheese, grated
2 tablespoons butter, softened

Sift together the flour, salt and cayenne pepper. Mix in the butter and the cheese until the mixture is mealy. Stir in the cream and with a fork form the pastry into a ball. Chill for several hours. On a lightly floured board roll out the dough. Cut into 2″ circles. Brush the circles with the egg and place on a cookie sheet. Bake in a preheated 450° oven for about 6 minutes or until they are lightly browned. Combine the Swiss cheese and butter. Spread the mixture on half the pastry circles. Cover them with the remaining circles and return to the oven for a few minutes until they are heated through. Makes about 20 rounds.

Potted Cheese

4 cups Cheddar cheese, grated
3 green onions, tops and bottoms, chopped
3 tablespoons fresh parsley, finely chopped
1 teaspoon Dijon mustard
2 tablespoons butter, softened
2 tablespoons dry sherry
    Dash Worcestershire sauce
    Dash Tabasco
    Salt and white pepper, to taste

Combine the first 4 ingredients. Beat in the remaining ingredients and mix until creamy. Pack in a crock and refrigerate. When ready to serve the cheese should be room temperature. Serve with crusty French bread.

Cheese-Onion Log

1   stick butter, softened
8   ounce package sharp Cheddar cheese, grated
1   cup flour
1/2 teaspoon salt
1   package Green Onion Dip Mix
2   teaspoons heavy cream

Blend the butter and the cheese. Add the other ingredients and form into logs about 1" in diameter. Wrap each log in foil and freeze. Slice thin while frozen and place on ungreased cookie sheet. Bake at 400° for 8 to 10 minutes.

Brie Quiche

9"   pie crust, partially baked*
1/2 stick butter
3   slices ham, cut into thin julienne strips
8   green onions, tops and bottoms, chopped
1   cup soft Brie cheese
1   cup grated Parmesan cheese
4   eggs, beaten
2   cups heavy cream
1/4 teaspoon nutmeg

*Line a pie pan with your favorite pie crust. Place a piece of foil over the crust and fill with rice. Bake for 10 minutes in a preheated 400° oven. Remove foil and rice and bake for 5 minutes longer or until lightly colored.

Preheat oven to 325°. In a skillet saute the ham in the butter until browned. Remove and set aside. Saute the onions until soft. Remove with a slotted spoon and combine with the ham. Spread on the bottom of the prepared pie shell. Spread the Brie over the ham mixture and sprinkle with the Parmesan cheese. Combine the eggs, cream and nutmeg and pour the custard over the cheese. Bake for 30 minutes or until set. Let cool slightly. Cut into thin wedges to serve.

In a Hurry Jalapeno Squares—Sprinkle 2 or 3 seeded and chopped jalapeño peppers in a well-greased 9" square pan. Cover with 1 pound grated sharp Cheddar cheese. Pour 6 beaten eggs over that and bake at 350° for 30 minutes. Cool and cut in 1" squares.

Cheese and Olive Appetizers

1   cup pimento-stuffed olives
3   green onions, finely chopped
3/4 cup Monterey Jack cheese, grated
3/4 cup Cheddar cheese, grated
1/2 cup Hellmann's mayonnaise
1/2 teaspoon chili powder
    Salt, to taste
    Honey Butter English Muffins

Combine ingredients and mix well. Spread on muffins and bake at 400° until bubbly. Cut muffins into quarters and serve hot.

Chili Cheese Snacks

8   ounces Old English cheese, grated
2   sticks butter, softened
2¹/4 cups flour
1   teaspoon salt
1   teaspoon Worcestershire sauce
1/2 teaspoon cayenne pepper
4   ounce can diced green chilies, drained

Preheat oven to 350°. Combine all the ingredients and mix well. Shape into small balls. Transfer to a baking sheet and flatten with a fork. Bake for 15 minutes. Makes approximately 8 dozen.

Brie Pate

8   ounce package ripe Brie cheese (remove the rind and bring to
     room temperature)
1   stick butter, softened
1/2 cup chopped walnuts
1   shallot, chopped
1   teaspoon chervil
1   teaspoon dill weed
1/4 cup dry vermouth
     Dash Tabasco

Combine all the ingredients and place in a blender or food processor. Blend until smooth. Spoon into a crock and chill, covered, for several hours. Serve at room temperature with assorted crackers.

Brie Cheese Spread

4   green onions, tops and bottoms, chopped
2   garlic cloves, minced
1   tablespoon chopped parsley
1/2 teaspoon capers, drained
1   teaspoon lemon juice
1   teaspoon Worcestershire sauce
1   teaspoon green or pink peppercorns, crushed
8   ounce package cream cheese, softened
4   ounces Brie cheese, softened
     Dash Tabasco

Preheat oven to 425°. In a blender or food processor puree the first 4 ingredients. Add the remaining ingredients and blend until smooth. Spread on party rye and bake until bubbly.

Camembert en Croute

     Frozen puff pastry, thawed
8   ounce round Camembert cheese
1   egg yolk mixed with 1 tablespoon water

Roll out the pastry on a lightly floured board to about 1/8″ thick. With a pastry wheel cut an 8″ circle. Place the cheese in the center of the pastry. Bring up the pastry around the cheese pleating to make it fit. Prick with the end of a knife to let steam escape. Refrigerate. Brush with the egg wash and bake in a preheated 450° oven for 20 minutes (be sure the pastry is thick enough, so it will not break during baking).

In a Hurry Cheese Spread—Combine 1 pound crumbled Roquefort cheese, 1/2 pound grated Cheddar cheese, 1/2 stick softened butter, 1/2 cup sherry and a few drops Tabasco. Serve on toast rounds.

Cheese Cake Crunchy

¼   stick butter, melted
¾   cup cheese crackers, crushed
½   cup chopped pimento-stuffed green olives
2   celery ribs, finely chopped
1   onion, finely chopped
2   tablespoons lemon juice
1   teaspoon salt
1   teaspoon Worcestershire sauce
2   cups sour cream
1   pound cream cheese, softened
     Dash Tabasco

Brush the bottom and sides of a 9″ spring-form pan with the butter. Cover the bottom of the pan with half the crackers. Combine the remaining ingredients and mix until well blended. Spread mixture over cracker crust. Sprinkle remaining crumbs over top. Cover and refrigerate overnight. When ready to serve remove spring-form from pan and place cake still on pan bottom on serving platter. Cut into wedges to serve.

Sauteed Camembert

8   ounce round Camembert cheese (do not remove rind)
1   egg, lightly beaten
1   tablespoon Worcestershire sauce
     Dash Tabasco
1   cup Italian style bread crumbs
½   stick butter
4   green onions, tops and bottoms, chopped

Combine the egg, Worcestershire and Tabasco. Dip the cheese in the egg mixture, then coat both sides with the bread crumbs. Repeat. In a skillet saute the cheese in ¼ stick butter over high heat until brown on both sides. Remove to a serving platter. Add the remaining butter to the skillet and saute the onions for 3 minutes. Pour over the cheese. Serve with crackers.

GOURMET HELPER—To keep finger sandwiches from drying out, cover them with a damp dish towel and refrigerate. Uncover 20 minutes before serving.

Toasted Cheese Rolls

2   cups grated sharp Cheddar cheese
1/2   teaspoon salt
1/8   teaspoon cayenne pepper
1   teaspoon Dijon mustard
3   tablespoons heavy cream
1   loaf white sandwich bread, not sliced
    Melted butter

Preheat oven to broil. Combine the first five ingredients and mix until well blended. Remove the crusts from the bread and cut in lengthwise slices 1/4" thick (most bakeries will do this for you). With a pastry brush dab a small amount of melted butter on slices. Spread with the cheese mixture and roll the slices lengthwise like a jelly roll. Wrap in a damp cloth and refrigerate for several hours. Just before serving cut the rolls in 1 1/2" lengths and broil until bubbly.

Cheese Wafers

6   ounce jar Old English cheese
1   cup flour
1   stick butter
1/4   teaspoon garlic salt
1/8   teaspoon cayenne pepper

Preheat oven to 350°. Combine all the ingredients and roll into balls the size of a marble. Place on a greased baking sheet and mash lightly with a fork. Bake for 15 minutes or until golden brown. TO FREEZE: Place the balls on a baking sheet and place in the freezer. Once frozen, remove and store in a plastic bag. When ready to use, place on a baking sheet and bake in a preheated 350° oven until browned.

In a Hurry Nachos—Open a package of tostados. Cover each one with a slice of Cheddar cheese. Open a can of frozen avocado dip and add a few dashes of Tabasco. Bake the tostados until the cheese melts, top with avocado and serve hot.

Marinated Crab Fingers

16 ounce carton crab fingers (must be fresh as the frozen ones
    tear apart)
2   sticks butter
1/2 cup olive oil
1   tablespoon lemon juice
1   garlic clove, crushed
1/4 cup dry white wine
    Soy sauce, to taste
    Seafood seasoning, to taste
    White pepper, to taste

In a double boiler melt the butter. Add all other ingredients and cook until well blended. Place crab fingers in a shallow enamel baking dish. Pour hot sauce over them and bake at 375° until heated through.

Crabmeat Concern

1/2 pound King Crabmeat, cut into bite-size pieces
6   ounce package Kraft's bacon cheese roll, softened
1   cup mayonnaise
4   ounce can diced green chilies, drained
1   teaspoon garlic salt
1   tablespoon Worcestershire sauce
    English muffins

Preheat oven to 375°. Combine all the ingredients and mix well. Spread on English muffins and bake until bubbly. Cut into quarters and serve.

In a Hurry Crabmeat Canapies—Combine 1 pound crabmeat; 14 ounce can artichoke hearts, drained and chopped; 1/2 cup Russian salad dressing; and 1/2 teaspoon dry mustard. Spread on English muffins and bake at 450° until bubbly. Cut muffins in quarters and serve.

In a Hurry Mushrooms with Sausage—Remove the stems from large fresh mushrooms. Fill with Owens Hot Sausage and bake at 375° for 30 minutes.

Mushrooms Stuffed with Crabmeat

50 large, fresh mushrooms, with stems removed
   Marinate mushrooms overnight in:
2 cups oil
3/4 cup tarragon vinegar
3 tablespoons sugar
4 tablespoons tarragon leaves

STUFFING

8 ounce package cream cheese, softened
8 ounce package Old English cheese, softened
1/2 cup sour cream
1/2 cup Hellmann's mayonnaise
1/2 onion, grated with juice
1/2 bunch green onions, tops only, chopped
2 garlic cloves, crushed
2 tablespoons lemon juice
1/2 pound King Crabmeat
   Salt and white pepper, to taste

Combine all ingredients, except mushrooms and crabmeat, and mix well. Gently fold in crabmeat. Drain the mushrooms. Stuff each mushroom cap with the crabmeat mixture. Chill before serving.

Hot Crabmeat Mornay

1 pound King Crabmeat
1 stick butter
1 bunch green onions, tops and bottoms, chopped
2 tablespoons flour
1 3/4 cups half and half cream
3 1/2 cups Swiss cheese, grated
   Dash cayenne pepper
   Dash Tabasco
1 teaspoon dry mustard
1 teaspoon dry sherry
   English muffins

In a saucepan melt the butter and sauté the onions. Blend the flour, cream, and cheese and heat, slowly, until the cheese has melted. Add all the seasonings, except the sherry. Gently fold in the crabmeat and continue stirring until the mixture is hot. Blend in the sherry. Spread on the muffins and bake at 400° until bubbly. Quarter the muffins and serve hot. Makes about 2 cups.

Campy Crabmeat

1   pound King Crabmeat, cut into bite-size pieces
8   ounce package cream cheese with chives, softened
1   cup grated Monterey Jack cheese
1/2   package Kraft's bacon cheese roll
1/4   cup bacon bits
1/2   teaspoon Worcestershire sauce
2   tablespoons brandy
1/8   teaspoon cayenne pepper
  Party rye bread

Preheat oven to 425°. Combine all the ingredients and spread on the rye bread. Place on a baking sheet and bake until bubbly.

Hot Crabmeat Cheese Puffs

1/2   pound King Crabmeat
4   green onions, tops and bottoms, chopped
1/2   cup Monterey Jack cheese, grated
1/2   cup Cheddar cheese, grated
1/2   cup Hellmann's mayonnaise
1   teaspoon lemon juice
1/4   teaspoon curry powder
5   ounce can water chestnuts, drained and chopped
1   package flaky-style refrigerator rolls

Combine all ingredients, except rolls, and mix well. Separate each roll into 3 layers. Place on ungreased cookie sheet and place crabmeat mixture on top. Bake at 400° for about 10 minutes or until golden. Makes 36 puffs.

Hot Crabmeat Wine Dip

1/2   pound King Crabmeat
8   ounces cream cheese, softened
1/3   cup white wine or sauterne
1   teaspoon Dijon mustard
1   tablespoon onion, grated
2   garlic cloves, crushed
2   tablespoons Worcestershire sauce
1   tablespoon chicken soup base
  Salt and white pepper, to taste

Combine all ingredients, except crabmeat, and heat in the top of a double boiler, stirring frequently. Fold in the crabmeat and transfer to a chafing dish. Serve with assorted crackers.

Crazy Crabmeat

1/2   pound King Crabmeat, cut into bite-size pieces
8   ounce package Old English cheese, softened
8   ounce package cream cheese, softened
1/2   cup mayonnaise
1/2   cup sour cream
4   green onions, tops only, chopped
2   garlic cloves, crushed
2   tablespoons chopped pimientos
2   tablespoons lemon juice
1   teaspoon garlic salt
1   teaspoon chervil
       Pepperidge Farm party rolls

Preheat oven to 375°. Combine all the ingredients and mix well. Split the rolls open and spread the cheese mixture on both tops and bottoms. Bake until bubbly.

In a Hurry Crab Cheesies—Combine 1 pound crabmeat, 8 ounce jar Cheese Whiz, 2 tablespoons dry mustard and 1/2 package any flavor salad dressing mix. Spread on toast rounds and bake at 450° until bubbly.

Hot Curried Crab Dip

1/2   pound King Crabmeat
8   ounces cream cheese with chives, softened
1   tablespoon Hellmann's mayonnaise
1/2   onion, grated
1   tablespoon horseradish
2   tablespoons milk
1   tablespoon Worcestershire sauce
1/2   teaspoon curry powder
       Salt and pepper, to taste

Combine all the ingredients and heat, in the top of a double boiler, until the mixture is hot. Transfer to a chafing dish and serve with assorted chips.

Curried Shrimp Dip

½	pound shrimp, peeled, deveined, and chopped fine
1	can cream of shrimp soup, undiluted
8	ounce package cream cheese, softened
½	teaspoon curry powder
4	ounce can chopped ripe olives
2	teaspoons lemon juice
	Dash garlic salt
	Salt and white pepper, to taste

Combine all the ingredients and refrigerate several hours before serving. Serve with assorted crackers or chips.

Mushrooms Stuffed with Shrimp and Spinach

24	large fresh mushrooms with stems removed
	Marinate mushrooms over night in:
1	cup oil
½	cup tarragon vinegar
2	tablespoons sugar
3	tablespoons tarragon leaves

STUFFING

½	pound shrimp, cooked and chopped
1	package frozen chopped spinach, thawed and drained (do not cook)
3	ounce package cream cheese with chives, softened
1	cup sour cream
4	green onions, tops and bottoms, chopped
4	slices bacon, diced and fried until crisp
¼	teaspoon nutmeg
	Dash Tabasco
	Seasoning salt and pepper, to taste

Combine shrimp, spinach, cream cheese, sour cream, onions, bacon, and seasonings and mix well. Drain mushrooms. Stuff each mushroom cap with the shrimp mixture. Chill before serving. Makes about 3 cups.

In a Hurry Herbed Mushrooms—Stuff 1 package Herbed Boursin cheese mashed in 6 canned mushrooms caps. Place a parsley sprig on top.

Hot Shrimp and Spinach Dip

1/2 pound shrimp, cooked and diced
1   package frozen chopped spinach, thawed and drained
     (do not cook)
1/2 bunch green onions, tops and bottoms, chopped
1   garlic clove, minced
1/2 stick butter
1   can Golden Mushroom soup
1   package Green Onion Dip Mix
1   tablespoon Parmesan cheese
3   ounce can mushrooms, pieces and stems
1/2 5-ounce can water chestnuts, sliced
1   tablespoon Worcestershire sauce
     Dash Tabasco
     Salt and pepper, to taste

Sauté the onions and the garlic in butter until the onions are soft. Combine all other ingredients and mix well. Add to the onion mixture and heat slowly, stirring frequently, until mixture is hot. Season to taste. Pour into a chafing dish and serve with assorted crackers.

Shrimp Stuffed in Artichoke Bottoms

     Large jar artichoke bottoms
1   pound shrimp, cooked and chopped
16   ounce package Kraft's Jalapeño Pepper Cheese Spread
8   ounce package cream cheese, softened
1   bunch green onions, chopped
1   cup sour cream
2   tablespoons mayonnaise
2   garlic cloves, crushed
2   tablespoon Worcestershire sauce
2   tablespoon lemon juice

Combine all the ingredients, except the shrimp, and mix well. Gently fold in the shrimp. Stuff in the artichoke bottoms and chill for at least 1 hour. Makes about 3 cups.

Shrimp and Cheese Appetizers

1   pound cooked chopped shrimp
4   green onions, tops and bottoms, chopped
½   cup mayonnaise
1   cup grated Gruyere cheese (or any white cheese)
½   teaspoon chicken soup base
1   tablespoon chopped pimientos
1   teaspoon Beau Monde seasoning
1   teaspoon dill weed
      Pepperidge Farm Party Rolls

Preheat oven to 400°. Combine all the ingredients and mix well. Spread on tops and bottoms of the split rolls and bake until bubbly.

Spicy Marinated Shrimp

½   pound jumbo shrimp, peeled and cooked (leave the shell on tails)
1½   cup oil
½   cup garlic flavored vinegar
1   bottle catsup
3   tablespoons Worcestershire sauce
3   tablespoons A-1 Sauce
1   garlic clove, crushed
      Dash Tabasco
      Juice of 2 lemons
      Salt and pepper, to taste

Combine all ingredients, except shrimp, and mix well. Place shrimp in a shallow enamel or glass bowl. Pour marinade over them, cover, and place in refrigerator overnight. Serve chilled.

GOURMET HELPER—Artichokes will turn a grayish color if cooked in aluminum or iron pots.

Marinated Shrimp New Orleans

1/2 pound jumbo shrimp, cooked and peeled (leave the shell on the tails and they can be picked up by the tails eliminating toothpicks)
1 onion, sliced thin
1 jar French dressing
2 tablespoons horseradish
2 tablespoons dry mustard
1 garlic clove, crushed
Dash thyme

Add all ingredients, except shrimp, and mix well. Place shrimp in a shallow enamel or glass dish. Pour marinade over them, cover, and place in refrigerator overnight. Serve chilled.

Easy Marinated Shrimp

1/2 pound shrimp, cooked, peeled and deveined
1 package Good Seasons Italian Dressing, mixed according to directions on package
6 green onions, tops and bottoms, chopped

Mix all the ingredients and place in a jar. Refrigerate marinade for 24 hours, turning the jar upside down several times. Serve on a chilled platter.

Tuna Stuffed Jalapeño Peppers

28 ounce can large whole jalapeño peppers
9 1/4 ounce can chunk light tuna
1/2 cup pecans, finely chopped
4 tablespoons lemon juice
1 package Garlic and Onion Dip Mix
1 tablespoon Worcestershire sauce
Hellmann's mayonnaise, to bind
Dash Spice Islands Pepper Seasonings with Bacon
Monterey Jack cheese, sliced

Cut jalapeño peppers lengthwise and remove seeds. Soak in ice cold water for 1 hour. Drain. Combine remaining ingredients and stuff peppers. Top each pepper with a slice of cheese and place on a lightly greased cookie sheet. Bake at 375° until hot. (These may be served cold by omitting the cheese.)

Meatballs in Mushroom-Sherry Sauce

2   pounds ground beef
1   cup bread crumbs
1/2   cup catsup
1/4   cup green pepper, finely chopped
2   packages Green Onion Dip Mix
2   eggs
1/2   teaspoon oregano
1/2   teaspoon garlic powder
    Salt and pepper, to taste

Combine all ingredients and shape into cocktail-size balls. Place on a lightly greased cookie sheet and bake 30 to 45 minutes at 350°.

SAUCE

2   cans cream of mushroom soup
2 1/2   cups sour cream
4   tablespoons sherry
1/4   cup onion, minced
1   tablespoon fresh parsley, minced
1/4   teaspoon oregano
1/2   teaspoon garlic powder

Combine the above ingredients and heat. Simmer, on low heat, for 45 minutes. Add meatballs and transfer to a chafing dish. Makes about 40 balls.

Party Beefballs

1 1/2   pounds ground beef
3/4   cup Hellmann's mayonnaise
3/4   pound Roquefort cheese, softened
2   tablespoons Worcestershire sauce
1   teaspoon prepared mustard
3   cups corn flakes, crushed
3/4   cup milk
1   egg, slightly beaten
    Salt and pepper, to taste

Mix cheese, mayonnaise, Worcestershire sauce and mustard. Add remaining ingredients and mold into cocktail-size balls. Bake, on lightly greased cookie sheet, for about 40 minutes. Serve hot with your favorite barbecue sauce. Makes about 30 balls.

Herbed Meatballs Stroganoff

1½ pounds ground beef
1 onion, minced
4 slices white bread, de-crusted
2 eggs, lightly beaten
1 package Onion and Bacon Dip Mix
  Seasoning salt, to taste
2 cans beef consommé, heated
4 garlic cloves, minced
½ stick butter
2 tablespoons dill weed
1 teaspoon tarragon
1½ cups sour cream

Soak the bread in cold water. Sauté the onion in butter until it is softened. Combine the ground beef, onion, the bread which has been squeezed of excess moisture, eggs, dip mix and seasoning salt. Form the mixture into cocktail-size balls. Drop into the consommé and boil, gently, for about 30 minutes. Drain them in a colander. Sauté the garlic cloves in butter. Add the dill weed and tarragon. Add the meatballs and sauté them until they are coated with the herb mixture and heated through. Stir in the sour cream and cook over low heat, stirring, until heated through. Transfer to a chafing dish. Makes abut 30 balls.

Beef Filled Crescent Rolls

1 pound ground beef
1 onion, finely chopped
½ stick butter
1 teaspoon cumin
1 teaspoon oregano
1 teaspoon chili powder
2 tablespoons tomato paste
8 ounce carton sour cream
1 cup Monterey Jack cheese, grated
  Garlic salt, to taste
2 cans Crescent dinner rolls

Sauté the beef and the onion in butter until beef is lightly browned. Add remaining ingredients, except rolls. Warm the mixture but do not boil. Remove from heat and cool to room temperature. Separate rolls and spread mixture on each roll. Roll into crescent shape and bake according to directions. Slice each roll into bite-size pieces and serve hot.

Hot Chili Dip

3 pounds ground beef
3 onions, chopped
3 tablespoons butter
1/2 cup flour
4 garlic cloves, mashed
1 tablespoon sugar
4 tablespoons Mexine chili powder
2 4-ounce cans green chilies, chopped
2 tablespoons cumin
1 teaspoon oregano
1 can beef consommé
8 ounce can tomato sauce
10 ounce stick Kraft Crackerbarrel Extra Sharp cheese
1 can tamales
1 bunch green onions, tops and bottoms, chopped (for garnish)

In a large skillet sauté the onions in the butter until they are soft. Add beef, breaking it into small pieces, and stir until it is no longer pink. Sprinkle with flour and continue cooking, stirring frequently, until the meat is lightly browned. Drain off excess grease. Add next 8 ingredients. Add salt and pepper, to taste. Cover and simmer for 3 hours, stirring occasionally. Cool and refrigerate, covered overnight. The next day remove the grease from the top and reheat. Add the tamales, which have been sliced, and cook until they fall apart. Add the cheese and cook until melted. Transfer to a chafing dish and top with green onions. Serve with round tostados. Serves 50.

Red Hot Sausage Balls

2 pounds Owens Hot Sausage
2 1/2 cups applesauce
1/3 cup candy Red Hots

Mold the sausage meat into cocktail-size balls. In a small amount of oil, fry the balls until they are well browned. In a saucepan combine the applesauce and the candies. Heat, stirring, until they are dissolved. Add the meat balls and put into a chafing dish.

Sausage Turnovers

CRUST

8   ounce package refrigerated crescent dinner rolls

Shape dough into a ball and roll out on a floured board. Cut into 3″ rounds.

FILLING

1/2   pound Owen's hot sausage (use regular if you do not like a
      highly seasoned taste)
2   eggs, lightly beaten
1   cup cottage cheese, drained well
4   green onions, tops and bottoms, chopped
1/2   cup grated Gruyere cheese (or any white cheese)

Preheat oven to 350°. In a heavy skillet saute the sausage until browned. Remove with a slotted spoon and drain. Combine with the other ingredients. Place a rounded teaspoon of sausage mixture on 1 side of the dough. Fold over and press edges together firmly. Prick top of turnovers with the tip of a knife. Brush with egg wash (mix 1 egg yolk with 1 tablespoon water). Place on a baking sheet and bake for 15 minutes or until golden brown.

Picadillo

3   pounds ground beef
1/4   stick butter
2   onions, chopped
2   tablespoons flour
3   tablespoons chili powder
1   tablespoon cumin powder
1/2   teaspoon cardamon seed, crushed
1/2   cup chili sauce
2   cans beef consommé
4   ribs celery, with leaves, chopped
1   green pepper, chopped
1   cup raisins
1   small can crushed pineapple, drained
1   large potato, peeled and cut into very small cubes
1   apple, peeled, cored and chopped
1   cup seedless grapes, diced
1   jalapeño pepper (remove seeds and chop)

In a large skillet sauté the onions in butter until soft. Add the beef breaking it into small pieces and stir until the beef is no longer pink. Sprinkle with flour and continue cooking, stirring frequently, until meat is lightly browned. Drain off excess liquid. Add the next 9 ingredients. Add salt and pepper, to taste. Cover and simmer for 1 hour. Add the potato and simmer for 1 hour. Add the remaining ingredients and simmer for 1 hour. Pour into a chafing dish and serve with jumbo Fritos or round tostados. (May be prepared the day before, refrigerated, and heated in the top of a double boiler.) Serves 50.

Fundido

6   slices bacon, fried crisp, drained and crumbled
3   tablespoons bacon drippings
1   onion, chopped
4   green onions, tops and bottoms, chopped
1   garlic clove, minced
2   ounces chorizo sausage, cut into small pieces
¼   cup canned tomatoes, drained
1   fresh jalapeno pepper, chopped
⅛   teaspoon sugar
1   teaspoon cilantro
2   cups grated sharp Cheddar cheese
½   cup grated Monterey Jack cheese
1   cup milk
3   egg yolks, lightly beaten
1   onion, grated
1   teaspoon Worcestershire sauce
1   teaspoon dry mustard
⅛   teaspoon cayenne pepper
    Tortillas

In a large heavy skillet saute the onions, garlic and sausage in the bacon drippings until the sausage is cooked. Pour off any excess grease and add the next 4 ingredients and simmer, covered, for 10 minutes. In the top of a double boiler melt the cheeses over a low heat. Add the milk, egg yolks and seasonings. Cook, over low heat, stirring constantly, until the sauce is thick and creamy. Add the tomato sauce and cook until heated through. Transfer to a chafing dish. Serve with soft heated tortillas. To serve put 2 tablespoons sauce into a tortilla and roll up.

Mexican Frittata

2   eggs, beaten
2   tablespoons flour
1/2 teaspoon garlic salt
1/2 teaspoon cumin
1/3 cup evaporated milk
4   ounce can diced green chilies, drained
1   cup grated Cheddar cheese
1   cup grated Jarlsberg cheese (or other Swiss-type cheese)

Preheat oven to 350°. Combine all the ingredients and turn into a greased 8″ square baking dish. Bake for 40 minutes or until set. Cool slightly and cut into bite-size squares.

In a Hurry Cheese Frittata—Combine 3 beaten eggs, 2/3 cup flour, 1/3 cup white wine, 2/3 cup milk, 2 chopped green onions, 1/2 teaspoon salt, 3/4 cup grated Swiss cheese and 1 tablespoon melted butter. Pour into a buttered pie pan and sprinkle with 1/4 cup grated Parmesan cheese. Bake at 425° for 30 minutes or until golden brown. Cut into wedges to serve.

Bourbon Liver Paté

2   sticks butter
1   pound chicken livers
1   onion, chopped
4   garlic cloves, crushed
1/2 cup Port wine
1   cup pecans, chopped
1/3 cup Bourbon
2   sticks butter, melted

Sauté the chicken livers in butter. Add the onion and garlic and sauté until the onion is soft. Add the wine and simmer until the livers are tender. Cool. Place in a blender and purée until smooth. Pour the remaining ingredients into the blender and purée. Pour into a crock and refrigerate. Serve with thinly sliced dark bread which has been toasted. This paté freezes well.

In a Hurry Taco Pizza—Spread Taco Pizza Quick on English muffins. Saute 1 pound Jimmy Dean's Seasoned Taco Mix until browned. Mix with 1 cup sour cream and 1 cup mozzarella cheese. Spread on muffins and bake at 400° until bubbly. Cut into quarters and serve.

Chicken Liver Apple Paté

1   onion, chopped
2   garlic cloves, crushed
2   sticks butter
1   pound chicken livers
2   apples, unpeeled, cored and chopped
½   cup dry sherry
½   cup Calvados brandy
4   hard-cooked eggs, chopped
    Salt and pepper, to taste

Sauté the onion and garlic in a skillet until the onion is soft. Add the chicken livers and sauté them until they are tender. Add the apples, sherry and brandy. Cook the mixture, covered, until the liquid is reduced by half. Add the eggs, salt and pepper and pour into a blender. Purée until smooth. Pack in a crock, pour butter on top, and chill. Serve the paté on thin slices of rye toast with lemon wedges and finely chopped onion. This paté freezes well.

Chopped Chicken Livers

1   pound chicken livers
1   onion, finely diced
4   tablespoons rendered chicken fat (available at most
    delicatessens or specialty food stores)
2   hard-cooked eggs, chopped
    Dash Worchestershire sauce
    Dash garlic salt
    Pepper, to taste

Sauté the onions and the livers in chicken fat until the livers are cooked. Pour the mixture, including fat, into a wooden bowl. Add all other ingredients, except the eggs, and cool. Chop until mixture is crumbly, and add the eggs. Mold into a mound and serve with party rye which has been sliced melba thin and slightly toasted in oven with butter.

GOURMET HELPER—Artichokes cooked in broth rather than water will have much more flavor.

Indian Chicken Balls

8   ounces cream cheese, softened
1   cup chicken, chopped fine
1   cup blanched slivered almonds
2   tablespoons Hellmann's mayonnaise
1   tablespoon chopped chutney
1   tablespoon curry powder
1/2 teaspoon Seasoning Salt
    Grated coconut

Chill the mixture and form into small balls. Roll them in grated coconut. Chill the chicken balls and serve them on toothpicks.

Chicken Rolls

3   ounce package cream cheese, softened
3   tablespoons melted butter
2   cups finely chopped cooked chicken (use breasts)
2   tablespoons milk
2   green onions, tops and bottoms, chopped
1   tablespoon chopped pimientos
1   cup crushed seasoned croutons
8   ounce can refrigerated Quick Crescent Dinner Rolls

Preheat oven to 350°. Combine cream cheese and butter and mix well. Add the next 5 ingredients and season with salt and pepper. Separate the dough into 8 triangles. Place chicken filling on each triangle and roll up jellyroll style. Cut each roll into 4 pieces and bake until lightly browned and bubbly.

GOURMET HELPER—Caviar should be added at the last minute if it is going to be mixed with other ingredients, otherwise the oil will discolor the other ingredients.

Chicken Chutney Canape

2   cups finely chopped cooked chicken (use breasts)
8   ounce package cream cheese, softened
1/2 cup mayonnaise
1   cup chopped walnuts
1   tablespoon chopped chutney
2   teaspoons curry powder
1/2 cup flaked, toasted coconut
     Rye crackers

Combine all the ingredients and season with salt and pepper. Spread on rye crackers and serve.

Hawaiian Ribs

4   pounds meaty spareribs (have butcher cut ribs into small pieces)
2   jars Junior apricot baby food
1/3 cup tarragon vinegar
1/3 cup catsup
1/2 cup brown sugar
2   garlic cloves, crushed
2   teaspoons ginger
     Salt and pepper, to taste

Combine all ingredients, except ribs. Put ribs, meat side up, in shallow baking dish. Bake at 450° for 15 minutes. Pour the sauce over the ribs. Reduce oven to 350° and bake for 1 1/2 hours, basting every half hour.

Oriental Ribs

2   9 1/2-ounce bottles La Choy Plum Sauce
2/3 cup barbecue sauce (not hickory flavored)
2   tablespoons lemon juice
5   pound rack spareribs, cut into bite-size pieces

Combine the first three ingredients. Place ribs in a shallow Pyrex dish and cover with the barbecue mixture. Marinate, covered, several hours or overnight. Preheat oven to 350° and bake, uncovered, for 1 hour or until tender.

Party Weiners

1   package all beef weiners
$1/2$ cup bourbon
$1/2$ cup chili sauce
$1/2$ cup brown sugar

Cut the weiners into bite-size pieces. Combine the other ingredients, pour over the weiners, and simmer for 1 hour. Pour into a chafing dish and serve hot.

Hot Sausage Appetizer

3   large links Kielbasa sausage, cut into bite-size pieces
1   egg
2   tablespoons lemon juice
$1/2$ teaspoon dry mustard
$1/2$ teaspoon salt
1   cup salad oil
1 or 2 jalapeño peppers (remove the seeds and chop)
1   large jar Cheez Whiz

Combine the egg, lemon juice, mustard and salt and put in a blender. Slowly add the salad oil until the mixture is the consistency of mayonnaise. In the top of a double boiler melt the Cheez Whiz. Add the mayonnaise mixture and cook, stirring, until heated through. Add the sausage and transfer to a chafing dish.

Cream Cheese-Chutney Mold

8   ounce package cream cheese with chives, softened
8   ounce package sharp Cheddar cheese, softened
2   tablespoons dry sherry
$1/8$ teaspoon Tabasco
1   teaspoon curry powder
1   small jar chutney
4   green onions, tops and bottoms, chopped

Mix the first 5 ingredients until the mixture is smooth. Grease a pie pan and fill with the cheese mixture. Chill for at least 1 hour. Unmold on serving platter. Spread chutney and green onions on top. Serve with assorted crackers. Serves 16.

Chutney Loaf

1   bottle catsup
1   bottle chili sauce
1   bottle A-1 sauce
1   bottle Worcestershire sauce
1   bottle chutney
8   ounce package cream cheese

Combine first 4 ingredients and mix well. Cut chutney into small pieces or purée in a blender. Add to the mixed sauce. Pour enough sauce over cream cheese loaf to cover generously.(Refrigerate the remaining sauce in a covered container and serve with roast beef or any meat of your choice.) Serve with crackers.

Peanut Butter and Chutney Rounds

Rounds of bread, cut with cookie cutter
Cayenne pepper
1   stick butter, melted
$1/2$ cup smooth-style peanut butter
$1/2$ cup chutney, chopped
Bacon chips

With a pastry brush spread melted butter on bread rounds. Sprinkle with cayenne pepper. Toast at 400° until lightly browned. Mix peanut butter with chutney and spread on toasted rounds. Top with bacon chips and bake at 350° until hot.

Crispy Cheese Puffs

2   cups Cheddar cheese, grated
$1/2$ pound butter, softened
$1/2$ teaspoon Worcestershire sauce
$1/8$ teaspoon Tabasco
4   cups corn flakes, finely crushed
$3/4$ cup flour, sifted
$1/4$ teaspoon paprika

In a bowl mix butter and cheese with a mixer until well blended. Add the Worcestershire and Tabasco. Combine the corn flakes with the flour and the paprika. Add to the cheese mixture and beat until thoroughly blended. Drop dough by generous teaspoons onto ungreased cookie sheet 2″ apart. Bake at 375° for about 10 minutes or until golden brown. Makes about 60 puffs.

Fresh Mushrooms Stuffed with Spinach

2   packages frozen chopped spinach, thawed
     (do not cook)
2   teaspoons dry onion flakes
¹/₄ cup bacon bits
1   cup sour cream
¹/₂ cup mayonnaise
1   teaspoon garlic powder
¹/₄ cup seasoned bread crumbs
2   eggs, lightly beaten
1   cup grated sharp Cheddar cheese
24   large fresh mushrooms, stems removed

Preheat oven to 350°. Combine all the ingredients except the cheese and mix well. Stuff into the mushroom caps and top with cheese. Bake until bubbly.

Oven Quesadillas

12   corn tortillas
¹/₂ stick butter, melted
12   slices Monterey Jack cheese
8   fresh jalapeno peppers, seeded and chopped

Preheat oven to broil. Brush tortillas with the butter. Cover with the cheese and sprinkle with the jalapenos. Broil until the cheese melts. Roll up the tortillas and place on a serving platter.

In a Hurry Spinach Quiche—Fill an unbaked pie shell with 1 pound fresh sliced mushrooms, 1 package thawed Stouffer's Spinach Souffle (spread to cover), ¹/₂ teaspoon salt and 1 cup grated sharp Cheddar or Monterey Jack cheese. Bake at 350° for 45 minutes or until set. Cool slightly. Cut into wedges to serve.

Hot Mexican Bean Dip

1   pound pinto beans
5   cups water
2   onions, chopped
1/3   cup tomato paste
3   ounce can green chilies (or 2 jalapeño peppers if you like a
      highly seasoned dip)
1   tablespoon bacon drippings
2   bay leaves
1/2   tablespoon cumin
2   tablespoons chili powder
1 1/2 teaspoon oregano
1   stick butter
1/2   pound sharp Cheddar cheese, grated
      Salt and pepper, to taste

Soak the beans, overnight, in the water. Simmer in the same water and add the
onions, tomato paste, chilies, bacon drippings, bay leaves and cumin. Simmer,
over a low heat, until the beans are soft. Add water if mixture is too dry. Add
chili powder and the oregano and put the beans through a sieve. Add the butter and the cheese and check for seasoning. When hot, transfer to a chafing
dish. Serve with corn chips.

Cucumber Dip

8   ounce package cream cheese, softened
1   package Hidden Valley Original Ranch Mix
2   tablespoons mayonnaise
1   teaspoon lemon juice
1/2   cup pecan pieces, chopped
1   cucumber, peeled and chopped
      Garlic salt, to taste

Combine all the ingredients and mix well. Refrigerate until serving time. Serve
with raw vegetables.

In a Hurry Spiced Olives—Pour off juice from bottled green olives. Pour in
Worcestershire sauce and turn upside down. Marinate overnight.

Black-Eyed Pea Dip

1   package frozen black-eyed peas
1/4   cup bacon drippings
1/2   onion, grated
1   can Ro-tel tomatoes, drained
1   avocado, cut into thin strips (dip in lemon juice to prevent
      from turning dark)

Cook peas according to directions on the package. Drain. Sauté onion in the
bacon drippings. Add the peas and mash with a potato masher to break the
skins. Add the tomatoes to the pea mixture and heat. Season with salt and
pepper. Pour into a chafing dish and garnish with avocado. Serve with chips.
(If dip is too highly seasoned for your taste add 1/2 cup grated sharp cheese and
cook until the cheese is melted. This will reduce the spiciness.)

Hot Cheese and Sausage Dip

2   pounds Velveeta cheese, melted
2   pounds Owens Hot Sausage, cooked and drained
1   tall can evaporated milk
1   package dried garlic salad dressing
      Tabasco, to taste

Mix all ingredients and serve hot with tostados.

Spiced Nuts

2   sticks butter
2   cups pecan halves
2   cups walnut halves
3   cups confectioners sugar
2   tablespoons cinnamon
2   tablespoons ground cloves
2   tablespoons nutmeg

In a saucepan saute the nuts in the butter over low heat, stirring frequently, for
about 20 minutes or until the nuts are lightly browned.

Sift together, into a brown bag, the sugar and the spices. Remove the nuts from the saucepan with a slotted spoon and drain them on paper towels. Add the nuts to the spiced sugar and toss until they are heavily coated. Transfer them to a colander and shake to remove any excess sugar. Spread the nuts on paper towels to cool.

In a Hurry Barbecued Water Chestnuts—Cut 1 pound bacon slices into thirds. Wrap the strips around 2 cans drained water chestnuts and secure with a toothpick. Place on a baking sheet and bake at 350° for 40 minutes or until very crisp. Drain off the bacon grease and pour 1 box brown sugar over the chestnuts. Add a 12-ounce bottle of catsup and several good shakes of Tabasco. Bake for 20 minutes.

SALADS

Artichoke Potato Salad

14   ounce can artichoke hearts, drained and sliced
1   pound new potatoes, cooked, peeled and sliced
1   bunch green onions, tops and bottoms, chopped
1   green pepper, chopped
3   ribs celery, chopped
3   garlic cloves, crushed
4   hard cooked eggs, chopped
1   cup mayonnaise
2   teaspoons Dijon mustard
1   tablespoon sugar
1   tablespoon chervil
1   tablespoon chopped parsley
1   teaspoon dill weed
     Juice of ½ lemon

Combine the artichokes and the potatoes. Combine the remaining ingredients and mix with the artichoke mixture. Season with salt and pepper and refrigerate for several hours before serving. Serves 8.

Artichoke Rice Salad

1   box chicken flavored Rice-A-Roni, cooked according to
     package directions
2   6-ounce jars marinated artichoke hearts, drained and chopped
     (reserve marinade)
4   green onions, tops and bottoms, chopped
2   ribs celery, chopped
1   green pepper, chopped
¼   chopped pimiento stuffed olives
2   cups mayonnaise
     Reserved artichoke marinade

Combine the first 6 ingredients. Combine the last 2 ingredients. Fold the mayonnaise mixture into the rice mixture. Season with salt and pepper and chill before serving. Serves 6.

GOURMET HELPER—Place individual salad plates in the freezer about an hour before using.

Artichoke Cherry Tomato Salad

1   pint box cherry tomatoes, sliced
2   14-ounce cans artichoke hearts, drained and cut in halves
1   small onion, chopped
1   cup tarragon vinegar
1/2   cup oil
2   tablespoons sugar
1/4   teaspoon salt
1/2   teaspoon vanilla flavoring

Combine the tomatoes, artichokes and onion. Combine the remaining ingredients and beat until well mixed. Pour over the tomato mixture and marinate in the refrigerator for several hours. Serves 8.

Fresh Asparagus Roquefort Salad

48   fresh asparagus spears, cooked and chilled
2   cups oil
1/2   cup white wine vinegar
2   teaspoons sugar
1/4   teaspoon salt
1   teaspoon Dijon mustard
1   tablespoon dill weed
3/4   cup crumbled Roquefort cheese

Combine all the ingredients, except the asparagus, and mix well. Pour over the asparagus and marinate, covered, in the refrigerator for several hours before serving. Serves 8.

GOURMET HELPER—To rid your hands of the odor of onions rub them with salt or vinegar, rinse with cold water and wash with soap and warm water.

Green Bean and Mango Salad

2   pounds fresh cooked green beans, or
2   16-ounce cans cut green beans, drained
1   onion, chopped
4   ribs celery, chopped
1/4   pound fresh mushrooms, thinly sliced
3   tablespoons chopped pimentos
1/2   cup sliced water chestnuts
1   mango, peeled and chopped

DRESSING

1/2   cup oil
1/2   cup red wine vinegar
1/4   cup catsup
1/2   cup sugar
2   tablespoons Worcestershire sauce

Combine all the dressing ingredients and heat until the sugar melts (DO NOT BOIL). Cool. Combine the salad ingredients and toss with the dressing. Chill before serving. Serves 8.

Spicy Green Bean Salad

3/4   cup oil
1/2   cup vinegar
1   package spaghetti sauce mix
2   16-ounce cans cut green beans, drained
3   cups shredded lettuce
6   slices bacon, diced and fried crisp

Combine the oil, vinegar, and spaghetti sauce mix. Add the green beans and chill. Just before serving, top with the lettuce and the crisp bacon. Serves 8.

GOURMET HELPER—Do not use metal bowls when mixing salads. Use wooden, glass or china.

Mediterranean Green Bean Salad

MARINADE

1/2 cup oil
1/8 cup tarragon vinegar
1 tablespoon lemon juice
1/4 teaspoon dry mustard
1 teaspoon dill weed
1 teaspoon garlic powder
1 1/4 pounds fresh green beans, steamed until barely tender or
2 16-ounce cans cut green beans, drained
1 onion, thinly sliced
1/2 pound fresh mushrooms, thinly sliced
2 tomatoes, peeled, seeded and quartered

DRESSING

1/4 cup mayonnaise
1/4 cup sour cream
1/4 cup crumbled Roquefort cheese

Combine the first 6 ingredients and pour over the next 4 ingredients. Refrigerate, covered, for several hours. Before serving drain the marinade from the bean mixture. Combine the dressing ingredients and fold in the green bean mixture. Serves 8.

Oriental Green Bean Salad

1 1/2 pounds fresh cooked green beans or
2 16-ounce cans cut green beans, drained
4 green onions, tops and bottoms, chopped
3 ribs celery, chopped
1 cup mayonnaise
3 tablespoons soy sauce
2 teaspoons curry powder
2 teaspoons lemon juice
1/2 cup slivered toasted almonds

Combine the first three ingredients. Combine the next 4 ingredients and mix gently with the green bean mixture. Chill. Top with the almonds before serving. Serves 8.

Broccoli Caesar Salad

2   packages frozen chopped broccoli, thawed and drained
    (do not cook)
1/4 cup chopped pimiento stuffed olives
1   onion, chopped
6   hard cooked eggs, chopped
15 ounce can sliced water chestnuts, drained
3/4 cup mayonnaise
1   package Caesar Garlic Salad Dressing Mix

Combine all the ingredients in the order given. Season with salt and pepper
and refrigerate for several hours before serving. Serves 8.

Little Mushroom Cauliflower Salad

2   heads cauliflower, separated and sliced thin
12 radishes, sliced
6   green onions

DRESSING

1   cup sour cream
1   cup mayonnaise
1   package Good Seasons Cheese Garlic Mix (or 1 tablespoon
    pure granulated garlic)
4   tablespoons sesame seeds

Combine cauliflower, radishes, and onions. Blend dressing ingredients and
pour over vegetables. Toss until vegetables are well-coated. Refrigerate for several hours before serving.

Cauliflower Bacon Salad

1   head cauliflower, finely chopped
1   head iceberg lettuce, finely chopped
4   green onions, tops and bottoms, chopped
1   pound bacon cooked crisp, drained and crumbled
1 1/2 cups sour cream
2   garlic cloves, crushed
2   tablespoons sugar
1/2 cup grated Parmesan cheese

Combine all the ingredients, except the cheese, and mix well. Top with cheese and chill before serving. Serves 8.

Layered Cauliflower Salad

1 head cauliflower, finely chopped
1 head iceberg lettuce, finely chopped
3 carrots, grated
1 onion, sliced
1 green pepper, chopped
2 15-ounce cans pineapple chunks, drained
1 pound bacon cooked crisp, drained and crumbled
$1/2$ cup grated Swiss cheese
$1/2$ cup mayonnaise
$1/2$ cup sour cream
$1/4$ cup sugar

In a 9″ x 13″ baking dish layer the first 8 ingredients. Season each layer with salt and pepper. Combine the remaining ingredients and spread on top. Cover and refrigerate overnight. To serve lift out portions with a salad spoon and fork picking up all the layers. Serves 8.

Busy Day Cauliflower Salad

2 heads cauliflower, finely chopped
1 cup mayonnaise
1 cup buttermilk
$1/2$ teaspoon garlic powder
$1/2$ teaspoon onion powder
$1/2$ teaspoon Spice Island cottage cheese seasoning

Combine all the ingredients and season with salt and pepper. Chill before serving. Serves 8.

GOURMET HELPER—For fresh onion juice squeeze half an onion with the skin on, just as you would squeeze a lemon.

Frozen Daiquiri Salad

2/3 cup mayonnaise
6 ounce can frozen Daiquiri Mix, thawed
4¹/2 ounce package egg custard mix
8 ounce package cream cheese, softened
1 cup crushed pineapple, drained
Whole strawberries (garnish)

Combine the mayonnaise and the Daiquiri and custard mix. Gradually add the cream cheese, mixing until well blended. Fold in the pineapple and pour into a 9″ pie pan. Freeze mixture until it is firm. Cut into wedges and top with strawberries. Serves 8-10.

Frozen Cranberry Salad

16 ounce can crushed pineapple, drained
1 pound can whole cranberry sauce
1 cup sour cream
¹/2 cup chopped walnuts
¹/2 2-ounce can shredded coconut

Combine all the ingredients and transfer to ice cube trays. Freeze. To serve, cut into squares.

Frozen Cole Slaw

1 head cabbage, cut fine
1 teaspoon salt
1 carrot, shredded
1 green pepper, finely chopped
1 red pepper, finely chopped
2 cups sugar
1 cup vinegar
¹/2 cup cold water
1 teaspoon celery seed
1 teaspoon mustard seed

Combine the first 5 ingredients and mix well. Let stand for 1 hour. In a saucepan boil together the remaining ingredients. Cool and pour over the cabbage mixture. Place in plastic freezer boxes and freeze. When ready to serve, let thaw about 2 hours in the bowl.

In a Hurry Pineapple-Cranberry Freeze—Combine 2 3-ounce packages softened cream cheese and 2 tablespoons sugar. Stir in 2 tablespoons mayonnaise and mix well. Fold in 1 16-ounce can jellied cranberry sauce, 1 cup drained crushed pineapple, ½ cup chopped pecans and ½ cup whipped cream. Pour into a 9″ x 5″ loaf pan and freeze until firm.

Creative Cole Slaw

1   head cabbage, shredded
3   carrots, peeled and shredded
1   small green pepper, chopped
2   garlic cloves, crushed
1   teaspoon dill weed
½   cup buttermilk
¾   cup mayonnaise
1   tablespoon tarragon vinegar
1   tablespoon sugar
1   package Hidden Valley Party Mix

Combine the first 4 ingredients. Combine the remaining ingredients and mix with the first ingredients. Season with salt and pepper and chill before serving. Serves 8.

Swiss Cole Slaw

4   cups shredded cabbage
1   package frozen peas and carrots, cooked and drained
1   cup diced Swiss cheese
⅔   cup sour cream
3   tablespoons prepared mustard
4   green onions, tops and bottoms, chopped
1   teaspoon salt
2   tablespoons sugar

Combine the first 3 ingredients. Combine the remaining ingredients and mix with the first ingredients. Chill before serving. Serves 8.

GOURMET HELPER—To keep celery crisp, stand it up in a pitcher of cold salted water and refrigerate.

Red Cabbage Slaw

1   cup cottage cheese, drained
1/2 cup mayonnaise
2   tablespoons honey
1   teaspoon poppy seeds
1   teaspoon dry mustard
1   tablespoon tarragon vinegar
4   cups shredded red cabbage
1   tablespoon chopped pimentos
1/4 cup slivered almonds
1/4 cup raisins
2   cups fresh peaches, peeled and sliced

Combine the first 6 ingredients and place in a blender or food processor. Blend until smooth. Mix with remaining ingredients and season with salt and pepper. Chill before serving. Serves 8.

Bibb Lettuce with Cream Dressing

4   heads bibb lettuce or 2 heads Boston lettuce
1/2 teaspoon salt
1/2 teaspoon white pepper
1   tablespoon lemon juice
1/3 cup heavy cream
2   tablespoons oil

In a bowl combine the salt, pepper, lemon juice and cream. Beat with a wire whisk about 20 seconds (mixture should be foamy and creamy in consistency). Add the oil and mix with a spoon to blend. At serving time toss the salad gently and serve on individual chilled salad plates. Serves 6.

GOURMET HELPER—To store salad greens which have already been cut, toss with a small amount of oil and refrigerate in a large plastic bag and they will stay crispy.

Caesar Salad

2   heads romaine, torn into salad-size pieces
1/2   pound bacon, diced and fried crisp (reserve drippings)
11/2 cup day-old bread, cut into 1/2" cubes
3   garlic cloves, minced
1   teaspoon salt
4   anchovy filets, drained
3/4   cup olive oil
1   tablespoon Worcestershire sauce
1   teaspoon dry mustard
1/2   teaspoon Tabasco
1   cup Parmesan cheese, freshly grated

Chill the romaine. Sauté the bread cubes in the bacon drippings until they are lightly browned. Drain on paper towels. Mash the garlic with the salt. Add the anchovies and 1/4 cup olive oil and mash mixture to a paste. Stir in remaining 1/2 cup olive oil, Worcestershire sauce, dry mustard and Tabasco. Blend the mixture until it is well combined. Add the romaine, bacon, croutons and Parmesan cheese. Salt and pepper to taste. Serve on chilled salad plates. Serves 6–8.

Easy Caesar Salad

2   heads romaine, torn into bite-size pieces and chilled
1   cup seasoned croutons

DRESSING
8   ounce bottle Caesar salad dressing
1   cup sour cream
1/4   teaspoon dry mustard
11/2 tablespoons Worcestershire sauce
1   cup grated Parmesan cheese
1/2   teaspoon anchovy paste
1   garlic clove, minced
1   teaspoon pepper

Combine all the dressing ingredients and puree in a blender or food processor. Toss with the lettuce and top with the croutons. Serves 8.

Mock Caesar Salad

Juice of 1 lemon
3   garlic cloves, crushed
³/₄ cup salad oil
1   teaspoon sugar
¹/₂ teaspoon tarragon
¹/₄ pound bacon, diced
2   heads of romaine, torn into pieces
2   cups cherry tomatoes, halved
1   cup Swiss cheese, grated
²/₃ cup slivered almonds, toasted
¹/₃ cup freshly grated Parmesan cheese

Combine the first 5 ingredients and salt and pepper, to taste and let the dressing stand, covered, for 3 hours. Sauté bacon until crisp and drain on paper towels. In a salad bowl combine the remaining ingredients, including the bacon. Toss with the dressing and add salt and pepper, to taste. Serves 8.

Italian Tossed Salad

1   head romaine lettuce, torn into salad-size pieces
1   head iceberg lettuce, torn into salad-size pieces
4   green onions, chopped
1   green pepper, chopped
4   Italian sweet peppers, chopped
¹/₂ cup green olives, sliced
¹/₄ pound feta cheese, crumbled
¹/₂ cup slivered almonds
¹/₄ cup Parmesan cheese, freshly grated

DRESSING
³/₄ cup oil
¹/₄ cup wine flavored tarragon vinegar
1   tablespoon lemon juice
1   teaspoon oregano
1   garlic clove, crushed
     Dash honey, to sweeten
     Salt and pepper, to taste

Mix dressing ingredients and chill. Combine the lettuce, onions, green pepper, sweet peppers and olives. Add the feta cheese and almonds to the dressing. Toss the salad with the dressing and place on chilled salad plates.

Marinated Mushroom Salad

3/4   pound fresh mushrooms, thinly sliced
3   ribs celery, chopped
1   green pepper, chopped
1   red onion, chopped
1   small jar pimentos, drained and chopped
1/3   cup red wine vinegar
2   garlic cloves, crushed
1   teaspoon Worcestershire sauce
1   cup olive oil
1   teaspoon oregano
     Salt and pepper, to taste

Combine the first 5 ingredients and set aside. Combine all the other ingredients and mix well with a wire whisk. Toss the dressing with the mushroom mixture. Refrigerate, covered, for several hours or overnight. Serves 6–8.

Marinated Cucumber Salad

4   cucumbers, peeled, seeded and thinly sliced

MARINADE
3/4   cup white wine vinegar
1/4   cup oil
1/2   cup sugar

ROQUEFORT MUSTARD DRESSING
1/2   cup oil
1 1/2 tablespoons red wine vinegar
1   teaspoon Dijon mustard
1/4   cup crumbled Roquefort cheese
2   tablespoons grated onion

Combine the marinade ingredients and mix well. Add the cucumbers and marinate several hours in the refrigerator. Drain. Combine the dressing ingredients and toss with the cucumbers. Chill before serving. Serves 8.

In a Hurry Cucumber Pea Salad—Combine 2 packages frozen peas, thawed and drained; 2 peeled and chopped cucumbers; 1 cup mayonnaise; and 2 tablespoons jalapeno jelly. Chill before serving. Serves 8.

Cucumber and Cheese Salad

³/₄   cup sour cream
2   tablespoons dill weed
2   tablespoons white wine tarragon vinegar
1   tablespoon chopped chives
1   tablespoon olive oil
1   garlic clove, crushed
¹/₈   teaspoon cayenne pepper
4   cucumbers, peeled and diced
1¹/₂ cups Swiss cheese, coarsely chopped
6   green onions, tops and bottoms, chopped
6   radishes, thinly sliced
4   hard-cooked eggs, chopped
¹/₄   cup fresh parsley, finely chopped
4   slices bacon, diced and fried crisp

Combine the first 7 ingredients and chill. Combine the remaining ingredients, except the bacon, and chill. Pour the dressing over the salad, toss, and top with bacon. Serves 6–8.

24-Hour Salad

1   pound spinach, torn into pieces
¹/₂   teaspoon salt
¹/₄   teaspoon pepper
2   teaspoons sugar
¹/₂   pound bacon, diced and fried crisp
6   hard-cooked eggs, chopped
1   head iceberg lettuce, torn into pieces
10 ounce package frozen peas (thawed, but not cooked)
1   onion, sliced
2   cups Hellmann's mayonnaise
1   cup sour cream
1   cup Swiss cheese, grated

Layer the first 7 ingredients in a shallow enamel or Pyrex dish. Spread the next 4 ingredients, mixing the mayonnaise and sour cream, on top. Sprinkle with cheese. Cover tightly and refrigerate 24 hours. Serve without tossing. Serves 10.

24-Hour Spinach Salad

1   pound fresh spinach, de-stemmed and torn into bite-size pieces
1   cucumber thinly sliced
4   green onions, tops and bottoms, chopped
1/2   cup thinly sliced radishes
1   cup Roquefort dressing
6   slices bacon cooked crisp, drained and crumbled
1/2   cup peanuts

Layer the spinach on the bottom of a shallow enamel or glass baking dish. Sprinkle with salt and pepper. Add the next 3 ingredients and sprinkle with salt and pepper. Pour the dressing on top and refrigerate, covered, for 24 hours. Top with the bacon and nuts. To serve lift portions out with a salad spoon and fork, picking up all the layers. Serves 6.

Spinach Salad with Chutney Dressing

1   pound fresh spinach, de-stemmed and torn into bite-size pieces
1/2   pound fresh mushrooms, thinly sliced
1   cup sliced water chestnuts
6   slices bacon cooked crisp, drained and crumbled
1/4   cup thinly sliced red onion
1/2   cup grated Parmesan cheese

CHUTNEY DRESSING
1/4   cup white wine vinegar
1   garlic clove, minced
3   tablespoons chopped chutney
2   tablespoons prepared mustard
2   teaspoons sugar
1/2   cup oil

Combine the first 6 ingredients and place in refrigerator while preparing the dressing. In a blender or food processor combine the first 5 ingredients and mix until smooth. With the machine running, slowly pour in oil until mixture is thick and smooth. Season with salt and pepper and chill slightly before tossing with the spinach. Serves 6.

GOURMET HELPER—Store chopped onions in a screw-top jar in the refrigerator. They will retain their flavor for several days.

Spinach Salad

1   pound fresh spinach, torn into pieces
3   hard-cooked eggs, chopped
2   slices bacon, diced and sautéed until crisp

DRESSING

2   eggs
1   tablespoon Parmesan cheese, freshly grated
1   garlic clove, crushed
1¹/2 teaspoons Dijon mustard
¹/2 cup salad oil
¹/4 cup lemon juice
2   teaspoons sugar
     Salt and pepper, to taste

In a mixing bowl combine the dressing ingredients and with a wire whisk blend thoroughly. Chill. Combine the spinach, eggs and bacon. Add the dressing, toss the salad well and serve. Serves 4–6.

Sensational Spinach Salad

2   packages frozen chopped spinach, drained and squeezed dry
     (DO NOT COOK)
2   green onions, tops and bottoms, chopped
1   small onion, chopped
3   hard-cooked eggs, chopped
2   ribs celery, chopped
2   tablespoons chopped pimientos
¹/4 cup sour cream
¹/4 cup mayonnaise
1   tablespoon horseradish
1   cup grated sharp Cheddar cheese

Combine all the ingredients and mix well. Chill before serving. Serves 8.

GOURMET HELPER—Keep a small bottle of salad oil seasoned with your favorite herbs stored for ready use in making your favorite salad dressing.

Spinach Avocado Salad

1   pound fresh spinach, de-stemmed and torn into bite-size pieces
2   avocados, peeled and sliced
6   slices bacon fried crisp, drained and crumbled
1/2 cup chopped walnuts
1   cup oil
1/4 cup raspberry flavored vinegar*
1   teaspoon mustard with peppercorns*
2   tablespoons lemon juice
1   teaspoon salt
1   teaspoon sugar
1   teaspoon Worcestershire sauce
1/4 teaspoon basil
1/2 cup seasoned croutons

Combine the first 4 ingredients. Combine the next 8 ingredients and mix well. Toss with the spinach mixture and top with the croutons. Serves 6.

*Can find in specialty gourmet shops. You may substitute others if you cannot find the ones mentioned.

Spinach Mushroom Salad

1   pound spinach, torn into pieces
1/4 pound fresh mushrooms, sliced
5   slices bacon, diced and sautéed until crisp
2   hard-cooked eggs, chopped

DRESSING
1/4 cup white wine tarragon vinegar
2   tablespoons dry white wine
2   teaspoons soy sauce
1   teaspoon dry mustard
1   teaspoon sugar
1/2 teaspoon curry powder
1   garlic clove, crushed
2/3 cup salad oil

In a mixing bowl combine the first 7 ingredients of the dressing and beat until the mixture is well blended. Add the oil in a slow stream, beating until the dressing is well combined. Add salt and pepper, to taste. In a salad bowl combine the spinach and mushrooms. Toss the salad with the dressing. Top the salad with the bacon and eggs. Serves 4–6.

Wilted Spinach Salad

1   pound fresh spinach, de-stemmed and torn into bite-size pieces
10   slices bacon cooked crisp, drained and crumbled (reserve
     bacon drippings)
$^1/_2$ cup brandy
$^1/_4$ cup tarragon vinegar
2   tablespoons sugar
2   tablespoons Worcestershire sauce
2   teaspoons dry mustard

In a skillet heat the bacon drippings and pour over the spinach. In the same
skillet add the brandy and de-glaze the pan scraping up the bits of bacon clinging to the bottom. Add the remaining ingredients and pour over the spinach.
Cover for 5 minutes or until the spinach is slightly wilted. Serves 6.

Terrific Tossed Salad

1   head lettuce, shredded
1   avocado, peeled and sliced
1   tomato, peeled and quartered
1   hard cooked egg, sliced
6   slices bacon fried crisp, drained and crumbled
$^1/_4$ cup crumbled Roquefort cheese

DRESSING

$^3/_4$ cup oil
$^1/_4$ cup white wine vinegar
1   tablespoon lemon juice
$^1/_2$ teaspoon sugar
$^1/_4$ teaspoon dry mustard
1   teaspoon Worcestershire sauce
1   garlic clove, crushed

Combine the salad ingredients and toss lightly. Combine the dressing ingredients and toss with the salad mixture. Serves 6.

> **GOURMET HELPER**—If your homemade mayonnaise starts to curdle,
> put an egg yolk in a bowl and gradually whip the mayonnaise into it.

Garden Salad

2   heads bibb lettuce, torn into bite-size pieces
11   ounce can mandarin oranges, drained
2   avocados, peeled and sliced
1/4 cup toasted slivered almonds
4   slices bacon, diced and fried crisp

ROQUEFORT DRESSING

1   pint mayonnaise
1/2 pint sour cream
2   tablespoons lemon juice
2   teaspoons onion, grated
1/2 cup Roquefort cheese, crumbled
     Garlic salt, to taste
     Salt and pepper, to taste

In a salad bowl combine the first 5 ingredients. Combine the dressing ingredients until well blended. Place the salad on chilled individual salad plates and top with the dressing. Serves 8–10.

Cucumber Sour Cream Salad

3   large cucumbers, peeled, seeded and thinly sliced
1   onion, thinly sliced
12   radishes, thinly sliced
1/2 cup sour cream
1   cup mayonnaise
1   package Cheese Garlic Salad Dressing Mix
1   tablespoon dill weed

Combine the first 3 ingredients. Combine the remaining ingredients and toss with the first ingredients. Chill before serving. Serves 8.

GOURMET HELPER—Lettuce keeps better if you store in refrigerator without washing first so that the leaves are dry. Wash the day you are going to use.

Pickled Beet Salad

1   large can round beets, drain and reserve ½ cup liquid
1   onion, thinly sliced
½   cup white wine tarragon vinegar
½   cup sugar
¼   cup water
1½   teaspoon salt
6   whole cloves
3″   piece cinnamon stick

Combine the beets with the onion. In a saucepan combine the remaining ingredients (including the beet liquid) and bring to a boil. Cover and simmer for 10 minutes. Pour the hot liquid over the beet and onion mixture. Cover the bowl tightly, let the mixture cool, and refrigerate overnight or for several days. Serves 4.

Hot Pineapple Salad

2   large cans pineapple chunks, drain and reserve the juice
⅔   pound Velveeta cheese, cut in cubes
½   cup sugar
½   cup flour
     Juice of 1 lemon

Mix sugar, flour and the lemon juice. Add the pineapple and the cheese. Pour enough pineapple juice over the mixture to barely cover. Bake at 325° about 45 minutes or until thick (do not let boil or it will curdle).

In a Hurry Fruit Salad—Combine 1 small can lemonade concentrate with 2 lightly beaten eggs, and ½ cup sugar and cook, stirring until thick. Chill. When ready to serve fold in 1½ cups Cool Whip and 2 cups fruits for salad.

Fresh Fruit Salad with Honey Lemon Dressing

1 cup fresh pineapple chunks
1 cup apple slices
1 cup honeydew or casaba melon chunks
1 cup watermelon chunks
1 cup sliced seedless grapes

HONEY LEMON DRESSING

$^1/_2$ cup oil
$^1/_4$ cup lemon juice
$^1/_3$ cup honey
$^1/_2$ teaspoon salt
1 teaspoon celery seed
$^1/_4$ teaspoon cayenne pepper

Combine the fruits and chill. Combine the dressing ingredients and mix well. Pour over the chilled fruit and serve. Serves 8.

Fresh Fruit Salad with Yogurt Honey Dressing

1 melon (cantaloupe, casaba or honeydew) diced
2 bananas, sliced
1 cup sliced strawberries
2 peaches, peeled and sliced
1 apple, sliced
1 bunch seedless grapes, sliced

YOGURT HONEY DRESSING

8 ounces plain yogurt
2 tablespoons honey
1 teaspoon lemon juice
$^1/_4$ teaspoon vanilla flavoring

Combine the fruits and chill. Combine the yogurt and honey and beat with a wire whisk until well mixed. Add the lemon juice and flavoring and pour over the chilled fruit. Serves 8.

Fresh Fruit Salad with Honey Lime Dressing

1   apple, sliced
1   small pineapple, cut into spears
1   cantaloupe, cut into bite-size pieces
12   strawberries, sliced
2   peaches, peeled and sliced

HONEY LIME DRESSING

$^1/_2$ cup frozen limeade concentrate, thawed
$^2/_3$ cup honey
$^2/_3$ cup oil
1   teaspoon poppyseed

Combine the fruits and chill. Combine the dressing ingredients and beat with a mixer until the dressing is smooth and thickened. Toss with the chilled fruit and serve. Serves 8.

Fresh Fruit Salad with Sour Cream Dressing

4   cups fresh fruit, chopped into bite-size pieces
$^1/_2$ cup toasted coconut
1   cup miniature marshmallows
$^1/_2$ cup mayonnaise
$^1/_2$ cup sour cream
$^1/_2$ teaspoon vanilla flavoring
1   tablespoon sugar

Combine the first 3 ingredients. Combine the remaining ingredients and toss with the first ingredients. Chill before serving. Serves 8.

Fruit Basket Salad

2   apples, thinly sliced
2   bananas, sliced
1   orange, sliced
$^1/_2$ fresh pineapple, cubed
12   strawberries, sliced
1   package Dream Whip, whipped according to package directions
1   can lemon pie mix

Combine the first 5 ingredients and mix well. Combine the last 2 ingredients and toss with the fruit. Chill before serving. Serves 8.

Perfect Potato Salad

3   pounds new potatoes, cooked, peeled, sliced and still warm
2²/₃ cups mayonnaise
12   green onions, tops and bottoms, chopped
¹/₂   cup finely chopped parsley
4   hard-cooked eggs, sliced
¹/₂   teaspoon sugar
1   tablespoon Dijon mustard

Combine all the ingredients and toss well. Season with salt and pepper and refrigerate, covered, for 8 hours or longer. Serves 8.

Mexican Salad

1   head lettuce, chopped
1   large red onion, chopped
4   ripe tomatoes, peeled and chopped
2   cups grated Cheddar or Monterey Jack cheese
15   ounce can kidney beans, drained
1   ripe avocado, peeled and diced
1   pound ground beef, cooked, drained and crumbled
1   cup crushed corn chips
1   cup bottled French dressing

Combine all the ingredients, except the dressing, and mix well. Toss with the dressing and serve. Serves 8.

Jalapeno Pea Salad

1   cup jalapeno jelly
2   packages frozen peas, cooked and drained
4   green onions, tops and bottoms, chopped
3   ribs celery, chopped
2   tablespoons chopped pimentos

In a saucepan heat the jelly until melted. Pour over the remaining ingredients and chill. Serves 8.

Avocado Potato Salad

6   slices bacon, diced and fried crisp
2½ cups potatoes, cooked, peeled and diced
2   hard-cooked eggs, chopped
½   onion, finely chopped
2   green onions, tops and bottoms, chopped
1   tablespoon pimentos, drained and sliced
½   cup mayonnaise
2   tablespoons lime juice
2   avocados, peeled, seeded and cubed.

In a bowl combine the crisp bacon, potatoes, eggs, onions, pimentos and salt and pepper, to taste. Toss the mixture and chill, covered, for 1 hour. Combine the mayonnaise and lime juice. Fold the dressing into the potato mixture and gently mix until well blended. Add the avocados. Serves 6–8.

Party Potato Salad

1   cup sour cream
¼   cup Hellmann's mayonnaise
4   ribs celery, chopped
6   green onions, tops and bottoms, chopped
½   cup chopped cucumber, peeled and chopped
6   cups potatoes, cooked, peeled and diced
¼   cup chopped pimentos, drained
1½ teaspoon salt
½   teaspoon cayenne pepper
     Cucumber slices (garnish)
     Radish slices (garnish)
     Hard-cooked eggs (garnish)

In a bowl combine the sour cream and mayonnaise. Add remaining ingredients and mix well. Press firmly into a well-oiled tube pan. Chill thoroughly. Unmold carefully on a serving platter and garnish with the cucumbers, radishes, and eggs. Serves 6–8.

GOURMET HELPER—Store mayonnaise in the section of your refrigerator which is the warmest, preferably on the door shelf.

Apple and Potato Salad

¹/₄ cup heavy cream
¹/₄ cup white wine tarragon vinegar
2 tablespoons horseradish
1 tablespoon onion, grated
¹/₂ cup olive oil
1 pound apples, peeled, quartered and sliced ¹/₈" thick
2 pounds warm new potatoes, cooked, peeled and sliced ¹/₄" thick
¹/₄ cup dry white wine

In a jar combine the first 4 ingredients. Cover the jar tightly and shake the mixture until it is well blended. Add the olive oil, cover the jar, and shake the dressing again. Add salt and pepper, to taste. Put the potatoes in a serving bowl and toss them with the wine. Add the apples and toss with the dressing. Serve the salad warm. Serves 8.

Hot German Potato Salad

2 pounds new potatoes, boiled in salted water, peeled and cubed
¹/₄ stick butter, melted
6 strips of bacon, coarsely chopped and sautéed until crisp (reserve the drippings)
1 onion, chopped
1¹/₂ teaspoons flour
2 tablespoons sugar
¹/₄ teaspoon salt
¹/₄ cup white wine tarragon vinegar
¹/₂ cup water
Fresh parsley, chopped

Drain the cooked bacon on paper towels and then pour off about half of the bacon drippings. In remaining drippings sauté the onion until soft. Stir in flour, sugar, salt and pepper, to taste and simmer for a few minutes. Stir in the vinegar mixed with the water and cook over low heat, stirring constantly, until slightly thickened. Pour melted butter over the potatoes and shake pan to coat them. Season the potatoes with more salt, if needed. Pour the hot sauce over the potatoes and toss lightly. Transfer to a serving bowl and top with the bacon and parsley. Serve the salad warm. Serves 6-8.

Wild Rice Salad

3 cups cooked Uncle Ben's Wild Rice and White Rice Mix
4 green onions, chopped
1 garlic clove, crushed
1 cup peas, cooked
8 cherry tomatoes, cut in half
8$\frac{1}{2}$ ounce can artichoke hearts, drained and cut in half

SHERRY DRESSING

1 egg
$\frac{1}{2}$ teaspoon sugar
$\frac{1}{2}$ cup olive oil
2 cups salad oil
$\frac{1}{4}$ cup white wine tarragon vinegar
2 garlic cloves, crushed
$\frac{1}{4}$ cup sherry
Salt and pepper, to taste

Combine all ingredients and toss lightly. To make the dressing: combine the egg and sugar. Add remaining ingredients and heat until well blended. Toss rice mixture with the dressing. Serves 6–8.

Mushroom Rice Salad

2 cups cooked rice
1 cup fresh mushrooms, thinly sliced
4 green onions, tops and bottoms, chopped
2 ribs celery, chopped
1 small green pepper, chopped
1 tomato, peeled and chopped
1 cup mayonnaise
2 teaspoons tarragon vinegar
1 tablespoon sugar
$\frac{1}{2}$ cup Roquefort cheese

Combine the first 6 ingredients. Combine the remaining ingredients and toss with the first ingredients. Chill before serving. Serves 8.

Curried Rice Salad

2 cups cooked Uncle Ben's Long Grain and Wild Rice
4 green onions, tops and bottoms, chopped
1/2 cup raisins
1/2 teaspoon curry powder

DRESSING
1/4 cup olive oil
1/4 cup salad oil
1/2 cup tarragon vinegar
2 teaspoons sugar
1/4 teaspoon garlic salt
1/8 teaspoon pepper

Combine the first 4 ingredients and mix well. Combine the dressing ingredients and toss with the rice mixture. Chill before serving. Serves 8.

In a Hurry Curried Rice Salad—Combine 2 cups cooked rice, 1/2 cup mayonnaise, 1/4 cup plain yogurt or sour cream, 2 tablespoons chutney and 1 1/2 teaspoons curry powder. Chill before serving. Serves 8.

Chicken Rice Salad

2 cups cooked chicken breasts, torn into bite-size pieces
3 cups cooked rice
1 large green pepper, chopped
4 ribs celery, chopped
1/2 cup slivered almonds
2 hard-cooked eggs, chopped
2 cups mayonnaise
2 teaspoons Dijon mustard
1/4 cup white wine
1 package Green Onion Dip Mix or Onion Soup Mix
1 teaspoon crushed green peppercorns

Combine the first 6 ingredients. Combine the remaining ingredients and fold into the chicken mixture. Season with salt and pepper and chill before serving. Serves 8.

Little Mushroom Chicken Salad

8   halved chicken breasts, cooked and cut into large bite-size
     pieces
2   cups celery, chopped
1/2 cup toasted almonds, sliced
6   hard-cooked eggs, chopped
1/2 teaspoon chicken soup base
1   teaspoon white pepper
1   teaspoon sugar
1/2 cup mayonnaise

Mix first 4 ingredients until well blended. Mix next 4 ingredients until well
blended. Combine and toss gently. Chill until ready to serve. Serves 8.

Chicken Salad Supreme

1   stick butter, melted
2   cups mayonnaise
1/4 cup fresh parsley, minced
1/2 teaspoon curry powder
1/4 teaspoon pure granulated garlic
1/8 teaspoon marjoram
4   cups cooked chicken breasts, shredded
2   cups seedless green grapes, peeled
1/2 cup toasted slivered almonds

Let butter cool to room temperature. In a bowl combine the butter and the
mayonnaise with the parsley, curry powder, garlic, marjoram and salt and
white pepper to taste. Add the chicken, grapes and almonds and fold into the
dressing until well blended. Chill until ready to serve. Serves 6–8.

Exotic Chicken Salad

2   cups cooked chicken breasts, torn into bite-size pieces
4   green onions, tops and bottoms, chopped
4   ribs celery, chopped
1   apple, unpeeled and chopped
1   banana, sliced
15   ounce can pineapple chunks, drained
1   cup seedless white grapes, sliced
1   cup sliced water chestnuts
1   cup toasted coconut
1/2   cup mayonnaise
1/2   cup sour cream
1   teaspoon lemon juice
1/4   teaspoon chicken soup base
1   teaspoon curry powder
3   tablespoons chopped chutney

Combine the first 9 ingredients. Combine the remaining ingredients and toss lightly with the first ingredients. Season with salt and pepper and chill before serving. Serves 8.

Crabmeat Salad

1   pound King crabmeat, cut into bite-size pieces
2   ribs celery, chopped
1/4   cup heavy cream, whipped
3/4   cup mayonnaise
1   tablespoon Dijon mustard
1   teaspoon Worcestershire sauce
1/2   teaspoon tarragon
1/2   teaspoon seasoning salt
1/8   teaspoon Angostura bitters
1   tablespoon brandy

Combine all the ingredients except the crabmeat. Fold in the crabmeat and chill before serving. Serves 8.

Herbed Salmon Salad

2   7-ounce cans salmon, drained
4   green onions, tops and bottoms, chopped
2   ribs celery, chopped
1   apple, chopped
2   hard-cooked eggs, chopped
6   slices bacon cooked crisp, drained and crumbled
1   cup mayonnaise
1   tablespoon lemon juice
1   teaspoon fines herbs
1/2 teaspoon garlic powder

Remove the bones and skin from the salmon. Combine all the ingredients and mix well. Chill before serving. Serves 8.

Oriental Shrimp Salad

4   cups cooked chopped shrimp
2   cups pineapple chunks, drained
4   green onions, tops and bottoms, chopped
4   ribs celery, chopped
1/2 cup sliced water chestnuts
1   cup mayonnaise
1/2 cup sour cream
2   tablespoons chopped chutney
1   teaspoon curry powder

Combine the first 5 ingredients. Combine the remaining ingredients and fold in the shrimp mixture. Chill before serving. Serves 8.

Avocado Stuffed with Shrimp

4   cups cooked shrimp
4   avocados, peeled and halved

DRESSING

1½ cups mayonnaise
1   tablespoon lemon juice
2   green onions, tops and bottoms, chopped
1   garlic clove, crushed
2   tablespoons capers, drained
3   tablespoons catsup
2   teaspoons dill weed
⅛   teaspoon cayenne pepper

Combine the dressing ingredients and season with salt and pepper. Chill for several hours. When ready to serve fill the avocados with the shrimp and top with the dressing. Serves 8.

Little Mushroom Tuna Salad

12½ ounce can light chunk tuna, drained
4   green onions, tops and bottoms, chopped
3   ribs celery, chopped
¼   cup pimentos, chopped
2   hard-cooked eggs
½   cup sweet relish
⅛   teaspoon salt
⅛   teaspoon pepper
½   cup mayonnaise

Combine all ingredients and mix well. Taste for seasonings. Chill until ready to serve. Serves 8.

Tuna Salad

2 7-ounce cans tuna, drained
4 green onions, tops and bottoms, chopped
1 small onion, chopped
2 ribs celery, chopped
2 tablespoons chopped pimientos
1/2 cup sliced water chestnuts
1 cup mayonnaise
1/2 cup sour cream
1 package green onion dip mix or onion soup mix

Combine the first 6 ingredients and mix well. Combine the last 3 ingredients and fold into the tuna mixture. Season with salt and pepper and chill before serving. Serves 8.

Curried Tuna Avocado Salad

2 7-ounce cans tuna, drained
6 ounce jar cocktail onions, drained and halved
1 apple, chopped
1/2 cup chopped pecans
1 cup mayonnaise
1 tablespoon lemon juice
1 teaspoon garlic salt
1 teaspoon curry powder
2 avocados, chopped

Combine the first 4 ingredients and mix well. Combine the remaining ingredients, except for the avocados, and toss lightly. Gently fold in the avocado. Chill before serving. Serves 8.

Avocado Stuffed with Tuna

2 7-ounce cans tuna, drained
4 avocados, halved and pitted
1 cup chopped walnuts
2 cups heavy cream, whipped
1/4 cup catsup

Scoop the flesh from the avocado shells being careful not to tear the shells. Cut into bite-size pieces and toss with the tuna. Fold in the remaining ingredients and pile into the shells. Serves 8.

Marinated Vegetable Salad I

1   head cauliflower, chopped
1   bunch broccoli, chopped
1   cucumber, sliced
2   zucchini, sliced
1/2 pound fresh mushrooms, sliced
1   green pepper, chopped
4   ribs celery, chopped
1/2 cup salad oil
1/2 cup olive oil
3   cups tarragon vinegar
3/4 cup sugar
3   garlic cloves, crushed
1   tablespoon salt
1   tablespoon prepared mustard
2   teaspoons tarragon

Combine the first 7 ingredients. Combine the remaining ingredients and pour over the vegetable mixture. Chill, covered, for 24 hours before serving. Serves 8.

Zucchini and Rice Salad

4   cups shredded raw zucchini
2   cups cooked rice
4   green onions, tops and bottoms, chopped
2   ribs celery, chopped
4   ounce can diced green chilies, drained

GARLIC CHEESE DRESSING
1   cup sour cream
3/4 cup mayonnaise
1/2 teaspoon garlic powder
1   teaspoon garlic salt
1/4 teaspoon cayenne pepper
1/2 cup grated Parmesan cheese

Combine the first 5 ingredients and mix well. Combine the dressing ingredients and fold in zucchini mixture. Season with salt and pepper and chill before serving. Serves 8.

Zucchini Salad with Dill Dressing

4   medium zucchini, peeled and thinly sliced
1   onion, thinly sliced
1   large tomato, peeled and diced

DRESSING

2/3 cup oil
1/2 cup lemon juice
1   garlic clove, crushed
1   teaspoon Dijon mustard
1/4 teaspoon cayenne pepper
1   teaspoon dill weed

Combine the first 3 ingredients and mix well. Combine the dressing ingredients and pour over the zucchini mixture. Refrigerate, covered, for several hours before serving. Serves 8.

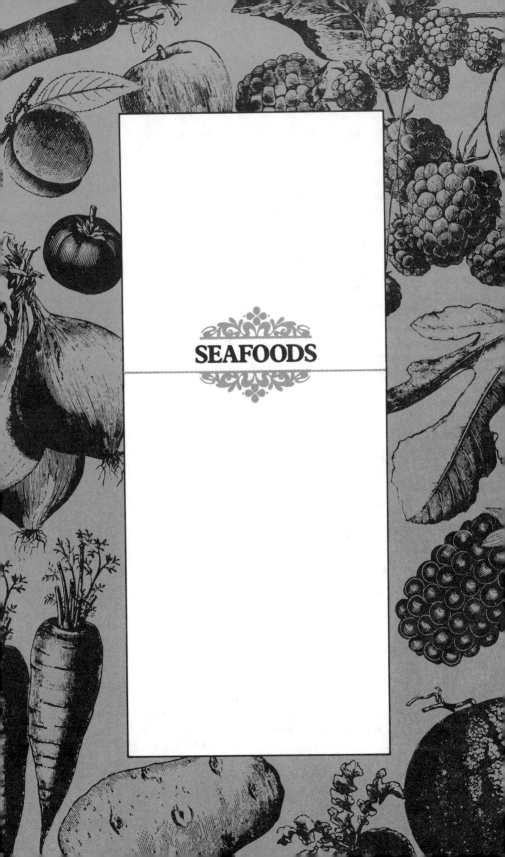

SEAFOODS

Deviled Crab

2   pounds King crabmeat, cut into bite-size pieces
6   tablespoons butter
1   cup flour
3/4   cup half and half cream
6   hard-cooked eggs, chopped
2   tablespoons Dijon mustard
1   tablespoon dry mustard
2   ounce can chopped pimentos, drained
1/4   cup Worcestershire sauce (or more)
    Dash Tabasco
    Salt and pepper, to taste
1   cup Parmesan cheese, freshly grated

In a saucepan melt the butter and add the flour, stirring constantly, until mixture thickens. Add the cream and stir with a wire whisk until mixture is consistency of a thick cream sauce. Add the remaining ingredients, except the cheese, and transfer to a lightly greased baking dish. Sprinkle with the cheese and bake at 400° for 15 to 20 minutes. Serves 6–8.

Little Mushroom Crabmeat Crêpes

1   pound King crabmeat, cut into bite-size pieces
1/2   stick butter
4   green onions, tops and bottoms, chopped
1   small yellow onion, chopped
4   ribs celery, chopped
1   small green pepper, chopped
4   cups milk
4   tablespoons cornstarch
2   teaspoons chicken soup base
1   cup Velveeta cheese
1/2   cup Parmesan cheese, freshly grated

In a skillet sauté the onions, celery and green pepper in butter until soft. In a saucepan heat the milk. Add the cornstarch and soup base stirring constantly with a wire whisk until mixture thickens to a cream sauce consistency. Reduce the heat and add the Velveeta cheese. Simmer until cheese is melted. Combine the crabmeat and the onion mixture. Add enough sauce to bind. Place a small amount of filling in each crêpe and roll. Place in a lightly greased shallow baking dish side by side. Top with the remaining sauce and sprinkle with Parmesan cheese. Bake at 350° for about 20 minutes or until heated through.

CRÊPE BATTER

1   cup flour
     Dash salt
2   eggs
2   tablespoons butter, melted
2   cups milk

In a bowl sift the flour and the salt together. Add the eggs, butter and milk and beat with a mixer until smooth. Lightly butter a small skillet or crêpe pan with a pastry brush. Pour a small amount of batter into the pan and roll it out to the edge of the pan. Cook like pancakes, turning once until lightly browned.

Little Mushroom Crabmeat Divan

1   pound King crabmeat, cut into bite-size pieces
1   cup Hellmann's mayonnaise
3   cups cream of chicken soup
1   tablespoon curry powder
1   cup Cheddar cheese, grated
1/2 cup seasoned bread crumbs
2   packages frozen chopped broccoli

Cook broccoli according to the directions on the package. Drain and place on the bottom of a lightly greased casserole dish or on the bottom of individual oval au gratin dishes. Combine crabmeat, mayonnaise, soup and curry powder. Pour over broccoli and top with cheese and bread crumbs. Bake at 350° for about 30 minutes or until bubbly. Serves 8.

GOURMET HELPER—To freeze fresh mushrooms, wash and dry quickly, place in a plastic bag and place in freezer. Do not defrost before using—you can't tell by the taste that they have been frozen.

Crabmeat Lasagna

8   ounce package lasagna noodles
1   tablespoon oil
2   cups cream of mushroom soup
1   pound King crabmeat
2   16-ounce cartons cream-style cottage cheese
8   ounce package cream cheese, softened
1   onion, chopped
1   egg, slightly beaten
1   teaspoon basil
1   teaspoon salt
1/4 teaspoon white pepper
2   teaspoons sugar
4   ripe tomatoes, peeled and sliced
1   cup Cheddar cheese, grated

Slide noodles, a few at a time, into boiling water. Add oil and cook 15 minutes. Drain in colander under running cold water. In a saucepan combine the soup and crabmeat and heat until bubbly. In a bowl combine the cottage cheese, cream cheese, onion, egg, basil, salt and pepper and sugar. In a greased 13″ x 9″ x 2″ casserole dish place a layer of noodles; add half the soup mixture, a layer of tomato slices and half the cottage cheese mixture. Repeat layers and top with Cheddar cheese. Bake at 350° about 1 hour or until bubbly. Serves 8.

Crabmeat Nantucket

1   pound King crabmeat, cut into bite-size pieces
1/2 cup mayonnaise
8   ounce package cream cheese, softened
2   egg yolks, lightly beaten
1   onion, chopped
1/2 teaspoon prepared mustard
2   teaspoons chili sauce

Preheat oven to 350°. Combine the crabmeat and mayonnaise and mix well. Combine the remaining ingredients and fold into the crabmeat mixture. Transfer to a lightly buttered shallow baking dish and bake for 30 minutes or until bubbly. Serves 6.

Crabmeat Brie Souffle

1/2	stick butter
2	shallots, chopped
3	tablespoons flour
1	cup milk
1/2	teaspoon salt
	Dash dry mustard
	Dash cayenne pepper
4	egg yolks
1	cup Brie cheese, rind removed and grated (if too soft to grate, cut into small pieces)
1	pound King crabmeat, cut into bite-size pieces
5	egg whites
	Pinch cream of tartar
1/8	teaspoon salt
1/2	cup grated Parmesan cheese

Preheat oven to 400°. Butter a 1 quart souffle dish. In a heavy skillet saute the shallots in the butter until soft. Stir in the flour and cook for 3 minutes. Add the next 4 ingredients and stir until the sauce is thick and smooth. Remove from the heat and cool for 5 minutes. Beat in the egg yolks one at a time. Add the cheese and cook on a low fire until the cheese is melted. Fold in the crabmeat and cool. Beat the egg whites until frothy. Add the cream of tartar and salt and beat until stiff peaks form. Fold the souffle mixture gently into the egg whites and turn into the souffle dish. Sprinkle with the cheese and lower the oven to 375°. Bake for 30 minutes or until set.

GOURMET HELPER—Remove fish from the refrigerator at least 1/2 hour before cooking it.

Crabmeat Artichoke Bake

¹/₂   stick butter
¹/₂   pound fresh mushrooms, thinly sliced
2   tablespoons flour
1³/₄   cups half and half cream
¹/₂   teaspoon chicken soup base
¹/₂   cup dry sherry
2   cups grated Gruyere cheese
¹/₄   teaspoon thyme
¹/₄   teaspoon Worcestershire sauce
      Dash Tabasco
1   pound King crabmeat, cut into bite-size pieces
2   14 ounce cans artichoke hearts, drained and sliced
¹/₂   cup grated Parmesan cheese

Preheat oven to to 350°. In a large skillet saute the mushrooms in the butter until soft. Add the flour and cook, stirring, until the roux is lightly brown. Add the next 7 ingredients and cook, stirring, until the sauce is smooth and thick. Remove from the heat and fold in the crabmeat. Line a shallow baking dish with the artichoke hearts. Pour the crabmeat mixture on top and sprinkle with the cheese. Bake for 30 minutes or until bubbly. Serves 6-8.

In a Hurry Crabmeat Macaroni Bake—Combine 1 package frozen macaroni and cheese, thawed; 1 cup crabmeat; 1 teaspoon dried onion flakes; ¹/₄ cup sherry; and 1 can cream of shrimp soup. Season with salt and pepper and place in a baking dish. Top with buttered bread crumbs and bake at 350° for 20 minutes. Serves 2 generously.

Crabmeat Enchiladas

4   ounce can green chilies, drained
2   canned jalapeno peppers, seeded
2   10-ounce cans green tomatoes, drained (reserve liquid)
2   teaspoons cumin
2   teaspoons chili powder
2   teaspoons coriander (cilantro)
2   cups heavy cream
2   eggs, lightly beaten
1   pound King crabmeat, cut into bite-size pieces
1   pound cream cheese, softened
6   green onions, tops and bottoms, chopped
      Oil
12   corn tortillas
1   pint sour cream, at room temperature

Preheat oven to 350°. In a blender or food processor puree the first 6 ingredients. The mixture should be the consistency of heavy cream. If too thick dilute with the reserved tomato liquid. Transfer to a bowl and add the cream, eggs and salt to taste. Transfer to a saucepan and simmer, covered, over low heat until heated through. Combine the crabmeat, cream cheese and onions and mix well. In a large skillet heat the oil. Dip each tortilla in the oil until they are pliable but not crisp. Drain on paper toweling. Spread 1 tablespoon chili mixture and 3 tablespoons crabmeat mixture on each tortilla. Roll and place seam side down in the bottom of a shallow baking dish. Pour the remaining sauce over the tortillas and bake, uncovered, for 30 minutes. Top with sour cream and serve.

Crabmeat Thermidor

1/2   stick butter
4   green onions, tops and bottoms, chopped
1   small onion, chopped
4   ribs celery, chopped
1   small green pepper, chopped
3   tablespoons flour
1   can cream of shrimp soup
1   cup evaporated milk
1/4   cup sauterne
1/2   teaspoon thyme
1/2   cup grated Monterey Jack cheese
1   pound King crabmeat, cut into bite-size pieces
1/2   cup grated Parmesan cheese

Preheat oven to 350°. In a large heavy skillet saute the onions, celery and green peppers in the butter until soft. Add the flour and cook, stirring, until the roux is light brown. Add the next 5 ingredients and simmer, covered, until heated through. Fold in the crabmeat and season with salt and pepper. Top with the cheese and bake for 20 minutes or until bubbly. Serves 6.

GOURMET HELPER—To thaw frozen fish, thaw slowly in the refrigerator instead of at room temperature.

Crabmeat Sour Cream Quiche

9" partially baked pie shell (bake 10 minutes in a preheated 400°
     oven)
2   eggs, lightly beaten
1   tablespoon flour
1/2 cup mayonnaise
1/2 cup sour cream
1   pound King crabmeat, cut into bite-size pieces
2   cups grated Monterey Jack cheese
6   green onions, tops and bottoms, chopped
4   ounce can diced green chilies, drained
     Dash Angostura bitters
     Dash nutmeg

Preheat oven to 350°. Combine the eggs and flour and with a wire whisk beat
in the mayonnaise. Add the sour cream and mix well. Add the remaining ingredients and turn into the prepared pie shell. Bake for 45 minutes or until set.

Mexican Crabmeat Quiche

CRUST

1/2 package piecrust mix
1   teaspoon chili powder
2   tablespoons cold water

FILLING

1   cup grated sharp Cheddar cheese
1   cup grated Monterey Jack cheese
1   pound King crabmeat, cut into bite-size pieces
3   eggs, lightly beaten
1   teaspoon salt
1   teaspoon chili powder
1/2 teaspoon cumin
1 1/2 cups half and half
4   ounce can diced green chilies, drained
1/4 cup sliced ripe olives
4   green onions, tops and bottoms, chopped

Preheat oven to 350°. Combine the piecrust mix with the chili powder. Add
water and mix with a fork until dough holds together. Form into a smooth ball
and roll out on a floured surface until 1 1/2" larger than an inverted 9" pie pan.
Ease the dough into the pan and flute the edges. Combine the cheeses and

spread on the bottom of the shell. Sprinkle the crabmeat over the cheese. Combine the remaining ingredients and pour over the crabmeat. Bake for 40 minutes or until a knife inserted in the center comes out clean. Cool slightly and cut into wedges to serve.

In a Hurry Crabmeat in Pastry—Bake 8 frozen puff pastry shells according to package directions. Combine 1 pound crabmeat, 2 5-ounce jars Old English cheese spread, 1½ sticks softened butter and 1 tablespoon garlic powder in a saucepan and simmer until heated through. Fill shells with mixture and broil until bubbly.

Crabmeat Rice Bake

6   slices bacon cooked crisp, drained and crumbled (reserve
    bacon drippings)
1   onion, chopped
4   ribs celery, chopped
1   small green pepper, chopped
2   garlic cloves, minced
1   pound King crabmeat, cut into bite-size pieces
4   cups cooked rice
¼   teaspoon chicken soup base
½   cup mayonnaise
2   cups sour cream

Preheat oven to 350°. In a large heavy skillet saute the onion, celery, green pepper and garlic in the bacon drippings until soft. Add the crabmeat, rice and soup base and heat thoroughly. Remove from the heat and stir in the mayonnaise, sour cream and bacon. Season with salt and pepper and transfer to a baking dish and bake for 30 minutes or until bubbly. Serves 8.

GOURMET HELPER—To store fresh mushrooms, put them in a plastic bag, without washing them, and place in refrigerator.

Crabmeat Fettucine

1   pound carton sour cream or plain yogurt, at room temperature
1   cup cottage cheese, drained, at room temperature
6   green onions, tops and bottoms, chopped
1   garlic clove, minced
1   teaspoon dillweed
1/2 teaspoon oregano
1/2 teaspoon Worcestershire sauce
12 ounce package flat noodles, cooked and drained
1   pound King crabmeat, cut into bite-size pieces
1   cup grated Gruyere cheese (or any white cheese)

Preheat oven to 350°. In a blender or food processor puree the first 7 ingredients and season with salt and pepper. In a greased shallow baking pan layer half the noodles, half the crabmeat, and half the sauce. Repeat. Top with the cheese and bake for 20 minutes or until bubbly. Serves 6.

Crabmeat Florentine

2   packages frozen chopped spinach, thawed and squeezed dry
4   green onions, tops and bottoms, chopped
1   pound King crabmeat, cut into bite-size pieces
1 1/2 cups grated Monterey Jack cheese
1 1/2 cups sour cream
1/2 cup tomato puree
1   cup Pepperidge Farm Cheddar & Romano Cheese Croutons, crushed

In a shallow baking dish layer half the spinach, half the onions, half the crabmeat and half the cheese. Season with salt and pepper. Repeat. Refrigerate overnight. When ready to bake top with the sour cream, puree and croutons and bake for 45 minutes in a pre-heated 325° oven. Serves 6-8.

GOURMET HELPER—To slice mushroom caps, use an egg slicer.

Crabmeat Avocado Bake

½   stick butter
6   green onions, tops and bottoms, chopped
2   tablespoons flour
2   cups evaporated milk
1   package Creamy Buttermilk Salad Dressing Mix
½   teaspoon tarragon
½   cup toasted, chopped almonds
1   pound King crabmeat, cut into bite-size pieces
2   avocados, peeled, seeded and sliced

Preheat oven to 350°. Saute the onions in the butter until soft. Add the flour and cook, stirring, until roux is light brown. Add the next 4 ingredients and stir with a wire whisk until sauce begins to thicken. Remove from the heat and fold in the crabmeat. Layer the avocados in the bottom of a shallow baking dish and top with the crabmeat mixture. Bake for 15 minutes or until bubbly. Serves 6.

Oyster Casserole

1   stick butter
3   green onions, tops an bottoms, chopped
3   ribs celery, chopped
2   pints raw oysters
    Salt
    Dash cayenne pepper
    Soda crackers, crushed
1   cup half and half cream
1   cup Monterey Jack cheese, grated

In a saucepan sauté the onions and celery in the butter. Place a layer of oysters on the bottom of a 2 quart baking dish. Top each oyster with the onion and celery mixture. Sprinkle lightly with salt and cayenne pepper. Top with a thin layer of cracker crumbs. Repeat layers, ending with cracker crumbs on top. Insert a knife blade around the edge of the dish and in the center in several places, pouring cream around the blade until all the cream is used. Bake, covered, at 400° for 30 minutes. Uncover, top with cheese, and bake 10 minutes more. Serves 6–8.

Scalloped Oysters

3   individual packets of saltines from a 16-ounce box
     (approximately 120 crackers) broken into bite-size pieces
1/2 stick butter, cut into pieces
1   pint fresh oysters, drained
1/4 teaspoon nutmeg
     Dash Tabasco
1 1/2 cups milk

Preheat oven to 350°. Cover the bottom of a 2 quart casserole with the crackers. Place pieces of butter over the crackers. Arrange the oysters on top and season with salt, pepper, nutmeg and Tabasco. Repeat until casserole is filled. Pour the milk over the mixture to 1/4″ from the top of the dish. Let sit for 30 minutes. Cover and bake for 1 hour. Serves 4.

Lobster Thermidor

6   large frozen lobster tails
1 1/2 sticks butter
1/2 pound fresh mushrooms, thinly sliced
1/2 cup flour
1 1/2 cups evaporated milk
1/4 cup water
1   tablespoon lemon juice
1/8 teaspoon cayenne pepper
     Salt, to taste
2   egg yolks, lightly beaten
1/4 cup sherry
     Parmesan cheese, freshly grated

Boil lobster tails according to the directions on the package. Remove from pot and let cool. Remove the meat from the tails, dice, and reserve the shells. In the top of a double boiler melt the butter. Add the mushrooms and sauté them until soft. Add the flour and stir until smooth. Add the milk and water stirring with a wire whisk until the sauce thickens. Add the lemon juice, cayenne pepper and salt, to taste. Stir a little of the sauce into the egg yolks. Add the remaining sauce and stir until well blended. Add the lobster and the sherry and place mixture in the shells. Sprinkle with the cheese and bake at 450° about 15 minutes. Serves 6.

Dijon Salmon

3/4 cup vermouth
3/4 cup milk
4   green onions, tops and bottoms, chopped
1 1/2 teaspoons salt
8   salmon steaks

MUSTARD SAUCE
2   cups sour cream
1   small onion, grated
3   tablespoons Dijon mustard
2   tablespoons finely chopped parsley
2   teaspoons tarragon

Combine the first 4 ingredients and marinate the salmon, covered, in the refrigerator overnight. Drain and place in a buttered baking dish. Broil 6″ below
heat for 7 minutes. Combine all the sauce ingredients and spread on the salmon
on the side that was facing down. Broil for 7 more minutes or until fish flakes
easily when tested with a fork.

Coquilles St. Jacques

1   cup dry white wine
1/2 teaspoon salt
1/2 bay leaf, remove stem and crush
4   green onions, tops and bottoms, chopped
1   pound fresh scallops, sliced
1/2 pound fresh mushrooms, thinly sliced
3   tablespoons butter
4   tablespoons flour
3/4 cup milk
2   egg yolks
1/2 cup heavy cream
1   tablespoon lemon juice
     Salt and pepper white, to taste
     Swiss cheese, grated

In a saucepan simmer the wine, salt, bay leaf and onions. Add the scallops,
mushrooms and water to barely cover. Simmer for about 5 minutes. Remove
the scallops and the mushrooms and continue to boil until the liquid boils
down to 1 cup. In a saucepan melt the butter and add the flour stirring to a
smooth paste. Reduce the heat and add the wine mixture and the milk and boil

for 1 minute. Add egg yolks and cream and slowly beat in hot sauce mixture. Add lemon juice and salt and pepper, to taste. Strain the sauce and add the scallops and mushrooms. Pour into a lightly greased casserole dish, or individual ramekins, and top with the cheese. Bake at 400° until bubbly and lightly browned.

Scallops Vermouth

4   slices bacon cooked crisp, drained and crumbled
1/2 cup finely chopped parsley
3   shallots, chopped
2   garlic cloves, minced
1   teaspoon oregano
1 1/2 pounds scallops, seasoned with salt and pepper
1/4 cup olive oil
1/2 stick butter
1   cup dry vermouth

Combine the first 5 ingredients and mix well. In a large heavy skillet saute the scallops in the oil and butter, turning, for 5 minutes or until lightly browned on all sides. Add the bacon mixture and with a slotted spoon transfer the scallops to a heated platter and keep warm. Add the vermouth to the same skillet and cook the sauce at a high heat, stirring constantly, until the wine is reduced by half. Season with salt and pepper and pour over the scallops. Serves 4.

Baked Red Snapper

8   fresh red snapper fillets
2   tablespoons butter
1   bunch green onions, tops and bottoms, chopped
4   carrots, cooked and sliced thin
3   potatoes, cooked, peeled and sliced thin
     Juice of 1 lemon
2   8-ounce cans tomato sauce
2   8-ounce cartons sour cream

Season fish with salt and white pepper. Sauté the onions in the butter until soft and mix all the vegetables together in the butter. In a lightly greased shallow baking dish place the vegetables on the bottom of the dish. Place fish on top and sprinkle with lemon juice. Combine the tomato sauce and sour cream and pour the sauce over the fish. Bake at 350° for 40 minutes. Serves 8.

Acapulco Baked Red Snapper

¹/₂ stick butter
1   onion, thinly sliced
2   garlic cloves, minced
4   cups peeled, diced tomatoes
¹/₂ teaspoon crushed red pepper
1   tablespoon coriander (cilantro)
1   tablespoon cumin
1   bay leaf
8   red snapper fillets

Preheat oven to 350°. In a large skillet saute the onion and garlic in the butter until soft. Add the remaining ingredients, except the fish, and bring to a boil. Reduce heat and simmer, uncovered, for 10 minutes. Place fish in a shallow baking dish and season with salt. Pour sauce over the fish and bake for 30 minutes or until fish flakes easily when tested with a fork.

Red Snapper Vera Cruz

8   red snapper fillets
1   cup flour, seasoned with salt and pepper
1   stick butter
2   12-ounce jars green chili sauce
2   cups grated Monterey Jack cheese
2   tablespoons finely chopped parsley

Preheat oven to 350°. Coat the fish with the seasoned flour and saute in the butter until browned. Transfer to a shallow baking dish and top with the chili sauce. Sprinkle with the cheese and bake for 30 minutes or until fish flakes easily when tested with a fork. Sprinkle with parsley and serve.

In a Hurry Spicy Fillet of Sole—Spread 1 package Rondele Cheese spiced with Garlic and Herbs on 4 fillet of sole and roll up. Place in a baking dish and pour ²/₃ cup white wine over the fish and top with 4 slices of lemon. Bake for 30 minutes or until fish flakes easily when tested with a fork.

Fillet of Sole Gruyere

1   stick butter
1   onion, sliced
1/2   pound fresh mushrooms, thinly sliced
2   cups grated Gruyere cheese
8   fillet of sole
1/4   cup finely chopped parsley

Preheat oven to 400°. In a skillet saute the onion and the mushrooms in the butter until soft. Place half the mixture in the bottom of a shallow baking dish and sprinkle with half the cheese. Fold each fillet in half and place over the onion mixture. Season with salt and pepper. Top with the remaining onion mixture and remaining cheese and season with salt and pepper. Bake for 30 minutes or until fish flakes easily when tested with a fork. Sprinkle with the parsley and serve.

Busy Day Fillet of Sole

8   fillet of sole, seasoned with salt and pepper
1   onion, thinly sliced
1   stick butter
3   cups mayonnaise
1   cup Dijon mustard
1/2   cup dry vermouth

Preheat oven to 350°. Arrange the fish in a shallow baking dish and cover with the onion and the butter. Bake for 20 minutes or until fish flakes when tested with a fork. Combine the remaining ingredients and pour over the fish. Set the oven on BROIL and broil for 3 minutes or until bubbly.

In a Hurry Fillet of Sole—Beat 1 egg white until stiff. Combine 1/4 cup mayonnaise, 1 tablespoon Dijon mustard, 1/4 teaspoon salt, and a dash of cayenne pepper. Fold mixture into egg white. Place 4 fillet of sole in a lightly greased shallow baking dish and spread with the meringue mixture. Bake at 400° for 30 minutes or until golden brown.

Fillet of Sole with Bacon

6 slices bacon cooked crisp, drained and crumbled
4 green onions, tops and bottoms, chopped
1 pound can tomato sauce
1 teaspoon garlic salt
8 fillet of sole

Combine the first 4 ingredients. Arrange the fish in a shallow baking dish and cover with the tomato mixture. Broil for 5 minutes on each side or until fish flakes easily when tested with a fork.

Easy Fillet of Sole

8 fillet of sole, seasoned with salt and pepper
2 tablespoons lemon juice
1 cup grated Parmesan cheese
1 stick butter, softened
1/2 cup mayonnaise
4 green onions, tops and bottoms, chopped
  Dash Tabasco

Arrange fish in a shallow baking dish and sprinkle with the lemon juice. Broil the fish for 5 minutes on each side or until it flakes easily when tested with a fork. Combine the remaining ingredients and spread over fish. Broil for 2 minutes longer or until lightly browned.

Baked Fillet of Sole

6 fillet of sole
3 tomatoes, thinly sliced
1/2 cup seasoned bread crumbs
3/4 cup sauterne
3/4 stick butter
2 teaspoons lime juice
1/4 cup Parmesan cheese, grated

Season the sole with salt and white pepper. Arrange the tomato slices in a long shallow baking dish. Sprinkle with the bread crumbs. Place the sole on top. In a saucepan combine the wine, butter and lime juice and simmer until the butter is melted. Boil for about 5 minutes. Pour over the sole and sprinkle with the cheese. Bake at 400° until sole is flaky when tested with a fork.

Fillet of Sole Tarragon

1/2 stick butter
1/2 pound fresh mushrooms, thinly sliced
1   onion, chopped
1   tablespoon tarragon
8   fillet of sole, seasoned with salt and pepper
3   cups Italian style tomatoes
1   cup dry vermouth

Preheat oven to 350°. In a skillet saute the mushrooms and the onion in the butter until soft. Add the tarragon and mix well. Place fish in a buttered shallow baking dish and top with the onion mixture. Add the remaining ingredients and season with salt and pepper. Bake, covered, for 30 minutes or until fish flakes easily when tested with a fork.

Fillet of Sole Veronique

1/2 stick butter
1/2 pound fresh mushrooms, thinly sliced
48   seedless grapes, sliced
1   cup sour cream
1   cup mayonnaise
     Juice of 1 lemon
8   fillet of sole, seasoned with salt and pepper

Preheat oven to 350°. In a large skillet saute the mushrooms in the butter until soft. Remove from the heat and add the next 4 ingredients and mix well. Arrange the fish in a shallow baking dish and top with the sauce. Bake for 30 minutes or until fish flakes easily when tested with a fork.

Fillet of Sole Dijon

1   stick butter
1/2 cup wine vinegar
1   tablespoon Dijon mustard
2   teaspoons salt
2   teaspoons lemon juice
1   teaspoon savory
1/2 teaspoon pepper
1   garlic clove, crushed
     Dash Tabasco
8   fillet of sole, seasoned with salt and pepper

Preheat oven to BROIL. Combine all the ingredients, except the fish, and place in a saucepan. Simmer on low heat for 5 minutes. Place the fish in a shallow baking dish and pour the sauce on top. Broil the fish for 10 minutes or until fish flakes easily when tested with a fork.

Baked Fillet of Sole Parmesan

2   cups sour cream
1/2 package onion soup mix
2   cups Italian style bread crumbs
1/2 cup grated Parmesan cheese
1/4 cup finely chopped parsley
2   tablespoons Worcestershire sauce
8   fillet of sole, seasoned with salt and cayenne pepper
1/2 cup oil

Preheat oven to 500°. Combine the first 2 ingredients. Combine the next 4 ingredients. Dip the fish in the sour cream mixture, then in the bread crumb mixture and arrange in single layers in a greased shallow baking dish. Sprinkle the oil over the top and bake for 10 minutes. Turn and bake another 5 minutes or until browned.

Little Mushroom Italian Baked Shrimp

2   pounds shrimp, cooked and deveined
3   tablespoons olive oil
4   green onions, tops and bottoms, chopped
4   ribs celery, chopped
1   green pepper, chopped
3   garlic cloves, crushed
1   tablespoon fresh parsley, finely minced
1   tablespoon cornstarch
8   ounce can tomato sauce
1/2 teaspoon oregano
1/2 teaspoon sweet basil
1   cup Mozzarella cheese, grated
1/2 cup seasoned bread crumbs

In a saucepan sauté the onions, celery, green pepper, garlic and parsley in the olive oil until soft. Stir in the cornstarch and stir until well blended. Add the tomato sauce, oregano and basil and simmer for about 15 minutes. Taste for seasonings. In a lightly greased casserole layer the shrimp and the tomato sauce mixture. Top with cheese and bread crumbs and bake at 350° for about 30 minutes or until bubbly. Serves 8.

Little Mushroom Shrimp Florentine

2   pounds shrimp, cooked and deveined
1/2 stick butter
4   green onions, tops and bottoms, chopped
1   small onion, chopped
4   ribs celery, chopped
4   cups milk
4   tablespoons cornstarch
2   teaspoons chicken soup base
2   tablespoons dry sherry
2   packages frozen chopped spinach, cooked and drained
1/4 cup Parmesan cheese, freshly grated

In a skillet sauté the onions and celery in butter until soft. Set aside. In a saucepan heat the milk. Add the cornstarch and soup base stirring constantly with a wire whisk until mixture thickens to a cream sauce consistency. Reduce the heat and add the onion mixture and the shrimp. Simmer for about 20 minutes. Add salt and pepper, to taste, and the sherry. Place the spinach in a lightly greased casserole dish (or individual oval au gratin dishes) and pour shrimp mixture on top. Sprinkle with cheese and bake at 350° about 15 minutes or until bubbly. Serves 8.

Little Mushroom Curried Shrimp

2   pounds shrimp, cooked and deveined
½   stick butter
4   green onions, tops and bottoms, chopped
1   small yellow onion, chopped
4   ribs celery, chopped
1   small green pepper, chopped
4   cups milk
4   tablespoons cornstarch
2   teaspoons chicken soup base
1   tablespoon curry powder
2   tablespoons sherry
1   cup Velveeta cheese

In a skillet sauté the onions, celery and green pepper. Set aside. In a saucepan heat the milk. Add the cornstarch, soup base and curry powder stirring constantly with a wire whisk until mixture thickens to a cream sauce consistency. Reduce the heat and add the Velveeta cheese. Simmer until the cheese is melted and add the shrimp, onion mixture and sherry. Simmer for about 30 minutes. Taste for seasonings. Serve over rice with a variety of condiments such as shredded coconut, chopped peanuts, crisp bacon bits, raisins, dried ginger and, of course, chutney. Serves 8.

In a Hurry Shrimp Sherry Bake—Combine 1 pint half and half, 2 cups mayonnaise, 1 pound cooked shrimp, 2 tablespoons chopped onion, 3 chopped hard cooked eggs, ½ cup sherry, and an 8 ounce package prepared stuffing mix. Place in a greased baking dish and bake at 375° for 45 minutes. Serves 10 generously.

Quick Shrimp Curry

2   pounds shrimp, cooked and deveined
½   stick butter
1   onion, chopped
2   garlic cloves, minced
3   cans cream of mushroom soup
½   cup heavy cream
½   cup raisins
¼   teaspoon lemon juice
1   tablespoon curry powder
      Salt and pepper, to taste

In a saucepan sauté the onion and garlic until soft. Add the remaining ingredients, except the shrimp, and simmer for 30 minutes. Add the shrimp and simmer until heated thoroughly. Serve over rice with a variety of condiments. Suggested condiments: shredded coconut, chopped pecans, crisp bacon bits, and chutney. Serves 6–8.

Hurry Shrimp Curry

2   pounds shrimp, cooked and deveined
2   tablespoons butter
1   small onion, chopped
2   teaspoons curry powder
2   cans cream of shrimp soup
2   cups sour cream
      Salt and pepper, to taste

In the top of a double boiler sauté the onion and curry powder in butter until onion is soft. Add remaining ingredients and simmer until heated through. Serve over rice with condiments. Suggested condiments: shredded coconut, chopped pecans, crisp bacon bits, raisins, dried ginger and chutney. Serves 6–8.

Curried Shrimp

¹/₂   stick butter
1   tablespoon flour
1   tablespoon curry powder
¹/₂   cup catsup
1¹/₂ cups milk
¹/₄   cup sherry
2   pounds cooked shrimp

In a large heavy skillet melt the butter. Add the flour and curry powder and cook to a thick paste. Add the catsup and mix well. Add the milk stirring with a wire whisk until the sauce is smooth and thickened. Add the sherry and shrimp and season with salt and pepper. Heat through and serve over rice. Serves 6–8.

Shrimp Creole

1¹/₂ pounds shrimp, cooked and deveined
¹/₂   cup bacon drippings
4   green onions, tops and bottoms, chopped
1   onion, chopped
4   ribs celery, chopped
1   green pepper, chopped
4   garlic cloves, finely minced
¹/₄   cup fresh parsley, finely minced
2   tablespoons flour
2   6-ounce cans tomato puree
1   cup water
1   tablespoon sugar
1   tablespoon Worcestershire sauce
¹/₂   teaspoon thyme
1   bay leaf, remove stem and crush
¹/₄   teaspoon seafood seasoning
      Salt and pepper, to taste
¹/₈   teaspoon Tabasco
2   teaspoons gumbo filé

In a saucepan sauté the onions, celery, green pepper, garlic and parsley in the bacon drippings until soft. Add the remaining ingredients, except the shrimp and filé, and cook the sauce, uncovered, for about 30 minutes. Add the shrimp and heat thoroughly. Just before serving add the filé. Serve over rice. Serves 6.

Shrimp Jambalaja

2   pounds shrimp, cooked and deveined
2   tablespoons butter
1   onion, chopped
2   garlic cloves, finely minced
1   green pepper, chopped
1   tablespoon flour
2   tomatoes, peeled
1/2 cup water
1/2 teaspoon salt
1/4 teaspoon cayenne pepper
1/4 teaspoon thyme
1   tablespoon Worcestershire sauce
2   cups rice, cooked
1   cup tomato juice
1/2 cup Cheddar cheese, grated
2   tablespoons fresh parsley, chopped

In a saucepan sauté the onion, garlic and green pepper in the butter until soft.
Add the flour and blend thoroughly. Add the remaining ingredients, except
the cheese and parsley, and simmer for about 10 minutes. Transfer to a lightly
greased baking dish. Sprinkle with the cheese and parsley and bake at 350°
until bubbly. Serves 4–6.

Cheese Shrimp

1/2 stick butter
6   green onions, tops and bottoms, chopped
1   small green pepper, chopped
1   garlic clove, minced
2   tablespoons flour
2   fresh tomatoes, peeled and chopped
1/2 cup dry sherry or vermouth
2   cups heavy cream
1/4 teaspoon Tabasco
1/4 teaspoon dry mustard
1/2 cup grated Gruyere cheese
1   cup Mozzarella cheese
2   pounds cooked shrimp

Preheat oven to 350°. In a large, heavy skillet saute the onions, green pepper
and garlic in the butter until soft. Add the flour and cook to a thick paste. Add

the tomatoes and sherry and simmer for 10 minutes. Gradually add the next 3 ingredients and stir until smooth. Remove from the heat and add the cheeses and the shrimp. Transfer to a baking dish and bake for 20 minutes or until bubbly. Serves 6–8.

Oriental Shrimp

1/2	stick butter
2	ribs celery, sliced
1	green pepper, sliced
1	onion, sliced
1/2	pound fresh mushrooms, sliced thin
2	pounds raw shrimp
1/4	cup catsup
1/4	cup Worcestershire sauce
2	teaspoons sugar
1	tablespoon soy sauce
2	tablespoons dry sherry
1/8	teaspoon Tabasco sauce

In a large heavy skillet saute the celery, green pepper, onion and mushrooms in the butter until soft. Add the shrimp and saute until pink. Add the remaining ingredients and bring to a slow boil. Serve over steamed rice. Serves 6–8.

Shrimp Baked in Foil

8	ounce package cream cheese, softened
8	ounce package Roquefort cheese, softened
1	garlic clove, crushed
1	tablespoon finely chopped onion
1	tablespoon finely chopped parsley
1	tablespoon finely chopped chives
1/2	teaspoon tarragon
3/4	cup dry white wine
2	pounds raw shrimp
12	lemon slices

Preheat oven to 400°. Combine all the ingredients except the shrimp and lemon and mix well. Butter four 12″ square pieces of foil. Place fourth of the cheese mixture and fourth of the shrimp in the center of each piece. Cover with lemon slices. Bring the edges up and fold them together to make a tightly sealed package. Arrange on a baking sheet and bake for 20 minutes.

Sour Cream Shrimp Enchiladas

2   pounds shrimp, cooked, deveined and diced
2   tablespoons butter
1   onion, chopped
1   garlic clove, finely minced
16 ounces tomatoes, drained and chopped
8   ounce can tomato sauce
1/4 cup green chilies, chopped
1   teaspoon cumin
1/2 teaspoon oregano
1/2 teaspoon basil
1/2 teaspoon salt
1   package tortillas
2 1/2 cups Monterey Jack cheese
3/4 cup sour cream

In a saucepan sauté the onion and garlic in butter until soft. Add the next 7 ingredients and bring to a boil. Reduce the heat and simmer, covered, for 20 minutes. Remove from heat. Dip each tortilla in tomato mixture to soften. Place about 2 tablespoons diced shrimp and 2 tablespoons cheese on each tortilla. Roll up and place, seam side down, in a 13 1/2" x 8 3/4" x 1 3/4" baking dish. Blend sour cream into the remaining sauce mixture and pour over the tortillas. Sprinkle with remaining cheese and bake, covered, in a 350° oven for about 30 minutes or until heated through. Serves 6.

Shrimp and Green Chilies

1/2 stick butter
4   celery ribs, chopped
1   green pepper, chopped
1   cup tomato puree
1   can cream of shrimp soup
1/2 cup sour cream
4   ounce can diced green chilies, drained
1   cup grated Monterey Jack cheese
2   pounds cooked shrimp
3   cups cooked rice
1/2 teaspoon chili powder
1/2 teaspoon cumin
1   cup buttered bread crumbs

Preheat oven to 350°. In a large skillet saute the celery and the green pepper in the butter until soft. Add the next 5 ingredients and simmer, on low heat, until heated through. Add the shrimp and rice and transfer to a greased baking dish. Combine the chili and cumin with the bread crumbs and sprinkle on top. Bake for 30 minutes or until bubbly. Serves 6-8.

Shrimp Provencale

1   onion, chopped
1   small green pepper, chopped
2   ribs celery, chopped
1/2 stick butter
2   tablespoons flour
3   cups canned Italian tomatoes
1   cup plain barbecue sauce
2   pounds cooked shrimp

In a large skillet saute the first 3 ingredients in the butter until soft. Add the flour and cook to a thick paste. Add the next 2 ingredients and simmer, covered, for 30 minutes. Add the shrimp and heat. Serve over rice. Serves 6-8.

Shrimp in Mustard Sauce

1/2 stick butter
1   onion, chopped
1/2 pound fresh mushrooms, thinly sliced
2   tablespoons flour
2   teaspoons dry mustard
2   cups heavy cream
2   teaspoons prepared mustard
1   teaspoon salt
2   pounds cooked shrimp
2   ounce package Monterey Jack cheese with jalapenos, grated

Preheat oven to 350°. In a large heavy skillet saute the onion and mushrooms in the butter until soft. Add the flour and mustard and cook to a thick paste. Add the cream stirring with a wire whisk until sauce is smooth and thick. Add the remaining ingredients and transfer to a baking dish. Bake for 20 minutes or until bubbly. Serves 6-8.

Noodled Shrimp

2   shallots, chopped
6   green onions, chopped
1/2 pound fresh mushrooms, thinly sliced
2   garlic cloves, minced
1   stick butter
2   pounds raw shrimp
1   pound package medium flat noodles, cooked
1   cup grated Parmesan cheese
1   cup grated Romano cheese
1½ cups heavy cream
1/2 cup chopped parsley

In a large heavy skillet saute the first 4 ingredients in the butter until soft. Add the shrimp and cook until they turn pink. Transfer to a platter and keep warm. To the same skillet add the noodles, cheeses and cream and mix well. Combine the noodle mixture with the shrimp mixture and season with salt and pepper. Sprinkle with parsley and serve. Serves 6–8.

Shrimp and Mushroom Bake

1   onion, chopped
1   green pepper, chopped
2   ribs celery, chopped
1/2 pound fresh mushrooms, thinly sliced
1/2 stick butter
1   tablespoon flour
1   cup milk
8   ounce package cream cheese, softened
1   tablespoon garlic salt
1/8 teaspoon cayenne pepper
1   cup cooked rice
2   pounds cooked shrimp
2   cups grated Jarlsberg or Monterey Jack cheese

Preheat oven to 350°. In a large heavy skillet saute the first 4 ingredients in the butter until soft. Add the flour and cook to a thick paste. Add the milk and stir with a wire whisk until the sauce is smooth and thick. Remove from the fire and add the cream cheese stirring until the cheese is melted. Add the next 4 ingredients and transfer to a shallow baking dish. Top with the cheese and bake for 20 minutes or until bubbly. Serves 6–8.

Shrimp Fettucine

4   green onions, tops and bottoms, chopped
½   pound fresh mushrooms, thinly sliced
2   garlic cloves, minced
1   stick butter
2   pounds raw shrimp
2   teaspoons salt
12   ounce package flat noodles, cooked and drained
1   cup grated Parmesan cheese
1   cup grated Jarlsberg cheese
1½   cups heavy cream
¼   cup sour cream

In a large heavy skillet saute the onions, mushrooms and garlic in half the butter until soft. Add the shrimp and cook until pink. Season with the salt and transfer to a bowl. Cover to keep warm. In the same skillet melt the remaining butter. Add the remaining ingredients and heat slowly. Combine with the shrimp mixture and serve. Serves 6-8.

In a Hurry Shrimp Pot Pie—Combine 1 cup half and half, 3 ounce package softened cream cheese, 1 can peas and onions, drained, 1 package onion soup mix, 1 pound cooked shrimp, ¼ cup white wine, ⅛ teaspoon Tabasco, ½ teaspoon salt and ¼ teaspoon pepper. Top with a 1 pound package frozen tater tots. Bake at 425° for 30 minutes or until bubbly. Serves 4.

24 Hour Shrimp and Wine Bake

1   loaf day-old French bread, torn into small pieces
1/2 stick butter, melted
1   cup grated sharp Cheddar cheese
1   cup grated Monterey Jack cheese
2   pounds raw shrimp
8   eggs (seasoned with salt)
1³/₄ cups milk
1/4 cup dry white wine
6   green onions, tops and bottoms, chopped
1   tablespoon Dijon mustard
2   tablespoons Worcestershire sauce
     Dash cayenne pepper
1   cup sour cream
1   cup grated Asiago or Parmesan cheese

Spread the bread pieces on the bottom of a 9" x 13" shallow baking dish and drizzle with the melted butter. Layer with the cheeses and shrimp. Combine the next 7 ingredients and beat until the mixture is foamy. Pour over the shrimp and cover tightly with foil. Refrigerate for at least 24 hours. Remove from the refrigerator 1 hour before baking. Bake, covered, in a preheated 325° oven for 1 hour or until set. Uncover, spread with the sour cream and cheese and bake for 10 minutes longer. Serves 6–8.

Greek Shrimp

6   green onions, tops and bottoms, chopped
1   small green pepper, chopped
1   garlic clove, minced
2   tablespoons minced shallots
1/2   stick butter
1/2   cup dry vermouth
1   pound can Italian tomatoes
1   teaspoon oregano
1/2   teaspoon basil
8   ounces crumbled feta cheese
2   pounds raw shrimp
1/2   cup finely chopped parsley

In a large heavy skillet saute the first 4 ingredients in the butter until soft. Add the next 4 ingredients and simmer until the sauce is slightly thickened. Add the cheese and simmer for 15 minutes. Season with salt and pepper. Add the shrimp and simmer until the shrimp are cooked. Sprinkle with parsley and serve. Serves 6–8.

Roquefort Shrimp

1   stick butter
1   bunch green onions, tops and bottoms, chopped
1   small onion, chopped
4   ribs celery, chopped
3   tablespoons flour
1   can cream of asparagus soup
1   cup evaporated milk
1/4   cup dry white wine
1   package Roquefort or Blue Cheese Salad Dressing Mix
1/2   cup sliced water chestnuts
1   cup Roquefort cheese crumbles
1/2   cup grated Parmesan cheese
2   pounds cooked shrimp

Preheat oven to 350°. In a large heavy skillet saute the onions and the celery in the butter until soft. Add the flour and cook until the roux turns brown. Add the next 7 ingredients and simmer until sauce is thick and smooth. Add the shrimp and season with salt and pepper. Transfer to a baking dish and bake for 15 minutes or until bubbly. Serves 6–8.

Shrimp and Rice Bake

2   pounds raw shrimp
1   green pepper, chopped
1   onion, chopped
1   pound fresh mushrooms, thinly sliced
1/2 stick butter
3   cups cooked Uncle Ben's Long Grain and Wild Rice Blend
1/2 teaspoon thyme
1/2 teaspoon salt
1   teaspoon Worcestershire sauce
1/8 teaspoon Tabasco
1   can cream of shrimp soup
1/4 cup buttered bread crumbs
1/4 cup heavy cream

Preheat oven to 350°. In a large heavy skillet saute the first 4 ingredients in the butter until the shrimp are pink. Add the next 6 ingredients and mix well. Transfer to a baking dish and sprinkle with the bread crumbs. Pour the cream around the edges and bake for 30 minutes or until bubbly. Serves 6–8.

CHICKEN

Breast of Chicken with Artichoke Hearts

8   chicken breasts, boned and skinned
1/2 stick butter
1   onion, chopped
4   green onions, tops and bottoms, chopped
1   small green pepper, chopped
3   celery ribs, chopped
1   can cream of chicken soup
1/4 cup sauterne
1   tablespoon poultry seasoning
1/2 teaspoon chicken soup base
2   14-ounce cans artichoke hearts, drained
1   cup grated Swiss cheese

Preheat oven to 375°. Season chicken with salt and pepper. In a large heavy skillet saute the chicken in the butter until browned on both sides. Lower the heat and simmer, covered, for 30 minutes or until tender. Remove to a platter and keep warm. In the same skillet saute the next 4 ingredients, adding more butter if necessary, until soft. Add the next 4 ingredients and stir until well mixed and heated through. Place 2 artichoke hearts in individual ramekins or layer the bottom of a shallow baking dish with the hearts. Top with a breast and cover with the sauce. Sprinkle with the cheese and bake for 20 minutes or until bubbly.

Spicy Breast of Chicken

8   chicken breasts
2   envelopes Italian salad dressing mix
1/2 cup lime juice
2   sticks butter, melted
    Seasoning salt and pepper

Season chicken breasts lightly with seasoning salt and pepper and place in a shallow baking dish. Mix lime juice, salad mix, butter and pour over chicken. Cover and bake at 350° about 1½ hours or until chicken is tender. Remove cover 15 minutes before serving and brown.

In a Hurry Tipsy Chicken—Combine 1½ cups chili sauce, ½ cup currant jelly, 1 envelope French dressing, dash Worcestershire sauce, 1 bunch of chopped green onions, 2 minced garlic cloves and ¼ cup white wine. Place 1 fryer, cut into serving pieces, in a baking dish and cover with the chili sauce. Bake at 350° for 45 minutes or until chicken is tender.

Breast of Chicken in Chutney Sauce

8   chicken breasts
2   tablespoons flour (seasoned with salt and pepper)
2   tablespoons oil
2   pints heavy cream
2   tablespoons Worcestershire sauce
1/2   cup chutney
1/2   cup dry white wine

In the top of a double boiler mix the cream, Worcestershire and chutney. Cook over low heat for 1 1/2 hours stirring occasionally. Place the chicken breasts side by side in a baking dish. Sprinkle with the flour and the oil. Bake at 350°, uncovered, until browned. Add the wine and the hot sauce and pour over the chicken. Bake, covered, for 20 minutes longer or until chicken is tender.

Breast of Chicken Fiesta

8   chicken breasts, boned and skinned
1   cup crushed cheddar cheese crackers
2   tablespoons Taco Seasoning Mix
1   stick butter, melted
4   green onions, tops and bottoms, chopped
4   ounce can diced green chilies, drained
2   cups heavy cream
1   cup grated Monterey Jack cheese
1   cup grated Cheddar cheese
1/2   teaspoon chicken soup base

Preheat oven to 350°. Combine the crackers and taco mix. Dredge chicken in the mix and place in a shallow baking dish. Sprinkle half the melted butter over top. In a heavy skillet saute the onions in the remaining butter until soft. Add the remaining ingredients and mix well. Pour over the chicken and bake for 45 minutes or until tender.

In a Hurry Stuffed Chicken Breasts—Prepare 1/2 package Pepperidge Farm cube stuffing according to package directions. Add 1 teaspoon poultry seasoning and 1/8 teaspoon cayenne pepper. Season 6 boneless chicken breasts with salt and flatten. Stuff 2 tablespoons dressing in each breast and place seam side down in a baking dish. Pour 1 bottle "1890" salad dressing over the chicken and bake for 45 minutes or until tender.

Breast of Chicken Dijon

8   chicken breasts, boned and skinned
1½ sticks butter
6   tablespoons Dijon mustard
1½ cups ground pecans
2   tablespoons oil
1½ cups sour cream

Preheat oven to 350°. In a skillet melt 1 stick of butter. Remove from the heat
and whisk in 4 tablespoons of the mustard. Dip each breast into the butter
mixture then into the pecans. In a large heavy skillet melt the remaining butter
and the oil. Saute the chicken on both sides until golden brown. Remove
chicken to a shallow baking dish, cover with foil, and bake for 30 minutes or
until tender. Pour off the remaining butter and pecans from the skillet and de-
glaze with the sour cream, scraping up all the browned bits from the bottom of
the skillet. Whisk the remaining mustard into the sauce and season with salt
and pepper. Transfer the chicken to a serving platter and cover with the sauce.

Quick Breast of Chicken in Orange Sauce

8   chicken breasts
2   eggs, lightly beaten
¼   cup orange juice
     Sesame crackers, crushed to cracker crumb consistency
     Salt and pepper
2   sticks butter, melted

Season the chicken breasts with salt (very little as the crackers are salty) and
pepper. Combine the eggs and the orange juice. Dip the breasts in the egg
mixture and roll in the cracker crumbs. Transfer breasts to a baking dish and
pour butter on top. Bake at 400° for about 25 minutes on each side.

In a Hurry Sweet n' Sour Chicken Breasts—Combine a 9-ounce bottle of
La Choy Sweet n' Sour Sauce, 1 jar of plum jelly and ½ teaspoon dry mustard.
Place 4 seasoned chicken breasts in a baking dish and cover with the sauce.
Marinate for several hours. Bake, covered, at 350° for 45 minutes or until
chicken is tender.

Breast of Chicken Mexicana

8   chicken breasts, boned and skinned
½   stick butter
1   onion, chopped
4   green onions, tops and bottoms, chopped
½   pound fresh mushrooms, thinly sliced
1   small green pepper, chopped
4   ounce can diced green chilies, drained
2   cups canned tomatoes
1   cup catsup
¼   cup sauterne
1   teaspoon chicken soup base
1   tablespoon cumin
1   tablespoon basil

GARNISH

1   cup sour cream

Preheat oven to 325°. Season chicken with salt and pepper. In a large heavy skillet saute the chicken in the butter until browned on both sides. Transfer to a shallow baking dish. In the same skillet saute the onions, mushrooms and green pepper until soft, adding more butter if necessary. Add the remaining ingredients and simmer for 1 hour. Pour sauce over the chicken and bake, covered, for 30 minutes or until chicken is tender. Top with sour cream.

In a Hurry Chicken Pot Pie—Place 1 cup cooked chopped chicken in the bottom of a baking dish. Place 1 package frozen carrots and peas, cooked, over chicken. Add 1 can cream of chicken soup, ½ cup milk and ½ package Pepperidge Farm herb stuffing mixed with ½ cup warm water and ½ cup melted butter. Season with 1 teaspoon onion flakes, 1 teaspoon salt, ½ teaspoon thyme, ½ teaspoon garlic powder and ⅛ teaspoon cayenne pepper. Bake at 350° for 1 hour.

Little Mushroom Breast of Chicken Stuffed with Wild Rice

8   chicken breasts, boned and pounded thin
2   tablespoons oil
3   cups Uncle Ben's Long Grain and Wild Rice Blend, cooked
4   slices bacon
¹/₄ pound chicken livers
¹/₂ stick butter
3   ribs celery, chopped
4   green onions, tops and bottoms, chopped
1   yellow onion, chopped

SHERRY CREAM SAUCE

4   cups milk
4   tablespoons cornstarch
2   teaspoons chicken soup base
¹/₂ cup sherry

In a saucepan heat the milk. Add the cornstarch and the soup base stirring constantly with a wire whisk until mixture thickens to a cream sauce consistency. Add the sherry and keep warm. In a saucepan sauté the bacon until cooked, but not crisp. Remove and drain on paper towels. Sauté the chicken livers in the bacon drippings until they are cooked. Remove and set aside. Sauté the onions and celery in the butter until soft. Combine rice, bacon, livers and onion mixture. Add just enough Sherry Cream Sauce to bind the mixture together. Season chicken breasts with salt and pepper. Fill each breast with the rice dressing and roll up, securing with a toothpick. Place breasts in a baking dish and sprinkle with the oil. Bake at 350°, uncovered, until browned. Pour sauce over the chicken and bake covered, for 1 hour or until tender.

In a Hurry Chicken in Sour Cream—Combine 2 cups cooked, chopped chicken, ¹/₂ cup mayonnaise, ¹/₂ cup sour cream, 2 chopped shallots, ¹/₄ teaspoon chervil, ¹/₄ teaspoon thyme, 1 cup grated Gruyere cheese and ¹/₂ cup grated Parmesan cheese. Combine all ingredients and place in a baking dish. Bake at 350° for 30 minutes or until bubbly.

Breast of Chicken Provencale

8   chicken breasts, boned and skinned
1/2 stick butter or 1/4 cup olive oil
1   small onion, chopped
4   green onions, tops and bottoms, chopped
1   garlic clove, minced
1   pound can Italian tomatoes
1   bay leaf
1   teaspoon oregano
1   teaspoon cumin
1   teaspoon chili powder
4   ounce can diced green chilies, drained
1/4 cup chopped ripe olives
1/4 cup burgundy wine

Season chicken with salt and pepper. In a large heavy skillet saute the chicken in the butter or oil until golden brown on both sides. Transfer to a platter and keep warm. In the same skillet saute the onions and garlic until soft. Add the remaining ingredients and stir until well mixed. Add the chicken and simmer, covered, for 1 hour or until chicken is tender.

In a Hurry Stir Fry Chinese Chicken—Stir-fry 1/3 cup raw, chopped peanuts, 2 crushed garlic cloves, 2 chopped green onions and 1 dried chopped chili pepper in 2 tablespoons peanut oil in a wok for 1 minute. Push mixture aside and stir-fry 1 cup white meat chicken cut into 1/2" strips (add more oil if needed) until chicken is slightly browned. Add 2 tablespoons soy sauce and 2 tablespoons sherry and cook for 1 minute longer. Serve over rice.

Breast of Chicken with Cherries

8   chicken breasts, boned and skinned and seasoned
     with Garlic Pepper Seasoning
¹/₂   stick butter
2   16-ounce cans dark sweet pitted cherries, drained (reserve
     liquid)
1   cup Port wine
1   tablespoon cinnamon
1   tablespoon sugar
1¹/₂ cups heavy cream
1   cup toasted almonds

Preheat oven to 350°. In a large heavy skillet saute the chicken in the butter
until browned on both sides. Transfer to a baking dish and bake, covered, for
45 minutes or until tender. To the same skillet add the cherry liquid and the
wine and simmer for 15 minutes. Add the next 3 ingredients and cook over a
high heat, stirring constantly, until sauce is thickened. Add the cherries. Pour
over the chicken, top with the almonds, and serve.

Breast of Chicken with Bing Cherries

8   chicken breasts
1   bottle French dressing
2   tablespoons oil
1   jar currant jelly
2   20-ounce jars Bing cherries
4   tablespoons frozen orange juice concentrate (undiluted)
2   tablespoons sherry

Marinate chicken breasts in the French dressing overnight. Pour off dressing
and place chicken breasts in a casserole. Pour oil on top and bake at 350°,
uncovered, until brown. Melt jelly over low heat. Add orange concentrate,
Bing cherries with juice, and the sherry. Pour over chicken and bake, covered,
for 1 hour or until tender.

Little Mushroom Chicken Breast with Pitted Cherries

8   chicken breasts
    Garlic salt
    Freshly ground pepper
    Paprika
1   stick butter
2   tablespoons flour
1   teaspoon sugar
1/4 teaspoon cinnamon
1/4 teaspoon dry mustard
16 ounce can red sour pitted cherries, drain and reserve juice
1   small can crushed pineapple, with juice
2   tablespoons dark rum
1   chicken bouillon cube

Season chicken with garlic salt, pepper and paprika. In a saucepan sauté the chicken in the butter until browned. Remove and set aside. Combine the flour, sugar, cinnamon and dry mustard and mix into the butter remaining in the saucepan. Add the cherry juice, chicken breasts, pineapple with juice, rum and bouillon cube. Simmer at 350°, covered for 1½ hours. Add the cherries and simmer for 10 minutes longer.

Breast of Chicken Normandy

8   chicken breasts, boned and skinned
1/2 stick butter
1½ cups dry white wine
4   tart green apples, cored, peeled and sliced (sprinkle with lemon juice)
2   teaspoons sugar
2   teaspoons cinnamon
1/4 cup Calvados brandy (apple brandy)
1   teaspoon chicken soup base
2   cups heavy cream

Season chicken with salt and pepper. In a large heavy skillet saute the chicken in the butter until browned on both sides. Add the wine and simmer, covered, for 30 minutes or until chicken is tender. Transfer to a platter and keep warm. To the same skillet add the apples, sugar and cinnamon and saute for 10 minutes. Add the brandy and de-glaze scraping up all the brown bits from the bottom of the pan. Cook for 5 minutes. Add the remaining ingredients and cook on medium heat until mixture turns a rich, ivory color. Season with salt and pepper and pour over chicken.

Breast of Chicken with Peanut Butter

8   chicken breasts, boned and skinned
1/2 stick butter
1   onion, chopped
1   small green pepper, chopped
1   pound can Italian tomatoes
1   cup smooth peanut butter
1/2 teaspoon thyme
     Dash Tabasco
1   cup chicken broth
2   bananas, peeled and cut into diagonal slices (cover with
     lemon juice)

Preheat oven to 350°. In a large heavy skillet saute the chicken in the butter until browned on both sides. Transfer to a shallow baking dish. In the same skillet saute the onion and green pepper until soft, adding more butter if necessary. Add the remaining ingredients, except the bananas, and heat slowly, stirring frequently. Season with salt and pepper and pour over the chicken. Bake, covered, for 45 minutes or until tender. Add the banana slices and bake 5 minutes longer.

Breast of Chicken Pina Colada

8   chicken breasts, boned and skinned
1   garlic clove, minced
1/2 stick butter
20   ounce can pineapple chunks, drained (reserve liquid)
1/4 cup dark rum
1/4 cup soy sauce
1/8 cup cream of coconut
1   teaspoon ginger
2   cups heavy cream
1   cup toasted coconut

Preheat oven to 350°. In a large heavy skillet saute the chicken and the garlic in the butter until the chicken is golden brown. Add the reserved liquid and the

next 4 ingredients and simmer, covered, for 30 minutes or until chicken is
tender. Remove the chicken to a platter and keep warm. To the same skillet add
the cream and cook over a high heat until the sauce is reduced by one-half.
Season with salt and pepper and add the pineapple. Pour over the chicken, top
with the coconut and serve.

Breast of Chicken with Honey

8   chicken breasts
1/2 cup oil
1/2 cup honey
1/2 cup white wine tarragon vinegar
1/2 cup chili sauce
2   tablespoons Worcestershire sauce
1   envelope dry onion soup mix

Preheat oven to 350°. Season chicken with seasoning salt and pepper. In a jar
place all other ingredients. Shake well. Place chicken in a single layer in a
shallow baking pan. Pour sauce over chicken and bake, uncovered, for 1 hour
or until tender.

Breast of Chicken Stuffed with Broccoli

8   chicken breasts, boned and skinned
1/2 stick butter
1   onion, chopped
1   package frozen chopped broccoli, cooked and drained
8   ounce package cream cheese, softened
1/2 cup grated Parmesan cheese
1/4 cup toasted and chopped walnuts
1/4 cup lemon juice
1   cup chicken broth
1/2 cup white wine
1   cup heavy cream
1   tablespoon flour
1   tablespoon butter

Preheat oven to 350°. In a large heavy skillet saute the onion in the butter until
soft. Add the broccoli and cream cheese and stir until well mixed. Transfer to a
mixing bowl and let cool. Add to the broccoli mixture the next 3 ingredients,
season with salt and pepper, and mix well. Season the chicken with salt and
pepper and place 2 tablespoons of the broccoli mixture in the center of each

breast. Fold over forming an oval. Place in a shallow baking dish, seam side down, and cover with the chicken broth and wine. Cover with foil and bake for 30 minutes or until tender. Transfer to a serving platter and keep warm. Pour the stock from the chicken into a skillet and over a high heat reduce the liquid by half. Add the cream and reduce the sauce by half again. Mix the butter and flour together and whisk into the sauce. Simmer until slightly thickened. Season with salt and pepper and pour over the chicken.

Breast of Chicken in Sour Cream Sauce

8   chicken breasts
1   tablespoon cinnamon and sugar mixture
1   teaspoon pure granulated garlic
1/4   teaspoon nutmeg
1   tablespoon soy sauce
1   tablespoon honey
1/4   cup sauterne
      Salt and pepper, to taste
2   shallots, sliced
1/4   pound fresh mushrooms, sliced
1/2   stick butter
4   tablespoons flour
2   cups half and half cream
2   cups sour cream

Season chicken breasts with cinnamon and sugar mixture, nutmeg and garlic. Cover with soy sauce, honey and wine. Season with salt and pepper. Bake covered, at 350° for 1 hour. Sauté shallots and mushrooms in the butter until they are tender. Add the flour, and the cream and stir until mixture thickens. Add the sour cream and warm but do not boil. Pour sauce over chicken and serve.

In a Hurry Chicken Breasts P.V.—Combine 2 10-ounce cans enchilada sauce, 1 4-ounce can green chilies, 1 teaspoon dried onion flakes, 1 teaspoon garlic powder and salt to taste. Place 4 chicken breasts in a baking dish and cover with the sauce. Bake at 350° for 45 minutes or until chicken is tender. (VERY SPICY).

Breast of Chicken in a Mustard Wine Sauce

8   chicken breasts, boned and skinned
1/2   stick butter
1   pound fresh mushrooms, thinly sliced
4   green onions, tops and bottoms, chopped
2   cups chicken stock
2   tablespoons Dijon mustard
1/4   cup white wine
1   tablespoon cornstarch
1   cup evaporated milk

Preheat oven to 350°. Season chicken with salt and pepper. In a large heavy skillet saute the chicken in the butter until golden brown on both sides. Transfer to a baking dish. In the same skillet saute the mushrooms and onions until soft, adding more butter if necessary. Add the next 3 ingredients and heat until bubbly. Pour over the chicken and bake, covered, for 30 minutes or until tender. Transfer chicken to a platter and keep warm. Pour stock from the chicken into the same skillet and heat. Combine the cornstarch with the milk and add to the sauce stirring constantly with a wire whisk until the mixture slightly thickens. Pour over the chicken and serve.

Breast of Chicken with Asparagus

8   chicken breasts
1   stick butter
1   pint sour cream
2   cans cream of asparagus soup
3   ounce can mushrooms, pieces and stems, drained
1/2   cup dry sherry
1   cup Parmesan cheese, freshly grated
19   ounce can whole asparagus spears

Season the chicken breasts with salt and pepper. In a sauce pan sauté the breasts in the butter until browned. Combine the sour cream, soup, mushrooms and sherry. Transfer the breasts to a baking dish and pour a fourth of the sauce over the breasts. Sprinkle 1/2 cup cheese over sauce. Place asparagus over cheese and add remaining sauce. Add the remaining cheese and bake at 350°, uncovered, for about 1 hour or until chicken is tender.

Breasts of Chicken with Sherry

8   chicken breasts
2   cans cream of chicken soup
2   cans sliced mushrooms
1   pint sour cream
1/2 cup sherry
1   tablespoon Worcestershire sauce
1/4 cup butter, melted
2   teaspoons salt
    Dash garlic powder

Place the chicken breasts in a lightly greased baking dish. Combine the remaining ingredients and pour over the chicken. Bake, covered, for 1 1/2 hours at 350°. Uncover and bake 30 minutes more.

Quick Marinated Chicken

8   chicken breasts
1   bottle dark Wish Bone Russian Dressing
1   package dry onion soup mix
10 ounce jar peach or orange marmalade preserves

Season the chicken breasts with salt and pepper. Combine the first 3 ingredients and mix until well blended. Layer half the sauce on the bottom of a shallow Pyrex dish. Place the breasts side by side on top. Pour remaining sauce over chicken, cover, and marinate in the refrigerator overnight. Bake, uncovered, at 325° for 1 hour or until chicken is tender.

In a Hurry Cranberry Chicken—Combine a 16-ounce can whole berry cranberry sauce, 1 package French dressing and 1 envelope onion dip mix (or onion soup mix). Place 1 fryer, cut into serving pieces, in a baking dish, and cover with the sauce. Bake at 350°, basting occasionally, for 45 minutes or until chicken is tender.

Breast of Chicken Caesar

8   chicken breasts, boned and skinned
1   cup flour, seasoned with salt and pepper
$1/2$ stick butter
1   onion, chopped
1   garlic clove, minced
    Juice of 1 lemon
$1/2$ cup apricot-pineapple preserves
1   cup chicken broth
1   teaspoon brown sugar
$1/2$ teaspoon nutmeg
$1/2$ teaspoon cinnamon
$1/2$ package Caesar Salad Dressing Mix

Preheat oven to 350°. Dust chicken lightly with the seasoned flour. In a large heavy skillet saute the chicken until golden brown on both sides. Transfer to a shallow baking dish. In the same skillet, adding more butter if necessary, saute the onion and garlic until soft. Remove from the heat and add the remaining ingredients stirring until well blended. Pour over the chicken and bake, covered, for 30 minutes or until chicken is tender.

Breast of Chicken Marsala

8   chicken breasts, boned and skinned
$1/2$ stick butter
$1/2$ pound fresh mushrooms, thinly sliced
$1/2$ teaspoon basil
$1/2$ teaspoon oregano
$1/2$ teaspoon rosemary
2   cups Marsala wine
10   ounce jar red currant jelly
2   cups sour cream

Preheat oven to 350°. Season the chicken with salt and pepper. In a large heavy skillet saute the chicken in the butter until browned on all sides. Transfer to a shallow baking dish. In the same skillet saute the mushrooms until soft. Add the next 4 ingredients and simmer, uncovered, for 10 minutes. Pour over the chicken and bake for 45 minutes or until tender. Transfer chicken to a platter and keep warm. In a saucepan melt jelly and stir in sour cream. Add sauce from chicken and mix well. Pour sauce over chicken and serve.

Breast of Chicken Mediterranean

8   chicken breasts, boned and skinned
1   cup flour, seasoned with salt, pepper and 1 teaspoon Italian
       seasoning
¼   cup crumbled feta cheese
3   ounce package cream cheese, softened
¼   cup finely chopped walnuts
¼   cup olive oil

SAUCE
½   cup olive oil
1   onion, chopped
4   ribs celery, chopped
½   pound fresh mushrooms, thinly sliced
1   garlic clove, minced
16   ounce can Italian tomatoes
1   cup dry red wine
½   teaspoon sugar
½   teaspoon chicken soup base
½   teaspoon oregano

Preheat oven to 350°. Pound chicken between pieces of wax paper to flatten.
Dredge in flour mixture. Combine cheeses and fold in walnuts. Place 2 tablespoons cheese mixture on each breast. Roll up and secure with toothpicks.
Close ends with toothpicks and saute in the olive oil until lightly browned on
both sides. Transfer to a shallow baking dish. In a large heavy skillet saute the
onion, celery and mushrooms in the oil until soft. Add the remaining ingredients and mix well. Pour over the chicken and bake, covered, for 30 minutes or
until the chicken is tender.

In a Hurry Chicken Stuffed Mushrooms—Combine 1 cup cooked,
chopped chicken, 3 ounce package cream cheese, ¼ cup mayonnaise, ½ cup
chopped walnuts, 1 tablespoon chopped chutney and 2 teaspoons curry powder. Stuff into 24 large mushrooms and bake at 350° until bubbly.

Little Mushroom Breast of Chicken Tarragon

8   chicken breasts
2   tablespoons flour, seasoned with salt and pepper
2   tablespoons oil
1/2 stick butter
4   green onions, tops and bottoms, chopped
1   yellow onion, chopped
3   ribs celery, chopped
4   cups milk
4   tablespoons cornstarch
2   teaspoons chicken soup base
4   tablespoons tarragon leaves
1   cup burgundy

Place chicken side by side in a baking dish. Coat with flour and sprinkle with the oil. Bake at 350°, uncovered, until browned. Sauté the onions and the celery in the butter until soft. Set aside. In a saucepan heat the milk. Add the cornstarch and the soup base stirring constantly with a wire whisk until mixture thickens to a cream sauce consistency. Add tarragon, burgundy and the onion mixture. Pour over the chicken and bake covered, for 1 hour or until tender.

Breast of Chicken with Port Wine

8   chicken breasts, boned and skinned
1/2 stick butter
1/2 cup raspberry flavored vinegar*
3/4 cup Port wine
2   tablespoons mustard with pink peppercorns*
2   cups heavy cream

Season chicken with salt and pepper. In a large heavy skillet saute the chicken in the butter until browned on both sides. Simmer, covered, for 30 minutes or until chicken is tender. Transfer to a platter and keep warm. In the same skillet cook vinegar and wine over a high heat until liquid is reduced by half. Add the mustard and beat with a wire whisk until dissolved. Add the cream and cook over a high heat until thick. Season with salt and pepper and pour over the chicken.

*Available in Gourmet and Specialty Food Shops. You may substitute regular vinegar and mustard or other flavors of your choice.

Breast of Chicken with Green Peppercorns

8   chicken breasts, boned and skinned
¹/₂ stick butter
2   shallots, minced
1   cup sauterne
2   cups heavy cream
1   teaspoon chicken soup base
2   tablespoons butter, softened
¹/₂ teaspoon Dijon mustard
4   teaspoons green peppercorns, drained and crushed

Season chicken with salt and pepper. In a large heavy skillet saute the chicken in the butter until browned on both sides. Add the shallots and saute for 5 minutes. Add the wine and de-glaze the pan. Simmer, covered, for 30 minutes or until the chicken is tender. Transfer to a platter and keep warm. To the same skillet add the cream and cook over a high heat, stirring constantly, until cream is reduced by half. Lower the heat and add the remaining ingredients. Season with salt and pepper and heat through. Pour over the chicken and serve.

Chicken Divan

2   packages frozen chopped broccoli, cooked according to the
     directions on the package
2   cups cooked chicken breasts, cut into large chunks
2   cans cream of chicken soup
1   cup Hellmann's mayonnaise
1   teaspoon lemon juice
¹/₂ teaspoon curry powder
¹/₂ cup Cheddar cheese, grated
¹/₂ cup soft bread crumbs
1   teaspoon butter, melted

In a lightly greased 2 quart baking dish, place a layer of broccoli. Combine the soup, mayonnaise, lemon juice and curry powder and spread on top of the broccoli. Place a layer of chicken on top of the soup mixture and sprinkle with the cheese. Mix the bread crumbs and butter and spread on top of the cheese. Bake, uncovered, at 350° for 30 minutes. Serves 6.

Breast of Chicken with Brandy

8   chicken breasts, boned and skinned
¹/₂ stick butter
2   cups dry vermouth
2   tablespoons brandy
2¹/₂ tablespoons peppercorn liquid
¹/₄ cup chicken stock
1   cup heavy cream
¹/₄ cup red wine vinegar
2   teaspoons sugar
¹/₄ cup Port wine
4   teaspoons green peppercorns
1   tablespoon chopped pimentos

Season chicken with salt and pepper. In a large heavy skillet saute the chicken in the butter until browned on both sides. Add 1 cup vermouth and simmer, covered, for 30 minutes or until tender. Transfer to a platter and keep warm. In the same skillet add the remaining vermouth and the brandy and bring to a boil. Boil for 5 minutes or until liquid is reduced by two-thirds. Add the next two ingredients and boil for 5 minutes. Add the cream, season with salt and pepper, and simmer until the liquid is reduced by one-third. While the sauce is reducing, combine the vinegar and sugar in a separate saucepan and boil for 1 minute or until mixture turns a dark caramel color and is the consistency of syrup. Add this mixture to the reduced cream sauce. Stir in the remaining ingredients and heat thoroughly. Pour over the chicken and serve.

In a Hurry Jalapeno Chicken—Combine 1 bottle Mexican style catsup, 1 package taco seasoning mix and ¹/₂ cup jalapeno jelly. Place 1 fryer, cut into serving pieces, in a baking dish and cover with the sauce. Bake at 350° for 45 minutes or until chicken is tender (VERY SPICY).

Curried Breast of Chicken

8	chicken breasts, boned and skinned
1	stick butter
1	onion, chopped
2	ribs celery, chopped
2	cups chicken stock
2	tablespoons flour
2	cups dry white wine
3	tablespoons curry powder
1	teaspoon salt
1/4	cup mango chutney
1/4	cup black currant jelly
2	apples, chopped
1/2	cup raisins

In a large heavy skillet saute the chicken, onion, and celery in the butter until the chicken is browned and the vegetables are soft. Add the stock and simmer, covered, for 45 minutes or until chicken is tender. Remove chicken to a platter and keep warm. Mix the wine gradually with the flour stirring to make a smooth paste. Beat into the chicken stock sauce with a wire whisk. Add the remaining ingredients and simmer until heated through. Pour over the chicken and serve.

Breast of Chicken with Roquefort

8	chicken breasts, halved, skinned and butterflied
8	ounce package cream cheese, softened
3/4	pound Roquefort cheese crumbles
1	stick butter
1/2	teaspoon thyme
8	slices Swiss cheese
4	egg whites, lightly beaten
1	cup flour, seasoned with salt and pepper
1	cup Italian seasoned bread crumbs
1	cup dry champagne
2	cups heavy cream

Combine the cheeses, 1/2 stick butter and thyme. Divide into 8 portions and pat into an oval shape. Wrap each oval into a slice of cheese. Place on one side of each breast, folding the other half over it and shaping chicken into an oval shape. Dip chicken into the egg whites, then dust with flour, then into the egg whites again, then into the bread crumbs. Repeat once more. In a large heavy skillet saute the chicken in the remaining ½ stick butter until golden brown on both sides. Lower the heat and simmer, covered, for 30 minutes or until the chicken is tender. Transfer to a platter and keep warm. To the same skillet add the champagne and cook over a high heat de-glazing the pan and scraping up all the browned bits from the bottom and sides of the pan. Cook until the champagne is reduced by half. Add the cream and cook over a high heat until reduced by half. Pour over the chicken and serve.

Chicken Stroganoff

8   chicken breasts, boned, skinned and sliced into julienne strips
    3″ x ¼″
1   cup flour, seasoned with salt, pepper, ½ teaspoon oregano and
    ½ teaspoon basil
½   stick butter
6   green onions, tops and bottoms, chopped
1   tablespoon chopped shallots
½   pound fresh mushrooms, thinly sliced
1   cup white wine
3   cups sour cream

Coat chicken with the flour and in a large skillet saute in the butter until opaque throughout and tender. Transfer to a platter and keep warm. To the same skillet add the next 3 ingredients and saute until soft, adding more butter if necessary. Add the wine and sour cream and season with salt and pepper. Simmer until heated through and pour over the chicken. Serve over rice or pasta. Serves 8.

Busy Day Breast of Chicken

8   chicken breast, boned and skinned
8   ounce bottle Russian salad dressing
1½   cups apricot-pineapple preserves
1   envelope onion dip mix or onion soup mix

Season the chicken with salt and pepper. Combine the salad dressing, preserves and mix and marinate the chicken in this mixture overnight, covered, in the refrigerator. Preheat oven to 350° and bake for 1 hour or until chicken is tender.

Garlic Chicken

40   garlic cloves, peeled (drop into boiling water for 1 minute;
     drain, rinse with cold water and peel)
1/2 cup oil
1   bunch green onions, tops and bottoms, chopped
4   ribs celery, chopped
1   cup finely chopped parsley
1   teaspoon thyme
2   fryers, cut into serving pieces
2   cups white wine

Preheat oven to 350°. Combine the first 6 ingredients and place on the bottom of a baking dish. Arrange chicken on top and season with salt and pepper. Cover with the wine and bake, covered, for 1 hour or until tender.

Chicken Munich

2   fryers, cut into serving pieces
1/4 pound bacon cooked crisp, drained and crumbled
     (reserve drippings)
1/4 cup olive oil
1/2 pound fresh mushrooms, thinly sliced
2   tablespoons chopped shallots
1/2 teaspoon thyme
1/4 teaspoon nutmeg
1   bay leaf
1 1/2 cups Port wine
1 1/2 cups heavy cream

In a large heavy skillet saute the chicken in the reserved bacon drippings and oil until browned on all sides. Add the mushrooms and cook for 5 minutes. Pour off all grease and add the next 5 ingredients. Simmer, covered, for 45 minutes or until chicken is tender. Add the bacon and the cream and cook until heated through. Season with salt and pepper and serve. Serves 8.

GOURMET HELPER—After stewing a chicken for diced meat for casseroles, etc., let cool in broth before cutting into chunks—it will have twice the flavor.

Orange Chicken

1/2 stick butter
2   tablespoons flour
12   ounce can frozen orange juice concentrate, thawed
1   cup honey
1/2 teaspoon sage
2   fryers, cut into serving pieces
1   cup flour, seasoned with salt, pepper and 1/2 teaspoon
     garlic powder

Preheat oven to 350°. In a saucepan melt the butter. Add the flour and cook to
a thick paste. Add the next 3 ingredients and heat through. Dust the chicken
with the flour and arrange in a baking dish. Cover with the honey mixture and
bake for 45 minutes, basting occasionally. Serves 8.

Sherried Chicken

2   fryers, cut into serving pieces
1   cup flour, seasoned with salt, pepper and 1 teaspoon poultry
     seasoning
1/2 cup oil
1   cup chicken stock
1/2 cup sherry
3   tablespoons dark brown sugar
1   teaspoon Angostura bitters

Preheat oven to 375°. Coat the chicken lightly with the flour and in a large
heavy skillet saute in the oil until browned on all sides. Transfer to a baking
dish. To the same skillet add the stock and sherry and bring to a boil, scraping
up all the brown bits from the bottom and sides of the pan. Add the sugar and
when it is dissolved remove from the heat. Add the bitters and pour over the
chicken. Bake, covered, for 45 minutes or until chicken is tender. Serves 8.

In a Hurry Chicken and Ham Roll-Ups—Place 6 slices cooked ham on 6
boneless chicken breasts. Roll up and secure with toothpicks. Put in shallow
baking dish and cover with 1/2 cup Durkee's and 1 can cream of mushroom
soup. Bake, covered, at 350° for 2 hours.

Chicken Oriental

1   cup chopped mango chutney
1   cup Dijon mustard
1   cup honey
3   tablespoons soy sauce
1   tablespoon curry powder
1   package Blue Cheese Salad Dressing Mix
2   fryers, cut into serving pieces
$1/2$ stick butter

Combine the first 6 ingredients and place in a plastic bag along with the chicken. Marinate for 24 hours turning the bag occasionally. Remove the chicken from the marinade and in a large skillet saute in the butter until browned on all sides. Simmer, covered, for 45 minutes or until tender. Transfer to a platter and keep warm. To the same skillet add the honey mixture and simmer until heated through. Pour over the chicken and serve. Serves 8.

Saffron Chicken

$1/8$ teaspoon saffron threads
1   garlic clove, crushed
$1/2$ teaspoon tumeric
$1/2$ teaspoon cumin
$1/2$ teaspoon ground ginger
$1/4$ cup olive oil
2   fryers, cut into serving pieces
$1/2$ stick butter
1   onion, sliced
1   cup chicken stock

Combine the first 6 ingredients and place in a plastic bag along with the chicken. Marinate for 24 hours turning the bag occasionally. Remove the chicken from the marinade and in a large heavy skillet saute in the butter until browned on all sides. Add the saffron mixture, the onion and the stock and simmer, covered, for 45 minutes or until chicken is tender. Serves 8.

GOURMET HELPER—For a brown crust on roasted chicken, rub mayonnaise generously over the skin before cooking.

Pineapple Walnut Chicken

1/2   stick butter, melted
1   tablespoon cornstarch
1   cup white wine
2   20 ounce cans pineapple chunks, drained (reserve liquid)
2   fryers, cut into serving pieces
1   cup flour, seasoned with salt and pepper
1   cup chopped walnuts

Preheat oven to 350°. Combine the butter, cornstarch, wine and pineapple liquid. Dust the chicken with the flour and arrange in a baking dish. Cover with the pineapple mixture and bake for 30 minutes. Add the pineapple chunks and walnuts and bake for 30 minutes longer or until chicken is tender. Serves 8.

Little Mushroom Chicken over Avocados

8   large, halved chicken breasts
2   celery stalks, including leaves
1   onion, quartered
2   cups mayonnaise
2   cups cream of chicken soup
1/2   teaspoon chicken soup base
1 1/2 tablespoons curry powder
2   or 3 avocados, peeled and sliced
2   cups Cheddar cheese, grated

In a large pot simmer the chicken breasts, in enough water to cover, with the celery, onion, and salt and pepper, until tender. Remove from the stock and cool. Debone and shred into bite-sized pieces. Strain the stock and refrigerate for another use. Combine the chicken, mayonnaise, soup, soup base and curry powder. Place a few avocado slices in each lightly greased individual au gratin dish. Pour chicken mixture over the avocados and top with the cheese. Bake about 20 minutes at 350° or until bubbly. Serves 8.

In a Hurry Barbecued Chicken—Combine 1 cup barbecue sauce, 1 cup orange marmalade, juice from 1 lemon, and several shakes of Worcestershire sauce. Place 1 fryer, cut into serving pieces, in a baking dish and cover with the sauce. Bake at 350° for 45 minutes or until chicken is tender.

Jalapeno Chicken Crepes

CREPE BATTER

4   eggs
2   cups milk
6   tablespoons melted butter
1/2 teaspoon salt
1   cup flour

In a blender or food processor combine the ingredients and blend until smooth. Chill. Brush a heated crepe pan with oil and pour about 2 tablespoons batter into the pan. Tilt to spread batter evenly. Cook for about 1 minute on each side. Makes 24 crepes.

FILLING

2   cups cooked chicken breasts, torn into bite-size pieces
2   tablespoons butter
2   tablespoons flour
1/2 teaspoon chicken soup base
1   teaspoon garlic powder
1   cup sour cream
2   tablespoons jalapeno peppers, seeded and chopped
1   cup grated Swiss cheese
2   8-ounce bottles mild taco sauce

Preheat oven to 350°. In a large heavy skillet melt the butter. Add the flour and cook to a thick paste. Add the remaining ingredients, except for the taco sauce, and stir until well mixed. Place about 3 tablespoons chicken mixture in each crepe and roll up. Place seam side down in a greased shallow baking dish. Cover with the sauce and bake for 30 minutes or until bubbly.

In a Hurry Onion Chicken with Sour Cream—Place one cut-up fryer in an oblong baking pan. Combine 1 can cream of mushroom soup, 1 cup sour cream, and 3 tablespoons dry onion soup mix. Spread over chicken and bake at 350°, covered, for about 2 hours.

GOURMET HELPER—When stuffing a turkey use the heel of a loaf of bread to hold the stuffing in the cavity.

Sour Cream Chicken Enchiladas

2   large chicken breasts
1/2 stick butter, melted
1   onion, chopped
1   garlic clove, minced
2   tablespoons butter
16   ounce can tomatoes, diced
8   ounce can tomato sauce
4   ounce can green chilies, drained
1   teaspoon sugar
1   teaspoon cumin
1/2 teaspoon salt
1/2 teaspoon oregano
1/2 teaspoon basil
1   teaspoon chili powder
1   package tortillas
2 1/2 cups Monterey Jack cheese, grated
3/4 cup sour cream

Preheat oven to 350° and bake chicken breasts with butter for about 1 hour. Remove skin and bones and sprinkle with a little salt. Cut into 12 strips and set aside. In a saucepan cook onion and garlic in the butter until soft. Add the next 9 ingredients and heat to a boil; reduce heat and simmer, covered, for 20 minutes. Remove from heat. Dip each tortilla in tomato mixture to soften. Place one piece of chicken and 2 tablespoons of cheese on each tortilla. Roll up and place, seam side down, in a 13 1/2" x 8 3/4" x 1 3/4" baking dish. Stir sour cream into the remaining sauce mixture and pour over the tortillas. Sprinkle with the remaining cheese and bake at 350°, covered, for 45 minutes or until heated through. Serves 6.

Chicken Mexicana

2 3-pound fryers, cut up into serving pieces
4 tablespoons oil
2 onions, chopped
2 garlic cloves, minced
1 tablespoon sesame seeds
1/2 teaspoon marjoram
1 cup burgundy
2 cups chicken consommé
1 cup blanched almonds
1/2 cup pimento-stuffed olives, sliced
2 teaspoons chili powder

Season chicken with salt and pepper. In a saucepan sauté the chicken pieces in oil until browned, turning 2 or 3 times. Remove and keep warm. Add the onions and garlic to the remaining oil and sauté until soft. Add the sesame seeds, marjoram and wine and simmer for about 10 minutes. Place the chicken, onion mixture and consommé in a baking dish. Sprinkle the almonds, olives and chili powder on top. Bake at 350°, covered, for 1½ hours. Uncover and bake 15 minutes longer. Serves 8.

Cream Chicken Tacos

8 large, halved chicken breasts
2 celery stalks, including leaves
1 onion, quartered
4 ounce can green chilies, chopped
1 onion, chopped
1/4 stick butter
2 tablespoons flour
2 cups tomato juice
1 tall can evaporated milk
2 cups Monterey Jack cheese, grated
3 tablespoons oil
1 package tortillas

In a large pot simmer the chicken breasts, in enough water to cover, with the celery, onion and salt and pepper, until tender. Remove from stock and cool. Debone and shred into bite-size pieces. Strain chicken stock and refrigerate for another use. Sauté the chilies and onion in butter until soft. Add flour and tomato juice and simmer until mixture is slightly thickened. In the top of a double boiler melt the cheese with the milk. Add to the tomato mixture and add the chicken. Place tortillas in hot oil and cook a few seconds, not allowing them to become crisp. Drain on paper towels. In a baking dish layer half the tortillas and half the tomato mixture. Repeat ending with the tomato mixture on top. Bake at 350° for 30 minutes or until bubbly.

Chicken and Tortilla Casserole

8   large, halved chicken breasts
2   celery stalks, including leaves
1   onion, quartered
1/2 can Ro-Tel tomatoes
1   can cream of mushroom soup
1   can cream of chicken soup
1/2 cup chicken stock
1   package tortillas, cut in strips
1 1/2 cups Cheddar cheese, grated

In a large pot simmer the chicken breasts in enough water to cover, with the celery, onion and salt and pepper, until tender. Remove from the stock and cool. Debone and shred into bite-size pieces. Strain the stock reserving 1/2 cup (refrigerate remaining stock for another use.) Combine the tomatoes, soups and stock. In a baking dish layer half the tortillas, chicken, tomato mixture and cheese. Repeat ending with cheese on top. Bake at 350° for 45 minutes or until bubbly. Serves 8–10.

Chicken Sour Cream Bake

4   cups cooked chicken breasts, torn into bite-size pieces
1   onion, chopped
3   ribs celery, chopped
2   cups toasted bread cubes
1 1/2 cups mayonnaise
1   cup sour cream
1   package Hidden Valley Ranch Dressing
2   cups grated Swiss cheese
1/2 cup sliced almonds

Preheat oven to 350°. Combine all the ingredients, except the almonds, and season with salt and pepper. Transfer to a baking dish, and bake for 30 minutes. Sprinkle with almonds and bake 15 minutes longer. Serves 8.

Chicken Macaroni Bake

4   cups cooked chicken breasts, torn into bite-size pieces
1   pound Jones sausage
1   onion, chopped
1   green pepper, chopped
2   tablespoons sugar
1   tablespoon chili powder
2   cups Italian plum tomatoes
2   cups buttermilk
2   cups uncooked macaroni

In a large heavy skillet brown the sausage. Saute the onion and green pepper in the drippings until soft. Add the remaining ingredients and simmer, covered, for 30 minutes, stirring occasionally, until macaroni is done. Season with salt before serving. Serves 8.

Chicken and Wild Rice Mix Casserole

3   cups cooked chicken breasts, large diced
1/2   stick butter
4   green onions, tops and bottoms, chopped
2   ribs celery, chopped
1   garlic clove, finely minced
1/2   pound fresh mushrooms, thinly sliced
1   cup Uncle Ben's Long Grain and Wild Rice Blend, cooked
1   can cream of celery soup
16   ounce can cut green beans, drained
1/2   cup mayonnaise
1   tablespoon pimento, chopped
5   ounce can water chestnuts, sliced
       Dash Tabasco
       Dash Worcestershire
1/2   cup Parmesan cheese, freshly grated
1/2   cup Monterey Jack cheese, grated

In a saucepan sauté the onions, celery, garlic and mushrooms in the butter until soft. Add to the cooked rice. Combine the remaining ingredients, except the cheeses, and mix until well blended. Combine the rice mixture and add the chicken. Transfer to a baking dish and top with the 2 cheeses. Bake at 350° for 30 minutes or until bubbly. Serves 6-8.

Chicken Lasagne

4	cups cooked chicken breasts, torn into bite-size pieces
3	cans cream of chicken soup
2/3	cup milk
1/4	teaspoon oregano
1/4	teaspoon Italian seasoning
1/4	teaspoon basil
1	onion, chopped
4	green onions, tops and bottoms, chopped
1	small green pepper, chopped
1	garlic clove, minced
3	ribs celery, chopped
1/2	stick butter
8	ounce package cream cheese, softened
1	cup cream-style cottage cheese
1/2	cup chopped pimiento stuffed olives
8	ounce package lasagne noodles, cooked according to package directions
1	cup grated Monterey Jack cheese

Preheat oven to 350°. Combine the first 6 ingredients and stir until well mixed. Season with salt and pepper. In a large heavy skillet saute the next 5 ingredients in the butter until soft. Add the soup mixture and mix well. Combine the next 3 ingredients. In a greased oblong baking dish layer half the noodles, half the soup mixture and half the cheese mixture. Repeat. Sprinkle with the cheese and bake for 30 minutes or until bubbly. Serves 8.

In a Hurry Cornish Game Hens—Combine an 8-ounce jar Dijon mustard with 3/4 cup bread crumbs. Spread over entire surface of 2 Cornish game hens. Spoon remainder into cavities and dot hens with a little melted butter. Bake in a pre-heated 350° oven for 1 1/2 hours or until hens are tender.

Chicken and Noodle Casserole

8   large, halved chicken breasts
2   celery stalks, including leaves
1   onion, quartered
8   ounce package thin noodles
1/2 stick butter
1   onion, chopped
3   ribs celery, chopped
1   green pepper, chopped
3   tablespoons fresh parsley, chopped
1   teaspoon poultry seasoning
1   teaspoon pure granulated garlic
1   can cream of chicken soup
1   package sour cream mix, prepared according to the directions
     on the package
1/2 cup Monterey Jack cheese
1/2 cup Cheddar cheese

In a large pot simmer the chicken breasts, in enough water to cover, with the celery, onion and salt and pepper, until tender. Remove from the stock and cool. Debone and shred into bite-size pieces. Strain the stock and return to the pot. Bring to a boil and add noodles; cook according to the directions on the package. Drain. In a saucepan sauté the onion, celery, green pepper, parsley, and seasonings in the butter until soft. Combine the soup and sour cream. Taste for seasonings. In a baking dish place the chicken, noodles, onion mixture, and soup mixture. Combine the cheeses and sprinkle on top. Bake at 350° for 30 minutes or until bubbly. Serves 8.

In a Hurry Cheddar Cheese Chicken Breasts—Combine 1 cup evaporated milk, 1 cup mayonnaise, 1 cup grated sharp Cheddar cheese and 1 teaspoon thyme. Place 4 seasoned chicken breasts in a baking dish and cover with the sauce. Bake at 350° for 45 minutes or until chicken is tender.

GOURMET HELPER—To truss a stuffed turkey, use dental floss to sew up the turkey—it won't tear the skin and holds better.

Chicken Broccoli Quiche

1   onion, chopped
3/4   stick butter
1¼   cups frozen chopped broccoli, cooked and drained
¼   teaspoon Worcestershire sauce
½   teaspoon basil
¼   teaspoon Italian seasoning
¼   teaspoon tarragon
⅛   teaspoon coriander (cilantro)
⅛   teaspoon cumin
⅛   teaspoon chili powder
⅛   teaspoon garlic salt
⅛   teaspoon cinnamon
3   eggs
2   cups half and half
½   cup grated Parmesan cheese
1   teaspoon nutmeg
1½   cups cooked, chopped chicken (use breasts)
2   cups grated Swiss or Jarlsberg cheese
1   partially baked pie crust (baked in a 10" x 2" quiche pan)

Preheat oven to 350°. In a large skillet saute the onion until soft. Add the next 10 ingredients and mix well. With an electric mixer beat the eggs until fluffy. Reduce speed and add the half and half, ¼ cup of the cheese and the nutmeg. Sprinkle the remaining cheese on the bottom of the pie crust. Layer the broccoli mixture, the chicken and the remaining cheese. Pour the egg mixture over the top and bake for 50 minutes or until set.

GOURMET HELPER—To turn a chicken when cooking use 2 wooden spoons rather than a fork so that the flesh will not be pierced.

Little Mushroom Hot Chicken Salad

8   large, halved chicken breasts
2   celery stalks, including leaves
1   onion, quartered
2   ribs celery, chopped
1   small onion, chopped
1/2 cup canned mushroom pieces and stems, drained
2   tablespoons pimentos, chopped
3   tablespoons almonds, chopped
3   hard-cooked eggs, chopped
2   cups mayonnaise
2   cups cream of chicken soup
1/2 teaspoon chicken soup base
2   cups seasoned bread crumbs
2   cups Cheddar cheese, grated

In a large pot simmer the chicken breasts, in enough water to cover, with the celery, onion, and salt and pepper, until tender. Remove from the stock and cool. Debone and shred into bite-size pieces. Strain the stock and refrigerate for another use. Combine the chicken and all other ingredients, except the bread crumbs and cheese, and transfer to a lightly greased baking dish. Sprinkle with the bread crumbs and top with the cheese. Bake at 350° for 30 minutes or until bubbly. Serves 8.

Quick Chicken Sesame

2   3-pound fryers, cut into serving pieces
1   stick butter
3   tablespoons oil
1/2 cup flour (seasoned with salt, pepper, poultry seasoning, and thyme)
    Sesame seeds
4   green onions, tops and bottoms, chopped
1   cup dry white wine

In a saucepan melt the butter and the oil. Dredge the chicken pieces in the flour, dip in the butter and coat heavily with sesame seeds. Marinate the onions in the wine and set aside. Transfer chicken to a baking dish and bake at 350° for 35 minutes. Pour the wine and onions over the chicken and bake 30 minutes longer. (A delicious gravy can be made from the residue in the bottom of the pan.)

Border Chicken

2   cans cream of chicken soup
1   onion, chopped
3   ribs celery, chopped
2   garlic cloves, minced
1/2 teaspoon chicken soup base
1 1/4 cups sauterne
12 tortillas, cut in strips
3   cups cooked chicken breasts, torn into bite-size pieces
7   ounce can diced green chilies, drained
2   cups grated Monterey Jack cheese

Preheat oven to 375°. Combine the first 6 ingredients and mix well. In a shallow baking dish layer the tortillas, chicken, chilies, cheese and soup mixture. Bake, uncovered, for 1 hour.

Chicken Curry

1   onion, chopped
2   garlic cloves, minced
1/2 stick butter
3   tablespoons flour
2   cups milk
3   cups cooked chicken breasts, torn into bite-size pieces
1/2 teaspoon chicken soup base
1   tablespoon curry powder
1/4 teaspoon garlic salt
1/4 teaspoon basil
1/4 teaspoon thyme
2   tablespoons lemon juice
1/4 cup apricot preserves
2   tablespoons sherry

In a large heavy skillet saute the onion and the garlic in the butter until soft. Add the flour and cook to a thick paste. Stir in the milk and beat with a wire whisk until mixture is smooth and thick. Add the remaining ingredients and simmer for 15 minutes or until heated through. Season with salt and pepper and serve over rice. Serves 6-8.

Chicken Curry II

2 5-pound stewing hens
6 cups chicken stock
1/2 cup raisins
3 tomatoes, unpeeled and quartered
1 stick butter
3 apples, cored, unpeeled and sliced
3 bananas, chopped
1 large onion, sliced
1/2 cup chutney
Curry powder, to taste

In a large pot simmer the hens, in enough water to cover, with salt, until tender. Remove the hens from the stock and cool. Remove the meat from the bones and shred into bite-size pieces. Strain the stock to measure 6 cups and pour into saucepan. Add the raisins and tomatoes and place on low heat. In a saucepan sauté the apples, bananas and onion and add to the stock mixture. Simmer, on low heat, for 3 to 4 hours. Put through a sieve or in blender. Let cool for several hours for seasonings to penetrate. When ready to serve add the diced chicken, curry powder and chutney and simmer slowly, about 30 minutes, until heated through. Serve over rice with condiments. Suggested condiments: shredded coconut, chopped peanuts, crisp bacon bits, raisins, dried ginger and chutney.

Chicken Rice Bake

1 package chicken noodle soup mix
2 cups water
1 cup raw rice
1/2 pound sausage
1 onion, chopped
1 green pepper, chopped
3 celery ribs, chopped
1/2 teaspoon chicken soup base
1 teaspoon curry powder
1 can cream of chicken soup
1/2 cup sliced almonds
3 cups cooked chicken breasts, torn into bite-size pieces

Preheat oven to 350°. Combine soup mix with water. Add rice and cook until tender. In a large heavy skillet saute the sausage. Add the next 3 ingredients and saute until soft. Add the remaining ingredients and simmer until heated through. Combine the sausage mixture with the rice mixture and season with salt and pepper. Transfer to a baking dish and bake for 30 minutes or until bubbly. Serves 6–8.

Quick Chicken and Rice

1/2   cup wild rice, uncooked
1/2   cup white rice, uncooked
1   can cream of mushroom soup
1   can cream of celery soup
1 1/2 cups milk
6   halved, chicken breasts
1/2   package dry onion soup mix

Sprinkle rice on the bottom of a lightly greased baking dish. In a saucepan combine the soups and the milk and heat. Pour over the rice. Top with the chicken and sprinkle with the onion soup mix. Cover and bake at 325° for 2 hours.

Chicken with Avocados

1/2   stick butter
4   tablespoons flour
1/4   teaspoon garlic salt
1/4   teaspoon onion salt
1/4   teaspoon basil
1/4   teaspoon marjoram
1/4   teaspoon thyme
1 1/2 cups milk
1   cup evaporated milk
2   tablespoons sherry
3   cups cooked chicken, torn into bite-size pieces (use breasts)
2   or 3 avocados, peeled and sliced
1   cup grated sharp Cheddar cheese

Preheat oven to 350°. In a large heavy skillet melt the butter. Add the flour and cook to a thick paste. Add the remaining ingredients, except for the avocados and cheese, and stir until well mixed. In the bottom of a shallow baking dish arrange the avocados. Cover with the chicken mixture and top with the cheese. Bake for 30 minutes or until bubbly. Serves 6–8.

Little Mushroom Chicken Madrid

8   large, halved chicken breasts
2   celery stalks, including leaves
1   onion, quartered
½   stick butter
½   bunch green onions, tops and bottoms, chopped
1   onion, chopped
2   cans cream of chicken soup
½   teaspoon chicken soup base
1   cup tomato puree
2   teaspoons chili powder
1   tablespoon cumin
1   tablespoon pure granulated garlic
1   package tortillas, diced
1   cup sour cream
1   cup sharp Cheddar cheese

In a large pot simmer the chicken breasts, in enough water to cover, with the celery, onion and salt and pepper, until tender. Remove from the stock and cool. Debone and shred into bite-size pieces. Strain the stock and refrigerate for another use. In a saucepan sauté the onions in butter until soft. Combine all the ingredients except the sour cream and cheese. Simmer until the tortillas are tender. Add the sour cream and transfer to a baking dish. Top with the cheese and bake at 350° until bubbly. Serves 8.

GOURMET HELPER—Rub chicken with a good brandy before roasting along with your other seasonings for extra flavor.

Chicken Spaghetti

1   5-pound stewing hen
1   onion, quartered
2   garlic cloves
2   bay leaves
1   stick butter
2   onions, chopped
4   ribs celery, chopped
2   green peppers, chopped
2   garlic cloves, minced
1   pound mushrooms, thinly sliced
2   cups tomato juice
1/2 cup stuffed olives
1/2 cup pimentos
3   tablespoons chili powder
    Salt and pepper, to taste
1   pound vermicelli spaghetti
2   cups Velveeta cheese
1/2 cup dry sherry

In a large pot simmer hen, with enough water to cover, with the onion, garlic, bay leaves, and salt and pepper, until tender. Remove from heat and let hen cool in the stock. When cool remove the hen and discard the skin and bones and shred into bite-size pieces. Strain broth and divide in half. In a saucepan melt the butter and sauté the next 5 ingredients until soft. In a large roasting pan combine the chicken, half the broth, onion mixture, tomato juice, olives, pimentos and chili powder. Taste for seasonings. Bake at 350°, covered, for 1 1/2 hours. In the remaining broth cook the spaghetti and drain. Fold in the spaghetti and the cheese and bake 30 minutes longer. Just before serving stir in 1/2 cup dry sherry.

In a Hurry Chicken and Rice—Combine 2 cups cooked, chopped chicken; 2 cups cooked rice; 1 cup mayonnaise; 1 cup cream of chicken soup; and 1 package onion dip mix. Place in a shallow baking dish and top with 2 cups grated Cheddar cheese. Bake at 350° for 30 minutes or until bubbly.

GOURMET HELPER—For a smoother and lighter textured crêpe, let batter stand in the refrigerator for an hour or more after mixing.

Easy Chicken Quiche

1½ cups milk
½ cup biscuit mix
¼ teaspoon poultry seasoning
½ teaspoon salt
¾ stick butter, softened
3 eggs
1 cup cooked chicken, torn into bite-size pieces
6 slices bacon cooked crisp, drained and crumbled
4 green onions, tops and bottoms, chopped
¼ pound fresh mushrooms, thinly sliced
1 cup grated sharp Cheddar cheese

Preheat oven to 350°. Combine the first 6 ingredients and mix in a blender or food processor until smooth. Pour into a 10″ pie or quiche pan. Add the chicken and the bacon and poke into the batter. Top with the onions, mushrooms and cheese. Bake for 45 minutes. Let cool slightly before serving.

Chicken Pie

3 cups cooked chicken, torn into bite-size pieces
2 cups grated Mozzarella cheese
2 cups tomato puree
2 teaspoons oregano
½ teaspoon basil
1 cup small curd cottage cheese
5 ounce package Bisquick
2 cups milk
4 eggs, lightly beaten
1 teaspoon salt
¼ teaspoon cayenne pepper

Preheat oven to 350°. Combine the chicken, 1 cup cheese, puree, oregano and basil. Set aside. Spread the cottage cheese on the bottom of a baking dish. Cover with the chicken mixture. Combine the next 5 ingredients and beat for 1 minute. Pour over the chicken mixture and bake for 30 minutes or until set.

Hot Chicken Salad Sandwich

3   cups cooked chicken, diced
2   hard-cooked eggs
1/2 cup canned sliced mushrooms, drained
1/4 cup stuffed olives, sliced
1/2 cup Hellmann's mayonnaise
12 slices Pepperidge Farm Thin Slice White Bread, de-crusted
1   can cream of chicken soup
1   cup sour cream
1   cup Cheddar cheese, grated

Combine first 5 ingredients and mix well. Spread on 6 slices of bread. Cover with the remaining slices and place in a baking dish. Combine the soup and sour cream and spread over the sandwiches. Refrigerate overnight. Bake at 325° for 20 minutes. Add cheese and bake until cheese is melted.

Chicken Livers with Apples

1   pound chicken livers
1/2 cup flour
1   stick butter
1/4 cup Madeira
1   onion, thinly sliced
1   large apple, peeled, cored and sliced into 4 rings
2   tablespoons sugar
1/4 teaspoon mace
3   tablespoons butter

In a saucepan saute the sliced onions in the butter, separating into rings, until golden. Remove them with a slotted spoon and keep them warm. Season livers with salt and pepper and dust with flour. Saute them in the butter remaining in the pan until they are tender. Add the Madeira and simmer for about 5 minutes. Add the onion rings and remove from heat, keeping warm. Sprinkle the apple rings with the sugar and mace and in another skillet saute them on both sides in the butter until they are glazed. Transfer the livers and onions to a heated platter and top with the apple rings. Serves 4.

Glazed Cornish Hens

6   cornish hens
1/2   cup 7-Up
1/2   cup honey

STUFFING

3/4   pound Owen's Hot Sausage
2   cups wild rice, cooked

Combine 7-Up and honey and with a pastry brush coat hens thoroughly, every hour, for 3 hours. (Allow the sauce to cling to the skin between coatings.) Lightly salt the cavities and stuff with the dressing. To make the dressing: In a saucepan crumble and sauté the sausage until cooked. Add to the rice and mix well. Bake hens at 325° for 1 hour. Turn to 350° and bake for 1/2 hour longer or until tender.

MEATS

Marinated Steak

8   8-ounce steaks of your choice, cut 1" thick
3   cups soy sauce
2   onions, chopped
3   garlic cloves
1/4 cup coffee
1   teaspoon Kitchen Bouquet
1   tablespoon Beau Monde Seasoning

SHALLOT SAUCE
1/4 cup finely chopped shallots
1   tablespoon Dijon mustard
2   cups port wine
1/2 cup heavy cream

Place the soy sauce, onions and garlic in a blender and puree. Add the next 3 ingredients and mix well. Place steaks in a shallow glass or enamel baking dish and cover with the sauce. Marinate for 2 hours at room temperature, turning frequently. Remove steaks and broil or cook in a skillet to the desired doneness. Remove to a platter and keep warm. Combine the shallots and mustard and place in a skillet. Add the port and cook over a high heat until sauce is reduced by half. Add the cream and cook until sauce begins to thicken. Season with salt and pepper and serve over the steaks.

Beer Marinated Steaks

4   8-ounce sirloin strips
3   cups beer
1   cup soy sauce
2   tablespoons orange marmalade
1   tablespoon coriander seed, crushed
2   teaspoons Dijon mustard
     Salt and pepper, to taste

Place the steaks in a shallow enamel or Pyrex dish. Combine all the ingredients and pour over the steaks. Marinate for 4 hours, turning every hour. Remove the steaks, reserving the marinade. Brush the steaks with the marinade while broiling.

Bourbon Steak

2   pounds thick prime sirloin
3   tablespoons butter, melted
1   tablespoon green onion, chopped
1   tablespoon fresh parsley, chopped
1¹/₃ cups bourbon, warmed

Season steak with salt and pepper. Broil the steak to desired doneness and brush on both sides with the onion and parsley mixed in the butter. Remove to a heat proof platter and pour warm bourbon over the steaks, ignite, and shake the platter until the flames die out.

Beef Bourbon Tenderloin

¹/₄ cup soy sauce
¹/₄ cup bourbon
¹/₄ cup firmly packed brown sugar
2   tablespoons red wine vinegar
2   tablespoons molasses
³/₄ cup orange juice
1   garlic clove, crushed
1   onion, sliced
1   beef tenderloin
¹/₂ package Brown Gravy Mix
     Dash Kitchen Bouquet

Combine the first 8 ingredients and pour over the tenderloin. Marinate, covered, in the refrigerator for 4 hours, turning meat frequently. Remove meat, reserving marinade. Preheat oven to 425° and bake the tenderloin on a rack in a roasting pan for 45 minutes or until the desired doneness. Remove the beef to a platter and keep warm. Pour off all but ¹/₄ cup beef drippings from the pan. Add the Brown Gravy Mix, the bourbon mixture, ¹/₂ cup water and Kitchen Bouquet. Season with salt and pepper. Cook over a low heat, stirring constantly, until sauce is smooth and thickened (If sauce is not thick enough add a little cornstarch). Serve the sauce over the beef slices.

GOURMET HELPER—Because veal is so delicately flavored, don't serve strongly flavored vegetables with it.

Filet of Beef Tenderloin

1　beef tenderloin
5　garlic cloves, cut in slivers
½　teaspoon Tabasco
1　cup soy sauce
½　cup oil
1　cup Port wine
1　teaspoon thyme
1　bay leaf, remove stem and crush leaves
　　Bacon slices

Season tenderloin with salt and pepper. Make small slits in beef and fill with the garlic. Place in a shallow enamel baking dish and pour remaining ingredients, except bacon, over beef. Marinate about 2 hours, turning frequently. Remove from marinade and place on a rack in a shallow roasting pan. Top with bacon slices and roast at 425° for 30 to 40 minutes.

Do Ahead Tenderloin

1　cup soy sauce
1　cup oil
1　cup dry white wine
4　large garlic cloves, crushed
¼　teaspoon Tabasco
1　beef tenderloin, 3–4 pounds

Combine the first 5 ingredients and mix well. Place the meat in a shallow baking pan and cover with the wine mixture. Marinate, covered, in the refrigerator for 24 hours, turning frequently. Remove from the refrigerator several hours before cooking. Remove meat and reserve marinade. Preheat oven to 475° and bake the tenderloin on a rack in a roasting pan for 45 minutes or until the desired doneness. Cool and cover with marinade. Chill. When ready to serve, drain meat and slice thinly. Serve chilled with a salad or on homemade bread as a sandwich.

GOURMET HELPER—To slice meat into thin strips, such as for stroganoff, partially freeze and it will slice easily.

Steak in a Mustard Sauce

8   8-ounce steaks of your choice, cut 1″ thick
½   cup Lea & Perrins Chef's Marinade
½   cup red wine
2   cups white wine
1   tablespoon Dijon mustard
1   teaspoon minced shallots
2   tablespoons butter, cut into pieces
1   tablespoon tarragon

Place steaks in a shallow glass or enamel baking dish. Combine the marinade and red wine and pour over the steaks. Marinate at room temperature for 2 hours, turning frequently. Remove the steaks from the marinade and cook in a heavy skillet to the desired doneness. Remove to a platter and keep warm. In the same skillet cook the white wine over a high heat, scraping up the brown bits clinging to the bottom and sides of the pan, until the wine is reduced by half. Stir in the mustard and shallots and whisk in the butter and tarragon. Pour over the steaks and serve.

Little Mushroom Beef Stanley

8   6-ounce filets
½   stick butter
1   small yellow onion, chopped
4   green onions, tops and bottoms, chopped
3   ribs celery, chopped
1   small green pepper, chopped
15   ounce can tomato puree
1   tablespoon smoke sauce
2   tablespoons burgundy
1   tablespoon seasoning salt (or more to taste)
     Pepper, to taste
4   large bananas, sliced lengthwise once then crosswise once

HORSERADISH SAUCE

1   cup sour cream
1½   teaspoons horseradish
½   teaspoon Worcestershire sauce

Season steaks with salt and pepper and broil over low heat for about 10 minutes. In a saucepan sauté the onions, celery and green pepper in butter until soft. Add the remaining ingredients, except the bananas, and pour over the steaks. Bake at 350° about 25 minutes. Top each steak with 2 slices of bananas which have been sprinkled with cinnamon and sugar and bake at 350° until bananas are soft. Combine the sour cream, horseradish and Worcestershire sauce and let stand at room temperature. Spoon over the steak.

Steak with Green Peppercorns

4   8-ounce sirloin strips (salted)
1/2 stick butter
1/4 cup Cognac, heated
2   tablespoons shallots, minced
1/2 cup burgundy
1/2 cup heavy cream
3   tablespoons beef stock
2   tablespoons butter, softened
1/2 teaspoon Dijon mustard
     Dash Madeira
     Salt and pepper, to taste
4   teaspoons green peppercorns, drained
1   tablespoon butter

In a skillet sauté the steaks in the butter over high heat for about 5 minutes on each side for medium-rare. Pour in the heated Cognac, ignite it, and shake the pan until the flames go out. Transfer the steaks to a heated platter and keep warm in a 175° oven. In the same skillet sauté the shallots for 2 minutes, stir in the burgundy, and reduce the liquid over high heat by half. Stir in the cream, stock, softened butter, mustard, Madeira and salt and pepper, to taste. Keep the sauce warm. In a small skillet sauté the peppercorns in the butter for 1 minute. Pour the sauce over the steaks and spoon the peppercorns over the sauce.

Chopped Sirloin with Peppercorns

2   pounds ground sirloin
1/4 cup onion, grated
2   garlic cloves, crushed with 1/2 teaspoon salt
4   tablespoons peppercorns, crushed
2   tablespoons butter
4   tablespoons good brandy, heated
1/2 cup beef stock
1/2 cup heavy cream

In a bowl combine the meat, onion and garlic and form into 4 half-inch thick patties. Press the peppercorns into the patties. In a skillet sauté them in butter over high heat until desired doneness. Add the heated brandy, ignite, and shake the pan until the flames die out. Transfer the meat to a heated serving platter and keep hot in a 175° oven. Add to the skillet the beef stock and cream, bring to a boil, stirring the brown bits clinging to the bottom and sides of the pan. Reduce the sauce by half and pour over the patties.

Beef with Roquefort Cheese

4   pounds sirloin or filet mignon, sliced in ¼" strips
2   cups flour (seasoned with salt and pepper)
½   cup oil
1   stick butter
4   cups beef stock
4   tablespoons sour cream
½   cup Roquefort dressing
½   cup Parmesan cheese, freshly grated

Dredge beef strips in flour, shaking off excess flour. In a saucepan sauté the strips in the oil and butter until lightly browned on all sides. Remove beef from the pan. Pour stock and sour cream into the pan and simmer over very low heat, until sauce is reduced by half. Stir in beef and remove from heat. Transfer to a lightly greased baking dish, top with Roquefort dressing and cheese and place under a pre-heated broiler until lightly browned. Serves 8.

Marinated Flank Steak

2   2-pound flank steaks
½   cup burgundy
½   cup olive oil
2   garlic cloves, sliced
1   bay leaf
¼   teaspoon rosemary
¼   teaspoon thyme
¼   teaspoon marjoram

With a sharp knife trim the membrane from the steaks and place them in a large shallow enamel container. Combine all the other ingredients and pour over the steaks. Refrigerate for at least 8 hours, turning them occasionally. Drain the steaks and broil them for about 5 minutes on each side for rare or broil them to your own preference. Season the steaks with salt and pepper and transfer to a carving board. With a sharp knife held diagonally and almost parallel to the meat, cut the steaks into thin slices.

Baked Brisket

4-6 pounds boneless beef brisket
2   onions, sliced
      Lemon Pepper Marinade
$^{1}/_{2}$ teaspoon garlic powder
10   ounce bottle Pepsi-Cola

Place the onions in the bottom of a roasting pan. Season brisket and place, fat side up, on top of the onions. Brown, uncovered, in a 450° oven for $^{1}/_{2}$ hour. Pour the Pepsi over the brisket and reduce oven to 325°. Cover and bake, basting with more Pepsi, about $3^{1}/_{2}$ hours or until tender.

Beer Brisket

4-6 pounds boneless beef brisket
2   onions, sliced
1   cup chili sauce
3   tablespoons brown sugar
2   garlic cloves, crushed
12   ounce can beer
3   tablespoons flour
$^{1}/_{2}$ cup water

Preheat oven to 350°. Season meat with salt and pepper and place in a roasting pan. Cover with the onion slices. Combine the next 4 ingredients and pour over the meat. Cover with foil and bake for 4 hours or until tender. Transfer meat to a platter and keep warm. Skim fat from liquid mixture and measure 1 cup (adding water if you need it). Blend flour and water and add to the mixture in the pan. Cook, stirring constantly, until the gravy is thick and bubbly.

In a Hurry Smoked Brisket—Pour 1 bottle liquid smoke over an 8 pound brisket. Season with garlic salt and cover with 2 chopped onions. Cover with foil and marinate in the refrigerator, covered, overnight. Sprinkle with $^{1}/_{4}$ cup Worcestershire sauce and bake, covered, in a preheated 300° oven for 6 hours. Uncover and pour 1 6-ounce bottle barbecue sauce over the meat and bake for 1 hour longer or until tender.

Sherry Brisket

4-6 pounds boneless beef brisket
2   garlic cloves, sliced
8   ounce bottle French dressing
12 ounce bottle chili sauce
1   cup dry sherry
3   onions, sliced

Season meat with salt and pepper. Make slits in the meat and push in the garlic slices. Combine the remaining ingredients and marinate the meat, covered, in the refrigerator overnight, turning the meat occasionally. Preheat oven to 350°. Cover the meat with foil and bake for 4 hours or until tender. Remove meat from pan and cool slightly. Slice and season with salt and pepper. Skim the grease off the top and puree the drippings in blender. Reheat and pour over the meat.

Spicy Pot Roast

4   pound rump roast
1/4 cup oil
1/2 cup horseradish, drained
1   cup whole cranberry sauce
1   cinnamon stick, broken into pieces
4   whole cloves
1   cup beef stock

In a heavy Dutch oven brown the roast in the oil on all sides over a high heat. Drain off any remaining oil. Combine the remaining ingredients and pour over the roast. Bring the mixture to a boil, cover tightly, and simmer gently for 4 hours or until meat is tender. Remove the meat from the pan and cool slightly. Slice and season with salt and pepper. Skim the grease off the top and puree the liquid in a blender until smooth. Reheat and add more beef stock if the mixture is too thick. Pour over the meat slices and serve.

In a Hurry Tipsy Pot Roast—Brown a 3 pound rump roast in 2 tablespoons oil until brown on all sides. Place in a heavy roasting pan and cover with 1 cup catsup, 2 12-ounce cans beer and salt and pepper to taste. Roast, uncovered, in a preheated 325° oven for 1 1/2 hours. Add 2 quartered potatoes, 1 quartered onion and 3 large sliced carrots. Cook, covered, for 1 1/2 hours longer.

Mexican Pot Roast

5   pound boned rump roast
3   tablespoons oil
2   garlic cloves, minced
3   onions, sliced
2   teaspoons salt
1/2   teaspoon cumin
1/2   teaspoon coriander (cilantro)
1 1/2   tablespoons chili powder
1/2   cup tomato puree
2   16-ounce cans tomatoes

Preheat oven to 325°. Season beef with salt and pepper. Place in a Dutch oven and saute in the oil until browned on all sides. Remove the meat while preparing the sauce. In the same skillet saute the garlic and onions until soft. Add the remaining ingredients and bring to a boil. Return the meat to the Dutch oven and cover with the sauce. Bake for 3 hours or until the meat is tender.

Quick Rump Roast

4   pound rump roast
1   package onion soup mix
1   cup burgundy

Sprinkle onion soup on roast and cover with the wine. In a roast pan bake at 275°, covered, until tender.

Marinated Chuck Roast

5   pound chuck roast
    Adolph's meat tenderizer
2   tablespoons sesame seeds, sautéed in 1 tablespoon butter
1   cup strong coffee
1   cup soy sauce
2   tablespoons Worcestershire sauce
1   tablespoon vinegar
1   large onion, chopped

Sprinkle meat with tenderizer. Combine all ingredients and pour over the roast. Let marinate at room temperature for 6 hours, turning several times. Charcoal broil the roast until cooked to desired doneness.

Rare Rib Roast

1   beef rib roast, any size

Let roast stand at room temperature for at least 30 minutes per pound before baking. Season with salt and pepper. Transfer the roast to a shallow baking pan, fat side up. Put in a thoroughly preheated 500° oven, uncovered. Bake 5 minutes per pound and turn off the heat. Leave the meat in the unopened oven for at least 2 hours. Roast will be crusty on the outside and rare inside (the roast may remain in the closed oven for up to 3 hours).

Quick Chuck Roast

4   pound chuck roast
¼   cup A-1 sauce
1   package onion soup mix
1   can cream of mushroom soup
     Heavy duty aluminum foil

Place roast in the center of a large piece of foil in a roasting pan. Brush meat with the A-1 sauce. Sprinkle with soup mix. Spread with the soup. Wrap loosely in foil and bake in a preheated 350° oven for 3 hours or until tender.

No Peek Beef Stew

4   pounds stew meat
2   potatoes, peeled and quartered
2   onions, sliced
1   pound carrots, sliced
2   cups beef stock
1½   cups Snap-E-Tom or other Bloody Mary Mix
1   tablespoon salt
1   tablespoon sugar
1½   tablespoons tapioca

Preheat oven to 275°. Season meat with salt and place in a heavy roasting pan. Add the other ingredients in the order given and cover with foil. Bake for 5 hours. DO NOT PEEK.

Spicy Beef Stew

3   pounds boneless chuck, cut into 1½" pieces
2   onions, chopped
¼   cup oil
1   cup finely chopped parsley
6   ounce can tomato paste
½   cup white wine
¼   cup red wine vinegar
3   cups water
1   teaspoon cumin
1   teaspoon cinnamon
1   teaspoon oregano
½   teaspoon sugar
1   bay leaf
¼   pound feta cheese, crumbled*

Preheat oven to 325°. In a large heavy skillet saute the meat and onions in the oil until the meat is browned on all sides and the onions are soft. Add the remaining ingredients, except the cheese, and transfer to a heavy Dutch oven. Bake, covered, for 2 hours or until the meat is tender. Season with salt and pepper. Transfer to a serving platter and top with the cheese.

*If you're not a feta cheese lover, omit the cheese and enjoy!

In a Hurry Beer Beef Stew—Combine 1½ cups catsup, 12 ounce bottle beer, ½ cup brown sugar, 2 chopped onions, 2 minced garlic cloves and salt and pepper to taste. Pour over 4 pounds lean stew meat in a baking dish and bake at 300°, covered, for 3 hours or until tender.

All Day Oven Stew

28   ounce can Italian tomatoes
1   cup beef consomme
1/2 cup white wine
1/4 cup Tapioca
1   tablespoon brown sugar
1   bay leaf
2   teaspoons salt
1/2 package Au Jus Gravy Mix
1   teaspoon Beau Monde seasoning
     Dash Kitchen Bouquet
1/2 cup prepared bread crumbs
3   potatoes, peeled and quartered
3   pounds stew meat
4   carrots, sliced

Preheat oven to 250°. Combine the first 12 ingredients and stir until well mixed. Transfer to a heavy casserole. Place the meat and carrots on top (do not stir). Cover with a tight lid and bake 8 hours. Serves 8.

Round Steak Provencale

2   pounds round steak, cut into 3" x 1½" strips
1   onion, thinly sliced
2   garlic cloves, minced
1/2 pound fresh mushrooms, thinly sliced
1/4 cup oil
1   pound can Italian tomatoes
1/2 cup finely chopped parsley
1/2 teaspoon oregano
1/2 teaspoon Italian seasoning
1   cup red wine
1/2 cup grated Parmesan cheese

Season meat with salt and pepper. In a large heavy skillet saute the meat, onions, garlic and mushrooms in the oil until the meat is browned on all sides and the vegetables are soft. Add the remaining ingredients and simmer, covered, for 2 hours or until the meat is tender. Serve over noodles or rice. Serves 6.

Round Steak with Cheese

2 pounds round steak, cut into 3″ x 1½″ strips
½ pound fresh mushrooms, thinly sliced
¼ cup oil
2 cups rosé wine
8 ounce can tomato sauce with cheese
2 tablespoons Pot Roast Seasoning Mix
¾ cup grated sharp Cheddar cheese

Season meat with salt and pepper. In a large heavy skillet saute the meat and the mushrooms in the oil until the meat is browned on all sides. Add the next 3 ingredients and simmer, covered, for 1 hour. Add the cheese and cook for 30 more minutes or until the meat is tender. Serve over noodles or rice. Serves 6.

Beef Burgundy

3 pounds round steak, cut into serving pieces
1 cup flour, seasoned with salt and pepper
1 onion, thinly sliced
¼ cup oil
1 pound can Italian tomatoes
4 ounce can diced green chilies, drained
½ cup burgundy wine
1 tablespoon dark brown sugar
2 teaspoons salt
1 teaspoon garlic powder
½ teaspoon cumin
½ teaspoon thyme
½ teaspoon chili powder

Coat the meat lightly with the flour. In a large heavy skillet saute the meat and the onion in the oil until the meat is browned on both sides and the onion is soft. Add the remaining ingredients and simmer, covered, for 1½ hours or until meat is tender. Transfer the meat to a serving platter and keep warm. If the sauce is too thin boil briskly over a high heat, stirring, until the desired consistency. Pour over the meat and serve. Serves 8.

In a Hurry Baked Round Steak—Saute 2 thinly sliced onions and ½ pound thinly sliced mushrooms in ¼ stick butter until soft. Add 2 12-ounce bottles chili sauce and 1 cup beef stock. Pour over 2 pounds round steak, cut into serving pieces and bake, covered, for 2 hours or until meat is tender.

Italian Beef

2   pounds round steak, cut into serving pieces
1   teaspoon garlic powder
1   cup grated Parmesan cheese
2   tablespoons oil
1   cup beef stock
2   10-ounce cans tomato puree
1   teaspoon oregano
1/2 teaspoon basil
2   cups grated Mozzarella cheese

Preheat oven to 350°. Season meat with salt and pepper and with a meat pounder pound the garlic and 1/2 cup of the cheese into the meat. In a large heavy skillet brown the meat in the oil. Transfer to a baking dish. Combine the next 4 ingredients and pour over the meat. Bake for 1 hour. Sprinkle with the remaining Parmesan and Mozzarella cheese and bake for 30 minutes longer. Serves 6.

Round Steak with Green Peppers

2   pounds round steak, cut in 1″ long strips
1   cup oil
4   medium onions, sliced
4   medium green peppers, cut in 1/2″ julienne strips
1/2 pound fresh mushrooms, finely sliced
2   garlic cloves, minced
16   ounce can tomatoes
1/3 cup Worcestershire sauce
1/4 cup fresh parsley, chopped
1/4 teaspoon oregano
1/4 teaspoon basil
3/4 cup burgundy
1/4 cup Parmesan cheese, freshly grated
     Salt and pepper to taste

Season steak with salt and pepper. In a skillet sauté the strips in oil until browned on all sides. Remove. Add to the same skillet the onions, green peppers, mushrooms and garlic and sauté them until soft. Return the meat to the skillet and add the tomatoes and a tomato soup can of water. Add the Worcestershire and spices and simmer, covered, about 1 1/2 hours or until meat is tender. Add the wine and cheese and taste for seasonings. Continue cooking for about 15 minutes longer.

Little Mushroom Beef Roulade Stuffed with Jalapeño Rice Dressing

4   pound beef round
½   stick butter
1   small yellow onion, chopped
4   green onions, tops and bottoms, chopped
2   ribs celery, chopped
1   small green pepper, chopped
2   cups rice, cooked
½   cup soft bread crumbs
4   ounce can green chilies, chopped
     Sour cream to bind

MEXICAN SAUCE

2   10-ounce cans enchilada sauce
1   tablespoon chili powder
1   tablespoon cumin
2   garlic cloves, minced

Slice the beef into long thin slices for stuffing. Season with salt and pepper. In a saucepan sauté the onions, celery and green pepper until soft. Add the rice, bread crumbs, and enough sour cream to bind together. Place mixture in each beef slice and roll up, securing with a toothpick or tie each roll with a string. Transfer to a shallow baking dish and place side by side. Bake at 350° until browned.

While beef is baking prepare the sauce. In a saucepan combine all sauce ingredients until well blended and simmer for about 10 minutes. Remove beef from oven and add the sauce. Return to oven and bake, covered, for 1 hour or until beef is tender.

In a Hurry Russian Beef—Saute 1 pound round steak in 2 tablespoons oil until browned on both sides. Add 2 cups water and simmer, covered, for 1½ hours. Add 1 can vegetable soup and 1 package sour cream mix and simmer for 30 minutes longer. Season with salt and pepper and serve over noodles.

Spanish Round Steak

2   pounds beef round steak, cut 3/4" thick
1/3 cup flour (seasoned with salt and pepper)
1/4 cup oil
1   teaspoon cumin
1   teaspoon sugar
28 ounce can tomatoes, drained and chopped (reserve liquid)
2   tablespoons lemon juice
1   garlic clove, crushed
1   beef bouillon cube, dissolved in 1/2 cup boiling water
1   green pepper, chopped
1   onion, chopped
4   ounce can green chilies
1/3 cup fresh parsley, chopped
1/3 cup raisins

Cut steak in 1/4" thick strips (this will be easy to cut if steak is partially frozen). Dredge strips in the flour and in a saucepan brown on all sides in the oil. Pour off drippings and sprinkle the meat with cumin and sugar. Add tomato liquid and the next 8 ingredients. Stir until well blended and simmer, covered, for 45 minutes, stirring occasionally. Stir in the tomatoes and simmer, covered, for 15 minutes longer or until the meat is tender. Serve over rice. Serves 8.

Beef Stroganoff

4   pounds sirloin tips, sliced diagonally into thin strips 1 1/2" wide
    and 2" long
    Adolph's meat tenderizer
2   pounds fresh mushrooms, sliced
3   onions, chopped
1   stick butter
2   cans beef bouillon
1/2 cup flour
1   pint sour cream
1/2 cup Rhine wine
1   cup tomato juice

Sprinkle meat with tenderizer, toss and refrigerate. In a skillet sauté the onions in butter until soft. Remove to a 6 quart enamel roasting pan. Sauté mushrooms in same butter until tender and remove to roasting pan. In the same skillet brown meat (you may need to add more butter) until brown. Remove to roasting pan. Put 1 can bouillon and the flour in a blender and puree until smooth. Set aside. Pour remaining can of bouillon into same skillet and stir and scrape to de-glaze the pan. Add bouillon and flour mixture, stirring until smooth. Add tomato juice and wine. Pour over meat and vegetables in roasting pan. Season with salt and pepper to taste. About 1½ hours before serving, place roaster in a pre-heated 375° oven and bring to a simmer, stirring occasionally. Just before serving, add sour cream and a splash more of wine. Serve with buttered noodles or wild rice. Serves 10.

In a Hurry Round Steak Stroganoff—Saute 2 pounds round steaks, cut into 3″ x 1½″ strips, 1 chopped onion and 1 crushed garlic clove in ½ stick butter until meat is browned. Add 1 teaspoon salt, ½ teaspoon pepper, 1 teaspoon paprika, 2 cans cream of mushroom soup, and ½ cup vermouth. Simmer, covered, for 2 hours or until meat is tender. Combine 3 tablespoons Dijon mustard with 1½ cups sour cream and add slowly to meat mixture. Heat and serve over rice or noodles.

Easy Beef Tips in Mushroom Sauce

2   pounds lean chuck, cut into 1¾″ pieces
1   can cream of mushroom soup
1   package onion soup mix
1   cup 7-Up

Place meat in a 2 quart casserole. Do not season. Pour soup and soup mix over the meat. Add the 7-Up. Cover the casserole and bake at 275° for 4 hours. During cooking—DO NOT OPEN OVEN DOOR. After 4 hours remove meat from oven and let stand for 30 minutes before serving.

Texas Chili

2½ pounds ground chuck
1   onion, chopped
2   tablespoons oil
2   garlic cloves, crushed
1   jalapeño pepper, seeded and chopped
½   teaspoon oregano
2   tablespoons chili powder
1   can Ro-tel tomatoes
2   cans chili beans

In a large heavy saucepan sauté onion in oil until soft. Add the beef and sauté until lightly browned. Add the remaining ingredients and salt and pepper, to taste. Simmer, covered, for 2 hours.

Nancy's Chili

4   pounds lean ground chuck
3   onions, chopped
2   small green peppers, chopped
1   package Williams chili mix
2   tablespoons chili powder
2   tablespoons cumin
2   tablespoons garlic salt
1   tablespoon minced dried garlic
1/2 teaspoon thyme
1/2 teaspoon oregano
2   teaspoons picante sauce (omit, if you don't like hot chili)
46   ounce can tomato juice
18   ounce can tomato juice
2 1/2 cups water
2   15-ounce cans Ranch style beans
2 1/2 tablespoons cornstarch

In a large heavy skillet saute the first 3 ingredients until the meat is browned and the vegetables are soft. Drain off all fat and add the next 10 ingredients. Place the beans, 1/2 cup of the water and the cornstarch in a blender and puree. Add to the mixture along with the remaining 2 cups water. Simmer for 3 to 4 hours. Season with salt and serve.

In a Hurry Jailhouse Chili—Saute 2 pounds ground beef and 1 chopped onion until browned. Add 2 cans drained red beans, 1 package chili seasoning, 4 cups tomato juice, 8 ounce can tomato sauce, 1 tablespoon chili powder and salt and pepper to taste. Simmer, covered, for 3 hours.

GOURMET HELPER—Never cook a roast cold. Let it stand for at least an hour at room temperature and brush with oil before and during roasting—the oil will seal in the juices.

Hot Chili

4   pounds lean ground chuck
4   onions, chopped
2   green peppers, chopped
4   ribs celery, chopped
2   tablespoons canned pickled jalapeno peppers, chopped
3   15-ounce cans stewed tomatoes
2   8-ounce cans tomato sauce with tomato bits
2   6-ounce cans tomato paste
1   cup beer
¼   teaspoon Tabasco
6   tablespoons chili powder
2   tablespoons cumin
1   teaspoon garlic salt
1   teaspoon garlic powder
2   bay leaves

In a large heavy skillet saute the first 4 ingredients until browned (add oil if needed). Pour off excess liquid. Add the remaining ingredients and simmer, covered, for 3 to 4 hours. (Add water if mixture becomes too thick.) Season with salt and serve.

Beer Chili

4   pounds lean ground chuck
4   onions, chopped
4   16-ounce cans tomatoes
4   fresh jalapeno peppers
3   12-ounce cans beer
6   tablespoons chili powder
4   tablespoons cumin
6   tablespoons paprika
2   tablespoons cayenne pepper
2   teaspoons oregano

In a large heavy skillet saute the meat until browned. In a blender or food processor puree the next three ingredients and add to the meat. Add the remaining ingredients and simmer for 3 to 4 hours. Season with salt and serve.

Italian Chili

6   slices bacon
10 ounces hot Italian sausage, cut into 1" pieces
1   pound lean ground beef
1   onion, chopped
1   green pepper, chopped
2   garlic cloves, minced
1/2 fresh jalapeno pepper, seeded and sliced
1   cup burgundy
1/2 cup Worcestershire sauce
1   teaspoon dry mustard
1 1/2 tablespoons chili powder
6   cups canned Italian tomatoes
15 ounce can kidney beans

In a large heavy skillet saute the bacon until crisp. Remove and drain on paper toweling. In the same skillet saute the sausage in the bacon drippings. Remove and drain on paper toweling. In the same skillet saute the next 5 ingredients. Pour off excess liquid. Add the remaining ingredients, except the beans, and simmer, covered, for 1 hour, stirring occasionally. Add the bacon, sausage and beans and simmer, covered, for 1 hour. Season with salt.

In a Hurry Lazy Lasagne—Saute 1 pound ground beef until browned. Add a 16 ounce can tomatoes and 1 package Sloppy Joe Mix. In a baking dish layer 6 cooked lasagne noodles, the meat mixture and an 8 ounce package of cream cheese which has been whipped. Top with 1 cup grated sharp Cheddar cheese and bake at 350° for 30 minutes or until bubbly.

Italian Beef Crepes

16 prepared crepes

FILLING

1½ **pounds ground beef**
1   **onion, chopped**
2   **garlic cloves, minced**
½   **stick butter**
½   **cup dry sherry**
1   **teaspoon oregano**
1   **teaspoon cumin**
1   **bay leaf, crushed**
1   **cup sour cream**
3   **cups grated sharp Cheddar cheese**
1½ **cups grated Parmesan cheese**

TOPPING

2   **cups sour cream**
1½ **cups grated Mozzarella cheese**

Preheat oven to 400°. In a large heavy skillet saute the meat, onion and garlic in the butter until the meat is browned and the vegetables are soft. Pour off excess liquid. Remove from the heat and add the next 7 ingredients. Season with salt and pepper. Place 3 tablespoons mixture in each crepe, roll up and place seam side down in a greased baking dish. Spread with the sour cream and sprinkle with the cheese. Bake for 15 minutes or until heated through.

In a Hurry Ground Beef and Rice—In a skillet brown 1 pound ground beef and ½ cup chopped onion in 1 tablespoon oil. Drain off fat. Add a 16 ounce can of tomatoes, 1 can cream of mushroom soup, 1 cup Minute Rice, ⅛ teaspoon thyme, ⅛ teaspoon oregano, ⅛ teaspoon garlic powder and 1 cup Cheddar cheese. Salt and pepper, to taste, and cook until heated through.

In a Hurry Pizza Meat Loaf—Combine 2 pounds ground beef, 2 eggs, 1 cup raw Quaker Oats, 1 chopped onion, 1 chopped green pepper, 1 crushed garlic clove and ¼ cup chopped green olives. Add 3 tablespoons from a 14 ounce jar Ragu Pizza Quick and season with salt and pepper. Pack into a loaf pan. Bake for 30 minutes. Top with the remaining Pizza Quick and 1 cup grated Parmesan cheese.

Italian Beef Pie

6   ounce package spaghetti, cooked and drained
2   tablespoons melted butter
½   cup grated Parmesan cheese
2   eggs, beaten
1   pound ground beef
1   onion, chopped
1   small green pepper, chopped
8   ounce can tomatoes
6   ounce can tomato paste
1   teaspoon sugar
1   teaspoon oregano
½   teaspoon Italian seasoning
2   teaspoons garlic salt
1   cup cottage cheese, drained
1   cup grated Monterey Jack cheese

Preheat oven to 350°. Combine the spaghetti, butter, cheese and eggs. In a 10″ pie pan mold the spaghetti mixture into a nest. In a large heavy skillet saute the next 3 ingredients until the meat is browned and the vegetables are soft, adding a little oil if needed. Drain off any excess liquid. Add the next 6 ingredients and simmer, covered, for 20 minutes. Spread cottage cheese over the spaghetti and add the meat sauce. Bake for 20 minutes. Sprinkle with the Jack cheese and bake until cheese is melted.

Baked Beef and Pasta

2   pounds ground beef
2   onions, chopped
2   cloves garlic, minced
1/4 pound fresh mushrooms, thinly sliced
14   ounce jar spaghetti sauce
1   pound can Italian tomatoes
8   ounces macaroni, cooked
2   cups sour cream
1/2 pound Provolone cheese, grated
1/2 pound Mozzarella cheese, grated

Preheat oven to 350°. In a large heavy skillet saute the first 4 ingredients until the meat is browned. Add the next 2 ingredients and simmer for 20 minutes. In a baking dish layer half the macaroni, half the sour cream, half the meat mixture and all the Provolone cheese. Repeat, ending with the Mozzarella cheese. Bake, covered, for 40 minutes. Bake, uncovered, for 10 minutes longer. Serves 8.

Little Mushroom Beef Cannelloni

3   pounds ground beef
1   small onion, finely chopped
3   ribs celery, finely chopped
1/2 green pepper, finely chopped
1/2 teaspoon pure granulated garlic
1/2 teaspoon chili powder
1   teaspoon cumin
1/2 teaspoon seasoning salt
2   tablespoons burgundy
1/2 cup tomato puree
1/2 cup sour cream

SAUCE
4   cups milk
4   tablespoons cornstarch
2   teaspoons chicken soup base
1/2 cup Velveeta cheese
1   cup Parmesan cheese, freshly grated

In a saucepan sauté the beef, breaking it apart with a fork, until it is lightly browned. Add the remaining ingredients and simmer for about 30 minutes.

(Do not let mixture boil.) Place mixture, divided evenly, into 16 crêpes. Roll and place seam side down, side by side, in a lightly greased shallow baking dish. (For crepe recipe see Crabmeat Crepes). In a saucepan heat the milk. Add the cornstarch and soup base stirring constantly with a wire whisk until mixture thickens to a cream sauce consistency. Add the cheese and simmer until cheese is melted. Pour sauce over crepes. Sprinkle with Parmesan cheese and bake at 350° until bubbly. Serves 8.

Spaghetti and Meat Sauce

2   pounds ground round
1   pound ground lean pork
2   tablespoons butter
1   onion, chopped
4   ribs celery, chopped
1   green pepper, chopped
1/2 pound mushrooms, thinly sliced
1   garlic clove, crushed
1   tablespoon chili powder
2   teaspoons cumin
16   ounce can tomatoes
2   cups tomato puree
8   ounce can tomato sauce
1   tablespoon Worcestershire sauce
1/4 teaspoon thyme
2   teaspoons Italian Herb Seasoning (or more)
2   teaspoons oregano (or more)
1/2 teaspoon sugar
1   pound spaghetti, cooked and drained
1   cup Parmesan cheese, freshly grated

In a large heavy skillet saute the onion, celery, green pepper, mushrooms and garlic in the butter until soft. Add the beef, breaking it up with a fork, and saute until lightly browned. Add the chili powder, cumin and salt and pepper to taste. Add the remaining ingredients, except the spaghetti and cheese, and simmer, covered, for about 2 hours (add water if sauce is too thick). Serve over the spaghetti and sprinkle with the cheese. Serves 8.

In a Hurry Lasagna—In a skillet brown 1 pound ground beef. Drain off the fat and add 1 large jar Ragu spaghetti sauce and heat for a few minutes. Remove from heat. Cook 1 pound lasagna noodles and drain. In a casserole place a layer of noodles, a layer of grated Monterey Jack cheese, a layer of cottage cheese, a layer of tomato beef sauce and a layer of Parmesan cheese. Repeat several times and bake, covered, in a 350° oven for 1 hour.

Luscious Lasagne

SAUCE

1   pound lean ground beef
1   onion, chopped
1   small green pepper, chopped
4   ribs celery, chopped
2   garlic cloves, minced
3   tablespoons oil
1   pound can tomato puree
1   pound can Italian tomatoes
1/2 cup dry red wine
1   teaspoon Italian seasoning
1   teaspoon oregano
1   teaspoon basil
1 1/2 teaspoon salt

FILLING

1   pound Ricotta cheese
1   cup grated sharp Cheddar cheese
1   cup grated Mozzarella cheese
1   cup grated Parmesan cheese
4   green onions, tops and bottoms, chopped
4   egg yolks
1   teaspoon salt
    Dash cayenne pepper

Cook 16 lasagna noodles according to the package directions. Preheat oven to 350°. In a large heavy skillet saute the first 5 ingredients in the oil until the beef is browned and the vegetables are soft. Add the remaining ingredients and simmer, covered, for 1 hour. Combine the ricotta, 1/2 cup Cheddar, 1/2 cup Mozzarella, 1/2 cup Parmesan and the remaining ingredients. Spread 3 tablespoons mixture on each noodle. Roll up and arrange seam side down in a greased, shallow baking dish. Cover with the sauce and bake, uncovered, for 20 minutes or until bubbly. Sprinkle the remaining cheeses on top and bake for 5 minutes longer. Serves 8.

In a Hurry Ravioli Bake—Saute 1 1/2 pounds ground beef, 1 chopped onion, 1 chopped green pepper, 2 ribs chopped celery and 1 chopped garlic clove until meat is browned. Pour off excess liquid and transfer to a shallow baking dish. Add 15-ounce can mini ravioli and 1 can cream of chicken soup. Season with salt and pepper and top with 1 cup grated Mozzarella cheese. Bake at 350° for 30 minutes or until bubbly.

Manicotti

SAUCE

1   pound Italian sausage (remove outer casing)
$1/2$ pound lean ground beef
2   tablespoons olive oil
1   onion, chopped
6   garlic cloves, crushed
2   tablespoons sugar
1   tablespoon basil
2   teaspoons oregano
2   teaspoons fennel seed
2   teaspoons Italian seasoning
$1/4$ teaspoon cayenne pepper
$1/4$ teaspoon nutmeg
$1/3$ cup finely chopped parsley
3   16-ounce cans Italian tomatoes
2   6-ounce cans tomato paste
$1/2$ cup red wine
1   cup beef stock
$1^1/2$ teaspoon salt

FILLING

1   pound Ricotta cheese
$1/2$ cup grated Mozzarella cheese
$1/2$ cup grated Romano cheese
1   cup grated Parmesan cheese
2   eggs, beaten
2   shallots, minced
$1/4$ cup finely chopped parsley
$3/4$ teaspoon salt
1   tablespoon oregano
12   Manicotti shells, cooked according to package directions

Preheat oven to 350°. SAUCE: In a large saucepan place the sausage and meat. Barely cover with water and simmer until cooked. In a large heavy skillet saute the onion and garlic until soft. Add the remaining ingredients and mix well. Drain meats and add to the tomato mixture. Simmer, covered, for 3 hours. Season with salt and pepper.

FILLING: Combine all the ingredients and stuff in the manicotti shells. Place in a buttered shallow baking dish, cover with the sauce, and bake, covered, for 20 minutes or until heated through. Serves 6.

Acapulco Dish

1½ pounds ground beef
1   onion, chopped
2   garlic cloves, minced
2   tablespoons oil
1   pound can Italian tomatoes
1   package taco seasoning mix
1   teaspoon cumin
1   teaspoon chili powder
4   ounce can diced green chilies, drained
2   ounce can chopped black olives
6   ounce package cheese flavored tortilla chips, crushed
2   cups grated Monterey Jack cheese
1   pint sour cream
1½ cups grated sharp Cheddar cheese

Preheat oven to 350°. In a large heavy skillet saute the first 3 ingredients in the
oil until browned. Pour off any excess liquid. Add the next 6 ingredients and
simmer, covered, for 30 minutes. Layer half the chips in the bottom of a
greased baking dish. Spread meat mixture on top. Sprinkle with the Jack
cheese and cover with the sour cream. Add the remaining chips and sprinkle
with the Cheddar cheese. Bake for 30 minutes or until bubbly. Serves 6.

Mexican Tart

1   pound ground beef
2   teaspoons paprika
½   teaspoon chili powder
1   onion, chopped
1   garlic clove, minced
2   tablespoons oil
1½ cups grated Monterey Jack cheese
1   cup sour cream
6   green onions, tops and bottoms, chopped
½   cup chopped green chilies
3   eggs, beaten
     9″ partially baked pie shell (bake in a pre-heated 400° oven for
     10 minutes)

Preheat oven to 325°. Combine the first 3 ingredients and mix well. Saute the
meat mixture, onion and garlic in the oil until the meat is browned. Simmer,
covered, for 30 minutes. Pour off any excess liquid. Remove from the heat and

add the remaining ingredients. Season with salt and place in the prepared pastry shell. Bake for 55 minutes or until filling is set and crust is lightly browned.

Beef and Green Chili Casserole

1½ pounds ground beef
½   teaspoon garlic salt
2   tablespoons butter
1   onion, chopped
1   package sour cream sauce mix, prepared according to the
    directions on the package
1½ cups rice, cooked
2   4-ounce cans green chilies, drained
2   cups Monterey Jack cheese, grated

In a saucepan sauté the beef in the butter until lightly browned. Add the garlic salt, and onion and simmer for about 20 minutes. Combine the sour cream and rice. Place half the rice mixture in a lightly greased baking dish. Layer half the beef mixture, half the chilies, and half the cheese. Repeat, ending with the cheese on top. Bake at 350° for about 35 minutes.

Easy Enchiladas

2½ pounds ground beef
1   onion, chopped
1   green pepper, chopped
1½ dozen corn tortillas
½   stick butter
1   onion, chopped
2   tablespoons flour
16 ounce can stewed tomatoes
16 ounce can chili with beans, mashed
1   teaspoon salt
3   tablespoons chili powder
2   cups grated Monterey Jack cheese

Preheat oven to 350°. In a large skillet saute the first 3 ingredients until the meat is browned. Soften the tortillas in a little oil and fill with the meat mixture. Roll up and place seam side down in a shallow baking dish. Saute the onion in the butter until soft. Add the flour and cook to a thick paste. Add the next 4 ingredients and simmer for 15 minutes. Pour over the rolled tortillas, sprinkle with the cheese, and bake for 15 minutes or until bubbly. Serves 8.

Mexican Meat Loaf

1   pound lean beef
1   onion, chopped
8   ounce can red taco sauce
1   can chicken with rice soup
1   can cream of mushroom soup
4   ounce can diced green chilies, drained
6   ounce can tomato paste
2   teaspoons garlic salt
12   corn tortillas, torn into pieces
1   cup grated Monterey Jack cheese

Preheat oven to 350°. In a large skillet saute the beef and onion until the beef is browned. Add the remaining ingredients, except the tortillas, and simmer, covered, for 30 minutes. Line a baking dish with half the tortillas. Spread half the meat mixture on top. Repeat. Top with the cheese and bake for 30 minutes or until bubbly.

Italian Meat Loaf

2   pounds ground beef
2   eggs
1/2   cup corn flakes, crushed
1   small onion, chopped
1   garlic clove, minced
1   tablespoon fresh parsley, chopped
2   teaspoons salt
1/4   teaspoon pepper
1   teaspoon basil
1/2   teaspoon oregano
1/2   teaspoon Italian Herb Seasoning
1/2   cup tomato juice
4   squares sliced Mozzarella cheese, cut in half diagonally

Combine all ingredients except cheese. Mix well and shape into a round layer about 7″ in diameter. Place on a lightly greased baking pan and bake at 350° for about 1½ hours or until done. Arrange cheese slices on top of loaf in a spiral with ends overlapping at center top. Return to oven until cheese melts. Garnish center with a cherry tomato. Cut in wedges to serve. Serves 8.

Meat Loaf Supreme

1½ pounds ground beef
1 onion, chopped
½ green pepper, chopped
2 ribs celery, chopped
2 garlic cloves, crushed
1 teaspoon Italian Herb Seasoning
½ teaspoon oregano
½ package Meat Loaf Mix
3 eggs
½ cup flour

TOPPING

2 tablespoons butter
½ cup onion, chopped
2 ribs celery, chopped
¼ cup green pepper, chopped
8 ounce can tomato sauce
2 tablespoons brown sugar

Combine all the ingredients and place in a lightly greased loaf pan. Prepare the topping. In a saucepan sauté the onion, celery and green pepper until soft. Add the tomato sauce and sugar and simmer for a few minutes. Spread on top of the loaf and bake at 350° for about 1½ hours.

In a Hurry Mexican Beef Quiche—Saute 1½ pounds ground beef until browned. Add 1 package Taco Seasoning Mix and ½ cup water. Simmer for 5 minutes. Separate an 8 ounce package crescent dinner rolls into 8 triangles and place in a pie pan pressing to form a crust. On the bottom of the crust layer 1 cup crushed corn chips, the meat mixture, 1 cup sour cream and 1 cup crushed corn chips. Bake at 375° for 25 minutes or until crust is brown.

Meat Loaf with Green Chilies

2   pounds ground beef
3   chorizo sausage, mashed
2   eggs
1   onion, chopped
1   small green pepper, chopped
4   ounce can green chilies, drained
1   cup Pepperidge Farm Cornbread Stuffing Mix
1/2   cup sour cream or 1/2 cup creamy cottage cheese, 1 tablespoon
      milk, 1 teaspoon lemon juice and 1/8 teaspoon salt pureed in
      the blender
2   teaspoons salt
1   teaspoon garlic powder
1   cup Monterey Jack cheese

Preheat oven to 350°. Combine all the ingredients and mix well. Pack into a
loaf pan and bake for 1 hour.

Marvelous Meat Loaf

2   pounds ground beef
2   eggs
1/2   envelope onion soup mix
1/4   cup catsup
1/4   cup minced green pepper
1/2   cup sour cream
1/2   teaspoon garlic salt
1   teaspoon salt
1/2   teaspoon pepper
2   teaspoons Worcestershire sauce
3   slices bread soaked in 1/2 cup milk

TOPPING

1 1/2 cups catsup
1   cup brown sugar
3   tablespoons Dijon mustard

Preheat oven to 350°. Combine the first 10 ingredients and mix well. Add the
bread and pack into a loaf pan. Bake for 1 hour. Spread with topping and bake
for 15 minutes longer.

Mozzarella Meat Loaf

2 pounds ground beef
2 eggs
1 cup Pepperidge Farm crushed Cheddar & Romano
Cheese Croutons
1 onion, finely chopped
2 8-ounce cans tomato sauce with cheese
1½ teaspoons salt
1 teaspoon oregano
½ teaspoon Italian seasoning
¼ teaspoon pepper
2 cups grated Mozzarella cheese

Preheat oven to 350°. Combine the first 9 ingredients, using 1 can tomato sauce. Mix well and press half of mixture into a loaf pan. Sprinkle with the cheese and add the remaining meat mixture. Bake for 1 hour. Top with the remaining tomato sauce and bake for 30 minutes longer.

Ricotta Meat Loaf

2 pounds ground beef
2 eggs
½ pound Ricotta cheese
¼ cup oil
1 onion, chopped
1 small green pepper, chopped
8 ounce can tomato sauce
6 ounce can tomato paste
¼ teaspoon Tabasco
1 tablespoon Worcestershire sauce
½ teaspoon garlic powder
1 teaspoon oregano
1½ teaspoons sugar
1 teaspoon salt

Preheat oven to 350°. Combine the first 3 ingredients and mix well. In a skillet saute the onion and pepper in the oil until soft. Remove with a slotted spoon. Combine the remaining ingredients and mix well. Mix 1½ cups sauce with the onion mixture and meat mixture and place in a loaf pan. Top with the remaining sauce and bake for 1 hour.

Oriental Meat Loaf

1   pound lean beef
¹/₂   pound bulk sausage
1   garlic clove, crushed
1   onion, chopped
1   green pepper, chopped
2   ribs celery, chopped
8   ounce can crushed pineapple, drained and squeezed dry
³/₄   cup cooked brown rice
¹/₃   cup soy sauce
3   tablespoons brown sugar
1   teaspoon ground ginger
1   teaspoon thyme
1   teaspoon oregano
2   eggs, lightly beaten
¹/₂   cup chopped water chestnuts

TOPPING

1   cup light brown sugar
3   tablespoons tarragon vinegar
1   teaspoon Dijon mustard

Preheat oven to 350°. Combine all the ingredients in the order listed and mix well. Pack into a loaf pan and bake for 1 hour. In a saucepan combine the topping ingredients and bring to a boil. Boil for 2 minutes. Spread half the sauce on top the meatloaf and bake for 30 minutes longer basting with the remaining sauce once or twice during the final baking period.

Meat Loaf with Sherry Wine Sauce

2	pounds ground beef
1	cup Quaker Oats, pureed in a blender or food processor
2	eggs, beaten
2	teaspoons dry onion flakes
2	teaspoons salt
1/2	teaspoon pepper
3/4	cup tomato sauce
1	tablespoon cornstarch
1/2	cup brown sugar
1/2	cup tomato sauce
1/4	cup sherry
3/4	cup beef consomme
1	teaspoon prepared mustard
1	tablespoon wine vinegar

Preheat oven to 300°. Combine the first 7 ingredients and mix well. Shape into a loaf and bake for 1 hour. In a saucepan mix the cornstarch with the sugar. Add the remaining ingredients and cook over a medium heat until the sauce boils and thickens. Pour off the fat from the pan the meatloaf was cooked in and pour the sherry sauce over the loaf. Bake for 1/2 hour longer, basting frequently.

In a Hurry Beef Artichoke Bake—Saute 1 1/2 pounds ground beef, 1 chopped onion, 4 chopped green onions, and 1 chopped garlic clove in the marinade from 2 6-ounce cans marinated artichoke hearts. Add the artichoke hearts. Combine 1 pound Ricotta cheese 1/2 cup sour cream, 2 eggs, 1 teaspoon salt and 1/2 teaspoon tarragon. In the bottom of a shallow baking pan layer 1/2 the meat mixture and 1/2 the cheese mixture. Repeat and top with 1 cup grated Swiss cheese. Bake, uncovered, for 30 minutes or until bubbly.

GOURMET HELPER—A roast with the bone in will cook faster than a boneless roast—the bone carries the heat to the inside of the roast quicker.

Beef and Spinach Bake

1¹/₂ pounds ground beef
1   onion, chopped
6   green onions, tops and bottoms, chopped
2   8-ounce cans tomato sauce with tomato bits
¹/₃   cup chili sauce
12   corn tortillas, cut into quarters
¹/₂   cup red taco sauce
3   cups grated Monterey Jack cheese
1   cup sour cream
2   packages frozen chopped spinach, thawed and squeezed dry

Preheat oven to 375°. In a large skillet saute the meat and the onions until the meat is browned. Add the next 2 ingredients and simmer for 15 minutes. Season with salt and pepper. Dip tortilla quarters in the taco sauce, covering both sides. Place half the tortilla pieces in the bottom of a buttered baking dish. Spread meat mixture on top. Sprinkle with half the cheese. Place the remaining tortillas on top and spread with the sour cream. Cover with the spinach and top with the remaining cheese. Bake, covered, for 15 minutes. Bake, uncovered, for 15 minutes longer. Serves 8.

Baked Mexican Beef Spaghetti

1¹/₂ pounds ground beef
1   onion, chopped
1   green pepper, chopped
2   ribs celery, chopped
¹/₄   pound fresh mushrooms, thinly sliced
2   garlic cloves, minced
2¹/₂ cups tomato juice
¹/₂   package Enchilada Sauce Mix
¹/₄   cup chopped green olives
¹/₄   cup chopped pimentos
4   ounce can diced green chilies, drained
1   tablespoon chili powder
1   teaspoon oregano
1   teaspoon sugar
1   pound spaghetti, cooked and drained
2   cups Velvetta or Old English cheese

In a large heavy skillet saute the first 6 ingredients until the meat is browned and the vegetables are soft. Add the next 8 ingredients and simmer, covered, for 1 hour. Add the spaghetti and cheese and remove from the heat. Season with salt and pepper and refrigerate, covered, overnight. (YOU DO NOT HAVE TO CHILL OVERNIGHT BUT THE FLAVOR WILL IMPROVE IF YOU DO). Bring the mixture to room temperature before baking. Preheat oven to 325°. Bake for 1 hour or until bubbly. Serves 8.

Spiced Stuffed Peppers

1   pound ground beef
1   tablespoon butter
$^1/_2$ cup tomato puree
$^1/_2$ cup onion, finely minced
$^1/_4$ cup raisins
$^1/_4$ cup tomato, peeled, seeded and chopped
3   tablespoons dry sherry
2   tablespoon dark brown sugar
$1^1/_2$ tablespoons white wine tarragon vinegar
1   garlic clove, crushed
1   teaspoon salt
$^1/_2$ teaspoon cinnamon
$^1/_4$ teaspoon ground cloves
1   cup rice, cooked
6   large green peppers, cut off the tops and remove
     the seeds and ribs
6   slices Monterey Jack cheese

In a large saucepan sauté the beef in the butter until it is browned. Add the next 11 ingredients and cook over moderate heat for about 20 minutes, or until most of the liquid has evaporated. Let the mixture cool for 10 minutes and stir in the rice. Place the peppers cut side down on a rack in a roasting pan over 1" of boiling water. Steam them, covered, for about 10 minutes or until they are barely tender. Transfer them to a slightly greased baking dish and arrange them side by side. Sprinkle the cavities with salt and pepper and fill with the beef mixture. Place a slice of cheese on each pepper and cover dish loosely with foil. Bake at 375° for 20 minutes.

Sweet and Sour Stuffed Peppers

1   pound ground beef
1   onion, chopped
1   garlic clove, minced
3/4 cup tomato puree
1/4 cup raisins
3   tablespoons sherry
1 1/2 tablespoons red wine vinegar
2   tablespoons brown sugar
2   teaspoons salt
1/2 teaspoon cinnamon
1/4 teaspoon ground cloves
1   cup cooked rice
6   large green peppers, tops, ribs and seeds removed
1   cup grated Monterey Jack cheese

Preheat oven to 375°. In a large heavy skillet saute the beef, onion and garlic until the meat is browned and the vegetables are soft. Add the next 8 ingredients and cook over medium heat for 20 minutes. Cool mixture for 10 minutes and add rice. Steam the peppers, cut side down, on a rack in a pot of 1 inch boiling water, covered, for 10 minutes. Arrange the peppers, cut side up, in a buttered baking dish just large enough to hold them. Sprinkle with salt and pepper and fill with the meat mixture. Sprinkle with the cheese and cover loosely with foil. Bake for 20 minutes.

Artichoke Stuffed Peppers

2   pounds ground beef
6   green onions, tops and bottoms, chopped
1   package Uncle Bens Brown and Wild Rice with Mushrooms,
     cooked according to package directions
6   ounce jar marinated artichoke hearts, drained and chopped
     (reserve 1/4 cup marinade)
1/4 cup chopped green olives
1/4 cup mayonnaise
8   large green peppers, tops, seeds and ribs removed

Preheat oven to 375°. In a large heavy skillet saute the beef and onions until the beef is browned and the onions are soft. Remove from the heat and pour off excess liquid. Add the next 4 ingredients and the reserved marinade and mix well. Steam the peppers, cut side down, on a rack in a pot of 1 inch boiling water, covered, for 10 minutes. Arrange, cut side up, in a buttered baking dish just large enough to hold them. Sprinkle with salt and pepper and fill with the meat mixture. Cover loosely with foil and bake for 20 minutes.

Jalapeno Stuffed Peppers

1	pound ground beef
1	small onion, chopped
4	green onions, tops and bottoms, chopped
1	small green pepper, chopped
1	cup rice
4	ounce can diced green chilies, drained
1	tablespoon pimento
1	teaspoon chicken soup base
1/2	cup sour cream
6	large green peppers, tops, ribs and seeds removed
1	cup grated Monterey Jack cheese

Preheat oven to 375°. In a large heavy skillet saute the first 4 ingredients until the meat is browned and the vegetables are soft. Remove from the heat and add the next 5 ingredients. Steam the peppers, cut side down, on a rack in a pot of 1 inch boiling water, covered, for 10 minutes. Arrange, cut side up, in a buttered baking dish just large enough to hold them. Sprinkle with salt and pepper and fill with the meat mixture. Sprinkle with the cheese and cover loosely with foil. Bake for 20 minutes.

Taco Stuffed Peppers

2	pounds Jimmy Dean's seasoned taco mix
1	small onion, chopped
4	green onions, tops and bottoms, chopped
1	small green pepper, chopped
1	cup cooked rice
1/4	cup Ragu Pizza Quick
1/4	cup sour cream
1	cup grated Mozzarella cheese
8	large green peppers, tops, seeds and ribs removed

Preheat oven to 375°. In a large heavy skillet saute the meat, onions and green pepper until the meat is browned and the vegetables are soft. Remove from the heat and pour off any excess grease. Add the remaining ingredients and mix well. Steam the peppers, cut side down, on a rack in a pot of 1 inch boiling water, covered, for 10 minutes. Arrange, cut side up, in a buttered baking dish just large enough to hold them. Sprinkle with salt and pepper and fill with the meat mixture. Cover loosely with foil and bake for 20 minutes.

Loose Hamburgers

3   cups cooked roast beef or brisket, chopped fine
1   green pepper, chopped
1   onion, chopped
1   bottle catsup
3   tablespoons white wine tarragon vinegar
2   tablespoons Dijon mustard
1   tablespoon sugar
1   tablespoon Worcestershire sauce
1   teaspoon chili powder
    Dash Tabasco
    Salt and pepper, to taste

In a saucepan combine all the ingredients and simmer for 1 hour, stirring occasionally. Serve over buttered, toasted sesame buns. Serves 6–8.

Little Mushroom Beef Stuffed in Mushrooms

16 large, fresh mushrooms with stems removed
4   pounds ground beef
1   small yellow onion, chopped
4   green onions, tops and bottoms, chopped
1   small green pepper, finely chopped
1   teaspoon chili powder
1   teaspoon cumin
1   teaspoon pure granulated garlic
2   cups tomato puree
2   tablespoons burgundy
1   cup sour cream
3   cups Cheddar cheese, grated

In a saucepan sauté the beef, breaking it apart with a fork, until it is lightly browned. Add the remaining ingredients, except the cheese, and simmer for about 30 minutes. (Do not let mixture boil.) Place 2 mushrooms in lightly greased individual au gratin dishes. Cover with ground beef mixture and top with cheese. Bake at 350° about 15 minutes or until heated through. Serves 8.

Mock Pizza

1   pound ground beef
1/3   cup fresh bread crumbs
1/4   cup beef consommé
1   onion, finely chopped
1   garlic clove, minced
1   teaspoon salt
1/4   teaspoon fennel seed
3/4   cup Italian plum tomatoes, drained and chopped
1/4   teaspoon dried red pepper
1/4   pound Mozzarella cheese, sliced
3   tablespoons Parmesan cheese, freshly grated
1   tablespoon basil
1   tablespoon oregano
1   tablespoon parsley, chopped
    Salt and pepper, to taste

In a bowl combine the first 7 ingredients. Press the mixture into a 9″ pie plate to form a shell and bake in a 375° oven for 15 minutes. Pour off any fat that has collected and spread the shell with the tomatoes and red pepper. Arrange the sliced cheese on top and add the remaining ingredients. Bake for about 15 minutes longer and, to serve, cut in wedges.

Beef Noodle Casserole

2   pounds lean ground beef
1/2   stick butter
1   onion, chopped
1   green pepper, chopped
2   garlic cloves, crushed
1   tablespoon sugar
2   tablespoons Worcestershire sauce
15   ounce can tomato sauce
8   ounce package thin noodles, cooked
8   ounce package cream cheese, softened
16   ounce carton sour cream
4   green onions, tops and bottoms, chopped
1   cup Cheddar cheese, grated

In a large skillet sauté the onion, green pepper and garlic in butter until soft. Add the beef and, breaking up with a wooden spoon, sauté until lightly browned. Add sugar, Worcestershire, tomato sauce and salt and pepper, to taste. Simmer, covered, for about 1 hour. Drain off excess fat. In a mixing bowl combine the onions, cream cheese and sour cream and beat at low speed until well blended. In a lightly greased baking dish layer half the noodles, half the sour cream mixture, and half the meat sauce. Repeat. Sprinkle with the cheese and bake at 350° for 30 minutes or until bubbly. Serves 8.

Liver Provencale

6   slices bacon cooked crisp, drained and crumbled
1   pound calves liver, sliced thin
1   onion, thinly sliced
2   16-ounce cans Italian tomatoes
1/2   cup catsup
1/4   cup water
2   teaspoons Worcestershire sauce
      Dash Tabasco

In a large heavy skillet saute the liver and onion in the bacon drippings until the liver is browned on both sides and the onion is soft. Add the remaining ingredients and simmer, covered, for 30 minutes or until the liver is tender. Season with salt and pepper, top with the bacon, and serve.

Veal Vera Cruz

8   veal cutlets
1   cup flour
4   green onions, tops and bottoms, chopped
1/2   stick butter
2   12-ounce bottles chili sauce
2   tablespoons brandy
1/2   teaspoon cumin
1/2   teaspoon Italian seasoning
1/4   teaspoon coriander (cilantro)
1 1/2 cups grated Monterey Jack cheese
1/2   cup grated sharp Cheddar cheese
1/4   cup finely chopped parsley

Preheat oven to 350°. Season veal with salt and pepper and coat with the flour. In a large heavy skillet saute the veal and the onions in the butter until the veal is browned on both sides. Transfer the mixture to a shallow baking dish arranging the veal side by side. Combine the remaining 5 ingredients and pour over the veal. Top with the cheeses and bake, covered, for 30 minutes or until veal is tender. Sprinkle with parsley and serve.

Veal with Artichokes

8 veal cutlets
1 cup flour
4 green onions, tops and bottoms, chopped
3 ribs celery, chopped
2 tablespoons oil
1½ cups evaporated milk
1 cup sour cream
¼ cup white wine
14 ounce can artichoke hearts
1 cup grated Monterey Jack cheese

Season veal with salt and pepper and dust with flour. In a large heavy skillet saute the veal, onions and celery in the oil until the veal is browned on both sides. Transfer to a shallow baking dish arranging the veal side by side. Combine the next 4 ingredients and pour over the veal. Top with the cheese and bake, covered, for 30 minutes or until the veal is tender.

Little Mushroom Veal Parmesan

8 veal cutlets
1 cup Parmesan cheese, freshly grated
¼ cup oil

TOMATO SAUCE

2 cups tomato puree
½ cup currant jelly
½ cup Parmesan cheese, freshly grated
2 tablespoons burgundy

Bread the veal with seasoning salt, pepper and cheese. Place in a shallow baking dish and sprinkle with oil. Brown in a 350° oven. While veal is browning prepare the sauce. In a saucepan combine the sauce ingredients and simmer, stirring, for about 10 minutes. Pour sauce over veal and bake, covered, for about 40 minutes or until the veal is tender.

Veal with Chutney

8 veal cutlets
1 cup flour
2 tablespoons oil
2 cups heavy cream
2 tablespoons Worcestershire sauce
1/2 cup chopped chutney
1/2 cup white wine

Preheat oven to 350°. Season the veal with salt and pepper and dust with flour. In a large heavy skillet saute the veal in the oil until browned on both sides. Transfer to a baking dish arranging the veal side by side. In the top of a double boiler combine the cream, Worcestershire and chutney and cook over a low heat for 1 1/2 hours, stirring occasionally. Pour over the veal. Add the wine and bake, covered, for 30 minutes or until the veal is tender.

Veal Dijon

8 veal cutlets
1 cup flour
1/2 stick butter
1/4 pound fresh mushrooms, thinly sliced
4 green onions, tops and bottoms, chopped
2 cups chicken stock
2 tablespoons Dijon mustard
1/4 cup white wine
1 tablespoon cornstarch
1 cup evaporated milk

Preheat oven to 350°. Season veal with salt and pepper and dust with flour. In a large heavy skillet saute the veal in the butter until browned on both sides. Transfer to a baking dish arranging the veal side by side. In the same skillet saute the mushrooms and onions until soft. Add the next 3 ingredients and simmer until mixture reaches a boil. Pour over the veal and bake, covered, for 30 minutes or until veal is tender. Remove the veal and keep warm. Combine the cornstarch with the milk and blend into the mustard sauce cooking until thickened. Pour over the veal and serve.

Little Mushroom Veal in Mushroom Wine Sauce

8   veal cutlets
2   tablespoons oil
1/2 stick butter
4   green onions, tops and bottoms, chopped
1   can mushrooms, pieces and stems (reserve liquid)
2   cans cream of mushroom soup
2   tablespoons burgundy

Season the veal with seasoning salt and pepper. Place in a baking pan, sprinkle with the oil and brown in a 350° oven. In a saucepan saute the onions and mushrooms in the butter until soft. Add the remaining ingredients and pour over the veal. Bake 30 minutes longer or until veal is tender.

Veal Provencale

8   veal cutlets, cut in 1/2" x 2" strips
1   onion, sliced
1   green pepper, cut into thin strips
2   tablespoons oil
16 ounce can stewed tomatoes
1/2 teaspoon garlic powder
1/4 teaspoon oregano
1/4 teaspoon basil
1   cup grated Mozzarella cheese
1   cup white wine

Preheat oven to 325°. In a large heavy skillet saute the first 3 ingredients in the oil until the veal is browned on both sides and the vegetables are soft. Transfer to a baking dish arranging the veal side by side. Add the remaining ingredients, in the order given, and bake, covered, for 1 hour. Serve over noodles or rice.

In a Hurry Veal Marsala—Pound 1 cup grated Parmesan cheese into 8 veal cutlets. Season meat with salt and pepper and cut into 3" x 1" strips. Brown in 1/4 cup oil. Add 1 cup beef consomme, 1 cup Marsala, 1/2 teaspoon thyme and 1/2 teaspoon marjoram. Simmer, covered, for 30 minutes or until meat is tender. Serve with noodles.

Little Mushroom Veal Scallapini

8   veal cutlets
1   cup Parmesan cheese, freshly grated
¼   cup oil

SOUR CREAM SAUCE
2   cans cream of chicken soup
½   teaspoon chicken soup base
1   cup sour cream
2   tablespoons sherry

Slice veal diagonally into strips and coat with seasoning salt, pepper and cheese. Place in a shallow baking dish and sprinkle with oil. Brown in a 350° oven. While veal is browning, prepare the sauce. In a saucepan combine the sauce ingredients and simmer, stirring, for about 10 minutes. (Do not boil). Remove veal from oven and in a casserole place a layer of veal, a layer of sauce, a layer of veal, and the remaining sauce. Bake for about 35 minutes or until veal is tender. Serve over noodles or rice. Serves 8.

Veal in Sour Cream Sauce

4   veal cutlets
¼   cup flour (seasoned with ¼ cup Parmesan cheese)
2   tablespoons butter
1   onion, thinly sliced
2   cups sour cream

In a large heavy skillet saute the onion in the butter until soft. Dust the veal with the seasoned flour and saute on both sides until browned. (Add more butter if needed.) Season the meat with a little salt and pepper and on a low heat stir in the sour cream. Cover and simmer until the veal is tender. Do not allow the mixture to boil.

Little Mushroom Veal Milanese

8 veal cutlets
2 eggs
1 cup milk
1 cup bread crumbs
1 cup Cheddar cheese, grated
¹⁄₄ cup oil

CREAM SHERRY SAUCE

4 cups milk
4 tablespoons cornstarch
2 teaspoons chicken soup base
1 cup Cheddar cheese, grated
2 tablespoons dry sherry

In a bowl beat the eggs and the milk until well blended. Combine the bread crumbs and the cheese. Dip the veal in the egg mixture and then coat with the bread crumb mixture. Place in a shallow baking dish and sprinkle with oil. Bake at 350° for about 30 minutes or until tender. While the veal is baking, prepare the sauce. In a saucepan heat the milk. Add the cornstarch and soup base and stir constantly with a wire whisk until the mixture thickens to a cream sauce consistency. Add the cheese and sherry and simmer until the cheese is melted. Pour over the veal.

Little Mushroom Veal Normandy

8 veal cutlets
2 tablespoons oil

BRANDY SAUCE

2 cans cream of mushroom soup
2 tablespoons brandy, warmed
2 apples, peeled and sliced
2 tablespoons butter
¹⁄₄ cup sugar and cinnamon mix

Season veal with seasoning salt and pepper. Place in a shallow baking dish and sprinkle with oil. Brown in a 350° oven. Combine the soup and brandy and pour over the veal. Bake at 350° for about 40 minutes. Sauté apples in the butter until barely soft. Sprinkle with the sugar and cinnamon. Serve on top of each veal slice.

Roquefort Veal

3   pounds veal scallops, ¹/₈" thick
1   cup flour
¹/₂   cup oil
2   cups heavy cream
1   cup Roquefort cheese crumbles

Season veal with salt and pepper and dust with the flour. In a large heavy skillet saute the veal in the oil for 3 minutes on each side. Transfer to a platter and keep warm. To the same skillet add the cream and cook until slightly reduced. Add the cheese and stir until smooth. Pour over the veal and serve immediately.

Veal with Pears

16   3-ounce veal scallops
1   cup flour
4   fresh pears, peeled, cored and sliced
1   stick butter
¹/₂   cup pear brandy
2   cups heavy cream

Season veal with salt and pepper and dust with the flour. In a large heavy skillet saute the pears in the butter until barely cooked. Remove and keep warm. In the same skillet saute the veal 3 minutes on each side. Remove and keep warm. In the same skillet add the brandy and cook over a moderate heat, stirring frequently, scraping up all the bits from the bottom of the pan. Add the cream and continue cooking until mixture turns a rich, ivory color. Place the pear slices on top of the veal and cover with the sauce.

GOURMET HELPER—When storing ground beef in the refrigerator for a couple of days, flatten it—the cold can penetrate faster.

Veal Scallops with Apples and Brandy

16   veal scallops (about 3½″ to 4″ in diameter)
4   Golden Delicious apples, peeled, cored and sliced
    Juice of 3 lemons
½   cup flour
6   tablespoons sweet butter
3   tablespoons oil
½   cup Calvados brandy
2   cups heavy cream

In a bowl marinate the apples in the lemon juice. Season the veal with salt and pepper and dust with flour. In a large heavy skillet sauté the veal in the butter and oil for about 4 minutes on each side or until lightly browned. Transfer the veal to a heated platter and keep warm in a 175° oven. Add the apples, lemon juice and brandy to the same skillet and scrape up all the encrustations on the pan and cook over moderate heat, stirring frequently about 3 minutes. Add the cream and continue cooking until mixture turns a rich, ivory color. Reduce the heat and cook, stirring frequently, about 10 minutes or until the cream has reduced to about half and the sauce coats a spoon. Taste for seasonings. Pour sauce over veal.

Olived Veal

8   veal scallops, ¼″ thick
1   cup flour, seasoned with salt and pepper
1   cup oil
1   onion, chopped
1   garlic clove, minced
1   green pepper, chopped
½   pound fresh mushrooms, thinly sliced
16   ounce can Italian tomatoes
¼   cup finely chopped prosciutto ham
¼   cup finely chopped green olives
2   cups grated Mozzarella cheese

Dust the veal with the flour and in a heavy skillet saute in ½ cup oil until browned on both sides. Transfer to a platter and keep warm. In the same skillet saute the next four ingredients in the remaining oil until soft. Add the remaining ingredients and bring to a boil, stirring constantly. Cook over a high heat until mixture is thick enough to coat the back of a spoon. Pour over the veal and serve.

Veal Marsala

16   3-ounce veal scallops
1   cup flour
$^1/_2$ stick butter
4   green onions, tops and bottoms, chopped
3   tablespoons chopped shallots
$^1/_2$ pound fresh mushrooms, thinly sliced
$^1/_2$ cup dry sherry
1   cup dry Marsala
2   cups heavy cream
$^1/_2$ cup finely chopped parsley

Season veal with salt and pepper and dust with the flour. In a large heavy skillet saute the veal in the butter for 3 minutes on each side. Remove and keep warm. In the same skillet saute the next 3 ingredients until soft. Add the wines and boil until sauce is reduced by one-half. Add the cream and cook until reduced by one-half. Pour over the veal, sprinkle with parsley and serve.

Veal Scallops with Cheese

6   veal scallops, pounded lightly
2   eggs, lightly beaten (seasoned with salt and pepper)
$^1/_2$ cup lemon juice
1   cup bread crumbs
3   tablespoons butter
3   tablespoons oil
12   thin slices lemon
6   thin slices Swiss cheese
1   cup heavy cream

Dip the scallops into the eggs, then into the lemon juice and then into the bread crumbs. In a heavy skillet sauté the scallops on one side only until browned. Remove with a slotted spatula and place, cooked side down, side by side in a baking dish. Cover each scallop with 2 lemon slices and 1 cheese slice. Sprinkle with salt and pepper and pour the cream over the veal mixture. Bake at 400° about 15 minutes.

Veal and Sour Cream Bake

1/3	cup oil
2	garlic cloves, crushed
3	pounds veal round, pounded thin and cut into serving pieces
3/4	pound fresh mushrooms, thinly sliced
3/4	pound noodles, cooked
1 1/2	cups sour cream
3/4	pound Swiss cheese, sliced
6	tomatoes, sliced
1 1/2	cups dry white wine
1 1/2	cups Parmesan cheese, freshly grated

In a skillet sauté the garlic and the veal. Sprinkle with salt and pepper. Add the mushrooms and simmer, covered, for about 20 minutes. Toss the noodles with the sour cream. In a 3 quart baking dish place half the noodle mixture, half the veal and mushrooms and half the cheese and tomato slices. Repeat. To the same skillet add the wine and Parmesan cheese. Heat, scraping the brown bits from the bottom of the skillet. Pour over the casserole and bake, uncovered, at 400° about 30 minutes. Serves 8–10.

Roast Pork with Apple Brandy

5	to 6 pound pork loin roast (have butcher crack chops)
3/4	cup Calvados
1	teaspoon ground cloves
1	teaspoon allspice
6	potatoes, peeled and quartered
6	Golden Delicious apples, peeled and sliced
1/2	cup brown sugar
1/4	teaspoon cinnamon

In a shallow enamel or Pyrex dish marinate the pork roast in the brandy for several hours or overnight, turning frequently. Drain and reserve marinade. Rub pork all over with seasoning salt, pepper, cloves and allspice. Transfer the pork to a roasting pan and bake, covered, at 325° for 1 1/2 hours. Remove the pork and pour off the fat in the pan. Spread the apples in the bottom of the pan and sprinkle them with the sugar and cinnamon. In a shallow pan, warm the reserved marinade adding 1/4 cup Calvados. Ignite and pour over the apples. Place pork roast on top of the apples and the potatoes around the roast. Bake, covered, for 1 hour more or until roast is tender. Serves 8.

Pork Roast with Sauerkraut

5   to 6 pound pork loin roast
3/4   teaspoon salt
1/4   teaspoon pepper
2   pounds canned sauerkraut, drained
1   large yellow onion, chopped
1   garlic clove, sliced
6   ounce can frozen apple juice concentrate, thawed

Season the pork with salt and pepper, place on a rack in a roasting pan and brown in a preheated 500° oven for 10 minutes. Pour off any excess fat. In a saucepan heat the sauerkraut and onion. Pour over the roast. Place the garlic slices on top and pour in the apple juice concentrate. Reduce the oven to 200° and return the roast to the oven, tightly covered. Bake for 8 hours, or longer. Slice the pork in thick slices and serve with the sauerkraut mixture.

Hawaiian Pork Roast

5   pound boneless pork roast, tied for roasting
3   jars strained apricots (baby food)
1/2   cup honey
1/4   cup lemon juice
1/4   cup soy sauce
1   garlic clove, minced
1   onion, finely chopped
1   cup Ginger Ale
1/8   teaspoon ginger
1/8   teaspoon pepper

Place pork roast in a shallow enamel or Pyrex dish. Combine 2 jars of the apricots with the other ingredients. Pour over roast and marinate 4 hours, turning occasionally. Light grill and let coals burn down until they are covered with gray ashes. Remove pork from marinade. (Reserve marinade.) Place the roast on a spit or in a kettle type grill. Cook for about 3½ hours (meat thermometer will register 185° when done). During the last ½ hour baste every 10 minutes with the reserved marinade. Five minutes before removing from grill, spread the remaining jar of apricots over the roast. Serves 6.

Pork Caldia

4   pounds pork, cut into 1¹/₂″ cubes
1   onion, chopped
4   green onions, chopped
1   green pepper, chopped
1   jalapeño pepper, seeded and chopped
2   cups potatoes, peeled and cubed
16 ounce can tomatoes
¹/₂ teaspoon pure granulated garlic
¹/₄ teaspoon ginger
    Salt and pepper, to taste

Boil pork in water to cover. Lower heat and simmer, covered, for about 3 hours or until tender. Add the remaining ingredients and simmer, covered, for 1 hour. Serve over rice. Serves 8.

Mango Pork

3   pounds boneless pork filets, cut into 16 medallions
1   cup flour
¹/₂ stick butter
¹/₂ cup finely minced shallots
2   mangos, peeled and finely chopped
1   cup dry white wine
3   tablespoons Amaretto
2   tablespoons Cognac
1¹/₂ cups heavy cream

Season pork with salt and pepper and dust with the flour. In a large heavy skillet saute the pork in the butter until browned on both sides. Lower the heat and simmer, covered, until pork is cooked and is tender when tested with a fork. Transfer to a serving platter and keep warm. In the same skillet saute the shallots and the mangos for 10 minutes. Place in a blender or food processor and puree. To the same skillet add the next 3 ingredients and cook over a high heat reducing the sauce by half. Add the cream and continue cooking until the sauce turns a rich, ivory color. Reduce the heat and cook, stirring, until the sauce has reduced by half and coats the back of a spoon. Add the mango mixture, season with salt and pepper, and pour over the pork. Serves 8.

Chinese Pork and Rice

2   pounds pork, cubed
1   onion, chopped
2   garlic cloves, chopped
1   teaspoon marjoram
1   teaspoon basil
1   teaspoon oregano
1   teaspoon thyme
1   teaspoon Worcestershire sauce
1   teaspoon soy sauce
1   teaspoon pepper
1/2 teaspoon chili powder
2   tomatoes, diced
1/2 cup dry sherry
3   cups beef consommé
1 1/2 cups raw rice

In a saucepan brown the pork on all sides in its own fat. Add the onion and garlic and sauté until the onion is soft. Add all other ingredients except the rice and simmer for about 15 minutes. Stir in the rice and cook the mixture, without stirring, until rice is tender. Serves 8.

Pork Carbonnade

3   pounds lean pork, cut into 2" cubes
2   tablespoons oil
1   large onion, finely chopped
2   garlic cloves, crushed
1   large tomato, peeled, seeded and chopped
1   green pepper, chopped
2   tablespoons pimentos, chopped
1   jalapeño pepper, seeded and chopped
1   tablespoon coriander
1/2 teaspoon cumin
1/2 teaspoon oregano
2   cups beer

In a heavy skillet sauté the pork in the oil until lightly browned. With a slotted spoon remove the pork to a Dutch oven. Pour off all but 2 tablespoons of fat remaining in skillet. Sauté the onion and garlic until soft. Add the remaining ingredients, except the beer, and season with salt and pepper. Cook the mixture, stirring occasionally for about 10 minutes. Pour the sauce over the pork cubes and add the beer. Simmer the stew, covered, for about 2 hours or until meat is tender and sauce is thick. Serve over rice.

Acapulco Pork Stew

4   **pounds boneless pork, cut into 2″ pieces**
2   **tablespoons oil**
1   **onion, chopped**
1   **garlic clove, minced**
2   **cups canned tomatoes**
4   **ounce can diced green chilies, drained**
2   **fresh jalapeno peppers, seeded and chopped (omit if you don't like highly seasoned stew)**
1   **teaspoon oregano**
1/8   **teaspoon brown sugar**
1   **teaspoon cumin**
1/2   **teaspoon chili powder**
2   **chorizo sausages, skinned, sliced and browned**

In a large heavy skillet saute the pork in the oil until browned on all sides. Transfer to a large pot, add water to barely cover the meat and cook, covered, for 1 hour. Remove pork and set aside (reserve 1 cup stock). In the same skillet saute the onion and garlic until soft. Add the next 7 ingredients and cook for 10 minutes. Add the reserved stock, season with salt and pepper, and cook, stirring occasionally, until the sauce begins to thicken. Add the sausage and the pork and heat. Serve with rice or pasta. Serves 6–8.

In a Hurry Pork Chop Potato Bake—Saute 4 pork chops in 2 tablespoons oil until browned on both sides. In a baking dish layer 3 cups sliced potatoes, 1 thinly sliced onion, 1 teaspoon salt, 1/2 teaspoon pepper and 1/4 cup flour. Place the pork chops on top. Add 1 1/2 cups hot milk and bake, covered, at 350° for 45 minutes or until chops are tender. Bake, uncovered, for 15 minutes or until browned.

Pork Tender with Mustard Sauce

3   pounds pork tenderloin
1/4 cup bourbon
1/4 cup soy sauce
1/4 cup Worcestershire sauce
2   tablespoons brown sugar

SAUCE

1/4 cup sour cream
1/4 cup mayonnaise
1   tablespoon dry mustard
1   tablespoon chopped shallots
1   teaspoon tarragon vinegar

Preheat oven to 325°. Combine the bourbon, soy sauce, Worcestershire and brown sugar and marinate the pork in the mixture for several hours. Transfer the meat to a heavy roasting pan and bake, basting frequently with the marinade, for 1 hour or until tender. Carve the meat on the diagonal in thin slices and keep warm. Combine all the sauce ingredients and serve with the pork on the side.

Pork Chops Michelle

12 pork chops
1   onion, thinly sliced
1   bell pepper, thinly sliced
3   cups water
2   cups catsup
1/3 cup Worcestershire sauce
1   tablespoon chili powder
1   teaspoon salt
2   teaspoons brown sugar
     Dash Tabasco

Preheat oven to 350°. In a large heavy skillet saute the pork chops, onion and green pepper until the chops are browned on both sides. Transfer to a shallow baking dish. Combine the remaining ingredients and pour over the chops. Bake, covered, for 45 minutes or until tender.

Pork Chops in Orange Sauce

8   pork chops, seasoned with salt and pepper
3   tablespoons oil
1/4 cup packed dark brown sugar
1/4 cup orange marmalade
2   tablespoons vinegar
1   teaspoon dry mustard
1   cup orange juice

In a large heavy skillet saute the chops in the oil until browned on both sides. Combine remaining ingredients and pour over the chops. Simmer, covered, for 1 hour or until the chops are tender. Transfer to a platter and keep warm. Cook sauce over a high heat until it thickens. Pour over chops and serve.

Perfect Pork Chops

8   pork chops, seasoned with salt, pepper and 1 teaspoon thyme
2   tablespoons oil
2   potatoes, peeled and cubed
2   onions, thinly sliced
1   garlic clove, minced
3   cups sour cream
1/4 cup Dijon mustard

Preheat oven to 350°. In a large heavy skillet saute the chops in the oil until browned on both sides. In a greased baking dish arrange the potato slices. Place the chops on top, layer with the onions and sprinkle with the garlic. Combine the sour cream and mustard and season with salt and pepper. Spread over the top and bake, covered, for 1 1/2 hours or until chops are tender.

Apricot Pork Chops

8   pork chops, seasoned with salt and pepper
3   tablespoons oil
1/2 teaspoon thyme
17 ounce can apricot halves
1/2 cup maple syrup

Preheat oven to 350°. In a large heavy skillet saute the chops in the oil until browned on both sides. Transfer to a baking dish and add the remaining ingredients. Bake, covered, for 1 1/2 hours or until chops are tender.

Spicy Pork Chops

1   bottle catsup
1/2 cup jalapeno jelly
1/2 package Taco Seasoning Mix
8   pork chops

Preheat oven to 350°. Combine the first 3 ingredients and mix well. In a heavy skillet saute the chops until browned on both sides. Transfer chops to a baking dish, pour the catsup mixture over the chops and bake, covered, for 1 hour or until the chops are tender.

Quick Pork Chops with Rice

6   pork chops, 3/4" thick
1 1/2 cups rice, cooked
1   cup orange juice
1   can chicken rice soup

Season chops with salt, pepper and sauté in a small amount of oil until browned on both sides. Place rice in a 7" x 12" baking dish. Pour orange juice over rice. Arrange browned chops on rice and pour chicken soup over chops. Cover and bake at 350° for 45 minutes. Uncover and bake 10 minutes longer. Serves 6.

Chutney Pork Chops

8   pork chops, seasoned with salt and pepper
1   cup catsup
1/2 cup lemon juice
1/2 teaspoon dry mustard
1   tablespoon brown sugar
1   tablespoon Worcestershire sauce
1   cup water
1 1/2 cups mango chutney

Preheat oven to 350°. In a large heavy skillet brown the chops. Transfer to a baking dish. In a saucepan combine the remaining ingredients and simmer over a low heat for 20 minutes. Pour over the chops and bake for 1 1/2 hours or until the chops are tender.

Pork Chops with Rice

8   pork chops, seasoned with salt and pepper
1   cup uncooked rice
1½ cups orange juice
½   cup water
½   teaspoon salt
1   can Cheddar cheese soup

Preheat oven to 350°. In a large heavy skillet saute the chops in their own fat until browned on both sides. Place rice in the bottom of a flat baking dish. Add the next 3 ingredients. Arrange the pork chops on top and cover with the soup. Bake, covered, for 1 hour or until the chops are tender. Bake, uncovered, for 15 minutes longer.

Pork Chops with Sour Cream

8   pork chops, seasoned with salt and pepper
1   cup dry white wine
10 ounce jar red currant jelly
16 ounce carton sour cream

Preheat oven to 350°. In a large heavy skillet saute the chops until browned on both sides. Transfer to a shallow baking dish. Combine the remaining ingredients and pour over the chops. Bake, covered, for 1 hour or until the chops are tender.

Pork Chops with Honey

6   pork chops
1   tablespoon oil
1   cup brown sugar
1   cup pineapple juice, unsweetened
⅔   cup honey
1   tablespoon Dijon mustard
4   cloves

In a heavy skillet brown the pork chops in oil. Transfer them to a baking dish. Combine remaining ingredients and pour over the chops. Bake, uncovered, at 350° for 1½ hours or until chops are tender.

Burgundy Pork Chops

8   pork chops, seasoned with salt and pepper
3   tablespoons oil
1   onion, thinly sliced
1   pound can Italian tomatoes
4   ounce can diced green chilies, drained
1/2 cup burgundy wine
2   teaspoons salt
1/2 teaspoon cumin
1   tablespoon brown sugar

In a large heavy skillet saute the chops in the oil until browned on both sides. Add the remaining ingredients and simmer, covered, for 1 1/2 hours or until the chops are tender.

Italian Pork Chops

8   pork chops, seasoned with salt and pepper
1   teaspoon garlic powder
1   cup grated Parmesan cheese
3   tablespoons oil
1   cup beef stock
2   10-ounce cans tomato puree
1   teaspoon oregano
1   teaspoon Italian seasoning
2   cups grated Mozzarella cheese

Preheat oven to 350°. Combine the garlic powder and Parmesan cheese and spread on the chops. Pound with a wooden mallet. In a large heavy skillet saute the chops in the oil until browned on both sides. Transfer to a baking dish. Combine the next 4 ingredients and pour over the chops. Bake, covered, for 1 hour. Sprinkle with the cheese and bake, uncovered, for 30 minutes longer.

In a Hurry Drunken Pork Chops—Combine 1 1/2 cups chili sauce, 1/2 cup currant jelly, 1 envelope French dressing mix, dash Worcestershire sauce, 1 bunch chopped green onions, 1 teaspoon dried minced garlic and 1/4 cup dry white wine. Brown 4 pork chops in a skillet and transfer to a shallow baking dish. Cover with the sauce and bake, covered, for 1 hour or until the chops are tender.

Mexican Pork Chops

4   loin pork chops, 1½" thick
6   tablespoons oil
2   garlic cloves, minced
1   onion, minced
1   teaspoon cumin
1   teaspoon oregano
1   cup tomato sauce
2   tablespoons chili powder
2   tablespoons green chilies, chopped
    Spice Island Cilantro

Brown chops in oil on both sides. Pour off excess oil, reduce heat to medium and add garlic and onion. Cook until onion is soft. Add next 4 ingredients and simmer until tender. Taste for seasonings. Sprinkle with chopped chilies and cilantro, spooning sauce over top of chops.

Mexican Pork Chops II

8   pork chops, seasoned with salt and pepper
2   tablespoons oil
1   onion, chopped
4   green onions, tops and bottoms, chopped
1   small green pepper, chopped
4   ounce can diced green chilies, drained
2   cups canned tomatoes
1   cup catsup
¼   cup dry white wine
½   teaspoon beef soup base
1   tablespoon cumin
1   tablespoon basil

Preheat oven to 350°. In a large heavy skillet saute the chops until browned on both sides. Transfer to a shallow baking dish. In the same skillet saute the next 3 ingredients until soft. Add the remaining ingredients and simmer for 10 minutes. Pour over the chops and bake, covered, for 1 hour or until the chops are tender.

Ranch Pork Chops

1   cup chili sauce
10   ounce can Rotel tomatoes with green chilies
½   cup currant jelly
½   package Hidden Valley Ranch Dressing Mix
1   bunch green onions, tops and bottoms, chopped
2   garlic cloves, crushed
8   pork chops

Preheat oven to 350°. Combine the first 6 ingredients and mix well. In a heavy skillet saute the chops until browned on both sides. Transfer chops to a baking dish, pour the tomato mixture over the chops and bake, covered, for 1 hour or until the chops are tender.

Pork Chops in Tomato Sauce

6   pork chops
2   tablespoons oil
1   tablespoon chili powder
4   tablespoons flour
2   teaspoons salt
1   teaspoon Worcestershire sauce
2   teaspoons A-1 sauce
½   bottle tomato catsup
1   catsup bottle of water
     Dash Tabasco
1   onion, sliced
2   green peppers, sliced

Combine the chili powder, flour and salt and coat the chops with the mixture, shaking off any excess flour. In a heavy skillet brown the chops on both sides in the oil. Transfer the chops to a baking dish, placing them side by side. Place an onion and green pepper slice on each chop. In a saucepan heat the remaining ingredients. Pour over the chops and bake at 350°, covered, for 1 hour or until tender.

In a Hurry Preserved Pork Chops—Combine 1 bottle Kraft's Golden Blend Italian Dressing, 1½ cups peach preserves, and 1 envelope onion soup mix. Brown 4 pork chops in a skillet and transfer to a shallow baking dish. Cover with the sauce and bake, covered, for 1 hour or until the chops are tender.

Pork Chops and Corn

6   pork chops, 1/2" thick
2   tablespoons oil
2   tablespoons Dijon mustard
2   tablespoons butter
1/2   onion, chopped
4   green onions, tops and bottoms, chopped
2   ribs celery, chopped
1/2   green pepper, chopped
2   tablespoons pimentos, chopped
16   ounce can cream style corn
1   teaspoon salt
2/3   cup soft bread crumbs
1   cup water, heated

Spread the pork chops lightly with mustard and in a heavy skillet brown them on each side in the oil. With a slotted spatula remove pork chops to a baking dish placing them side by side. In a saucepan sauté the onions, celery and green pepper in the butter until soft. Combine the onion mixture, pimentos, corn, salt and bread crumbs and mix well. Taste for seasonings. Pour the heated water around the chops and top with the corn mixture. Cover and bake at 350° for 15 minutes. Uncover and bake 45 minutes longer or until chops are tender.

Pork Chops with Bing Cherries

8   pork chops, seasoned with salt and pepper
2   tablespoons oil
2   tablespoons flour
1   teaspoon sugar
1/4   teaspoon cinnamon
1/4   teaspoon dry mustard
20   ounce jar Bing cherries, drained (reserve juice)
2   tablespoons dark rum
1/2   teaspoon beef soup base

In a large heavy skillet saute the chops until browned on both sides. Remove chops and set aside. In the same skillet heat the oil, stir in the next 4 ingredients and cook to a thick paste. Add the reserved juice, rum, beef base, and the chops. Simmer, covered, for 1 hour or until chops are tender. Add cherries the last 10 minutes of cooking.

Pork Chops with Cheese

4   pork chops
1   tablespoon oil
1   cup Swiss cheese, grated
1   tablespoon Dijon mustard
1   tablespoon heavy cream
1   garlic clove, crushed
1   tablespoon green onion, finely chopped
1   egg yolk
2   tablespoons dry white wine
2   tablespoons water

Season the chops with salt and pepper. In a heavy skillet sauté the chops in the oil until browned on each side and cooked thoroughly. While the chops are cooking, combine the remaining ingredients, except the wine and water. Spread one side of the chops with the cheese mixture. Run the chops under a preheated broiler until the topping is browned. Pour off the fat from the skillet and add the wine and water, bringing to a boil. Stir to dissolve the brown bits clinging to the bottom and sides of the pan. Pour the hot wine over the chops.

Easy Spareribs

4   pounds spareribs
    Lemon Pepper Marinade
6   ounce can frozen orange juice concentrate, undiluted
2   teaspoons Worcestershire sauce
1/2 teaspoon garlic salt
1/8 teaspoon pepper

Season the ribs with the Lemon Pepper Marinade and place them, meaty side down, in a shallow roasting pan. Bake at 450° for 30 minutes. Drain off the fat, turn the ribs over and bake 30 minutes more. Drain off the fat. Combine the remaining ingredients and with a basting brush cover the ribs with the sauce. Reduce the heat to 350°, cover the ribs with foil, and bake for 1 hour or until ribs are tender. Baste, occasionally, during the last hour of baking. Serves 4.

Spicy Spareribs

$^1/_2$ cup chili sauce
3   tablespoons prepared mustard
$^1/_2$ teaspoon garlic powder
1   teaspoon Tabasco
4   pounds spareribs, cut into individual ribs
$^1/_2$ cup flour
1   teaspoon thyme
1   tablespoon salt
$^1/_2$ teaspoon pepper
$^1/_4$ cup oil

Preheat oven to 350°. Combine the first 4 ingredients and brush mixture on all sides of the ribs. Combine next 4 ingredients and shake the ribs in this mixture until well coated. In a large heavy skillet saute the ribs in the oil until browned on all sides. Transfer to a shallow baking dish and bake for 1 hour or until tender. Serves 4.

Honey Barbecued Ribs

$^1/_4$ cup sugar
3   tablespoons honey
3   tablespoons soy sauce
1   cup hot chicken broth
2   tablespoons catsup
1   teaspoon salt
4   4-rib racks country-style ribs

Preheat oven to 300°. Place ribs in a roasting pan. Combine the first 6 ingredients and pour over the ribs. Marinate, at room temperature, for 3 hours, turning ribs occasionally. Bake, uncovered, 3 hours, turning occasionally. Serves 4-6.

GOURMET HELPER—Save the juices from your spiced fruits and other canned fruits—use them to pour over ham slices while baking.

Barbecued Ribs I

2   cups Kraft's Barbecue Sauce (not hickory smoked)
2   tablespoons lemon juice
2   bay leaves
3   tablespoons chili powder
3/4 cup Worcestershire sauce
2   teaspoons garlic powder
1/2 cup packed brown sugar
2   teaspoons pepper
1 1/2 tablespoons salt
1/4 cup hickory smoke
1   tablespoon oil
1   pound can tomatoes, mashed
2   6-ounce cans tomato paste
18   ounce can tomato juice
8   pounds spareribs

Preheat oven to 350°. In a large saucepan combine all the ingredients, except the ribs, and simmer for 4 hours. Place the ribs in a baking dish and cover with the sauce. Bake, uncovered, for 1 hour or until tender. Serves 8.

Barbecued Ribs II

1/4 cup oil
1   onion, chopped
1   garlic clove, minced
6   ounce can tomato paste
1/4 cup white wine vinegar
1   teaspoon salt
1   teaspoon thyme
1/4 cup honey
1/2 cup beef stock
1/2 cup Worcestershire sauce
1   teaspoon dry mustard
4   pounds spareribs

Preheat oven to 400°. In a large skillet saute the onion and garlic in the oil until soft. Add the remaining ingredients and simmer, uncovered, for 15 minutes. Place the ribs in a shallow baking pan and brush with the sauce. Bake for 1 hour basting thoroughly with the sauce every 10 minutes. Cut into individual portions and serve. Serves 4.

Curried Spareribs

16 ounce jar smoke-flavored barbecue sauce
1/2 cup boiling water
1/2 teaspoon chicken soup base
1 cup catsup
1 tablespoon lemon juice
2 teaspoons curry powder
1 tablespoon Worcestershire sauce
1 teaspoon dry mustard
1/2 can beer
1/2 cup molasses
8 pounds spareribs

Preheat oven to 350°. In a large saucepan combine all the ingredients, except the ribs, and simmer for 15 minutes. Add more beer if sauce is too thick. Place the ribs in a baking dish and cover with the sauce. Bake, uncovered, for 1 hour or until the ribs are tender. Serves 8.

Sausage and Cheese Frittata

8 slices crustless whole wheat bread
2 pounds bulk sausage, browned, drained and mixed with 2 teaspoons prepared mustard
2 cups grated Swiss cheese
6 eggs, lightly beaten
2 1/2 cups milk
1 1/2 cups half and half cream
1 teaspoon salt
2 teaspoons Worcestershire sauce
Dash cayenne pepper

Preheat oven to 350°. Line the bottom of a 13" x 9" baking pan with the bread slices. Spread the sausage mixture over the bread and top with the cheese. Combine the remaining ingredients and pour over the cheese. Bake for 1 hour. Cool slightly before serving. Serves 10–12.

GOURMET HELPER—For a juicier hamburger, add cold water to the beef before grilling (1/2 cup to 1 pound of meat).

Spicy Sausage Quiche

1   pound HOT bulk sausage
1   onion, chopped
4   green onions, tops and bottoms, chopped
1   small green pepper, chopped
6   ounce package Kraft's Garlic Cheese Roll, softened
1/2 cup mayonnaise
1/2 cup sour cream
1   cup grated Jarlsberg cheese (or any white cheese)
1   partially baked 9" pie shell (bake for 10 minutes in a preheated
     400° oven)
2   eggs, lightly beaten

Preheat oven to 350°. In a large heavy skillet saute the first 4 ingredients until
the sausage is browned. Remove from the heat and add the next 3 ingredients.
Sprinkle the cheese on the bottom of the prepared pie shell. Spread the meat
mixture on top and cover with the eggs. Bake, uncovered, for 45 minutes or
until set. Cool slightly and cut into wedges to serve. Serves 6.

Sausage Souffle

1   pound Owen's Hot Sausage
6   slices white bread, de-crusted
6   slices Swiss cheese
1   cup milk
1   cup half and half cream
4   eggs, beaten
1/2 teaspoon salt
1/4 teaspoon rosemary
1/4 teaspoon thyme
1/4 teaspoon sage
1   teaspoon Worcestershire sauce
1   teaspoon mustard
     Fresh parsley, finely chopped

In a heavy skillet sauté the sausage until lightly browned. Drain on paper towels. In a buttered 13" x 9" x 2" baking dish place the bread slices; cover with
cheese. Top with the sausage. In a mixing bowl combine the remaining ingredients, except the parsley, and mix until well blended. Pour over the sausage, sprinkle with the parsley, and bake at 350° for about 1 hour, or until set.
Serves 6.

Sausage Cheese Crepes

12 prepared crepes

FILLING

1   pound bulk sausage
1   onion, chopped
6   ounce package Kraft's Cheese with Bacon, softened
3   ounce package cream cheese, softened
1/2 teaspoon marjoram

TOPPING

2   cups sour cream
1   cup grated Jarlsberg cheese (or any white cheese)

Preheat oven to 375°. In a large heavy skillet saute the sausage and the onion until the sausage is well cooked. Drain off excess fat. Add the next 3 ingredients and when the cheese has melted remove from the heat. Spread each crepe with the sausage mixture and roll up. Arrange seam side down in a baking dish. Cover and refrigerate for several hours. Bake, covered, for 40 minutes. Spread the sour cream over the crepes, sprinkle with the cheese, and bake, uncovered, for 5 minutes. Serves 6.

Sausage Noodle Pie

8   ounces flat medium noodles, cooked and drained
2   tablespoons melted butter
1/2 cup grated Parmesan cheese
3   eggs, beaten
1   pound Italian sausage, casing removed and sliced
1   onion, chopped
15   ounce can tomato sauce with herbs
1   teaspoon oregano
1/2 teaspoon Italian seasoning
2   teaspoons garlic salt
1   cup grated Mozzarella cheese
1   cup grated sharp Cheddar cheese

Preheat oven to 350°. Combine the first 4 ingredients and mold into a nest in a 10″ pie pan. In a large heavy skillet saute the next 2 ingredients until the sausage is browned. Pour off excess liquid. Add the next 4 ingredients and simmer, covered, for 20 minutes. Spread the Mozzarella cheese over the noodles and the tomato sauce over the cheese. Top with the Cheddar cheese and bake for 20 minutes or until bubbly. Serves 6–8.

Sausage Macaroni Casserole

1   pound hot bulk sausage
1/2   green pepper, chopped
1/2   onion, chopped
2   14-ounce cans tomatoes
1 1/2 cups uncooked macaroni
1/4   teaspoon Italian Herb Seasonings
     Salt and pepper, to taste
     Dash chili powder
1   cup Cheddar cheese, grated

Brown sausage in skillet and pour off the drippings. Add the remaining ingredients, except the cheese, and simmer, covered, for 30 minutes. Uncover and simmer for about 10 minutes. Transfer to a lightly greased casserole and sprinkle with cheese. Place under broiler until the cheese melts. Serves 4–6.

Sausage and Wild Rice Bake

1   pound bulk pork sausage
1   onion, chopped
1   small green pepper, chopped
4   ribs celery, chopped
1/4   pound fresh mushrooms, thinly sliced
6   ounce box Uncle Bens Long Grain and Wild Rice Mix, cooked
     according to package directions
4   ounce can chopped pimientos, drained
1/2   teaspoon thyme
1/2   teaspoon marjoram
1   can cream of mushroom soup
1   cup sour cream
2   cups grated Monterey Jack cheese

Preheat oven to 325°. In a large heavy skillet saute the first 5 ingredients until the sausage is browned. Remove from the heat and add the remaining ingredients, reserving 1 cup cheese for the topping. Transfer to a baking dish and bake for 30 minutes or until bubbly. Top with the remaining cheese and bake for 10 minutes more. Serves 8.

Sloppy Joes Italian-Style

1   large onion, chopped
2   garlic cloves, minced
1/2 cup olive oil
1   pound Owen's Hot Sausage
3   potatoes, peeled and cut into 1" cubes
2   green peppers, coarsely chopped
2   cups tomato sauce
1   bay leaf, remove stem and crush leaf
1/4 teaspoon oregano
     Salt and pepper, to taste
     Italian bread, thickly sliced

In a large skillet sauté the onion and garlic in the oil until soft. Add the sausage, stirring with a fork, and saute until lightly browned. Add the remaining ingredients, except the bread, and simmer, covered, for about 1 hour. Serve over the bread slices.

Baked Bacon

     Thick sliced bacon
     Dark brown sugar

Coat bacon slices with sugar. Place on a rack in a shallow baking pan and bake at 375° for 25 minutes or until crisp.

Baked Ham in Beer

8-10 pound precooked ham
1/2 cup dry mustard
1   cup brown sugar
12   bay leaves
1   quart beer

Combine the mustard and brown sugar with a little water to make a paste. (The paste should be the consistency of prepared mustard.) Smear paste over ham and fasten the bay leaves with toothpicks over the ham. Place the ham in a roasting pan and pour beer around the sides of the pan. Cover and bake at 350° for 30 minutes per pound of ham.

Apricot Glazed Ham

8　 pounds precooked ham
12　ounce jar apricot marmalade
½　box dark brown sugar

Season the ham and place on the spit of an electric grill. Cook the ham 20 minutes per pound. Heat the marmalade and sugar over a very low heat, stirring, so the mixture won't scorch the bottom of the pan. Baste the ham every 10 minutes during the last 15 minutes.

Orange Glazed Ham

8　 to 12 pounds precooked ham
3　 tablespoons Dijon mustard
1　 cup brown sugar
½　cup frozen orange juice concentrate, thawed
3　 tablespoons Grand Marnier

Rub the surface of the ham with the mustard and sugar. Place in a shallow roasting pan and bake at 350° for about 20 minutes or until the sugar begins to melt. Combine the orange juice and the Grand Marnier and with a large pastry brush coat the ham. Baste with the drippings in the bottom of the pan about every 15 minutes. Bake about 1½ hours or according to the directions on the ham package.

In a Hurry Orange Glazed Ham—Place an 8 pound pre-cooked ham on the spit of an electric grill and cook the ham 20 minutes per pound to desired doneness. Heat 1 12-ounce jar orange marmalade and ½ box dark brown sugar over a low heat, stirring constantly. Baste the ham every 5 minutes during the last 30 minutes.

Ham and Cheese Casserole

4   cups ham, cut into julienne strips
1   small onion, chopped
1   small green pepper, chopped
2   tablespoons butter
1   tablespoon Dijon mustard
1   tablespoon chutney
1   tablespoon onion soup mix
1   small jalapeño pepper, seeded and chopped
1   teaspoon fennel seeds
1   cup noodles, cooked
1   cup heavy cream
1   cup Monterey Jack cheese
$1/2$ cup cracker crumbs
2   tablespoons sherry
     Salt and pepper, to taste

In a saucepan sauté the onion and green pepper until soft. Remove with a slotted spoon and combine all the ingredients and toss well. Transfer to a lightly greased baking dish and bake at 350° for 30 minutes. Serves 8.

Baked Ham with Dijon Mustard

2   cups currant jelly
$1/2$ cup Dijon mustard
6   pound cooked ham, boned and cut into $1/4''$ slices, tied loosely

Preheat oven to 350°. In a shallow roasting pan place the ham fat side up. In a saucepan combine the jelly and mustard and heat until the jelly has melted and the mixture is smooth. Pour $1/2$ the mixture over the ham and bake for 1 hour, basting frequently with the reserved mixture. Transfer ham to a serving platter and cool slightly. Cut the string. Pour the pan drippings in a gravy boat and pass with the ham.

Ham Steak with Wine

4   pounds ham steak, cut 1½" to 2" thick
½   cup brown sugar
¼   cup prepared mustard
¾   cup Port wine
2   tablespoons Port wine (reserve for later use)

Preheat oven to 350°. Rub the brown sugar and then the mustard on both sides
of the ham. Place in a baking dish and pour the wine over the ham. Bake for 1
hour, basting occasionally. Remove ham to a platter and keep warm. Skim off
the fat and pour 2 tablespoons Port wine into the pan. Heat and serve sauce
over the ham.

Ham Loaf with Hot Mustard Sauce

2   pounds ground ham
2   pounds lean ground pork
2   eggs, beaten
2½   cups bread crumbs (toast bread and grind fine)
1   can tomato soup
2   soup cans water

HOT MUSTARD SAUCE

¼   cup dry mustard
¼   cup white wine tarragon vinegar
2   tablespoons sugar
⅛   teaspoon salt
1   egg
½   cup Hellmann's mayonnaise

Combine all the loaf ingredients and divide in half. Place in two lightly greased
loaf pans. Place the pans in a large shallow pan containing ½" water. Bake the
loaves at 275° for 3 hours. Prepare the sauce while the loaves are baking. In a
saucepan combine all the ingredients, except the mayonnaise. Cook over low
heat until mixture is thickened, stirring constantly. Refrigerate until cooled
and stir in the mayonnaise.

Pineapple Ham Quiche

9″ partially baked pie shell (bake in a preheated 400° oven for 10
     minutes)
1/2 stick butter
1   onion, chopped
1   small green pepper, chopped
8   ounce can crushed pineapple, drained (reserve juice)
1   cup cooked ham, cut into julienne slices
1   cup grated Monterey Jack cheese
1   cup grated sharp Cheddar cheese
4   eggs
1/2 cup half and half
1   tablespoon Dijon mustard
1/4 teaspoon beef base
1/8 teaspoon cayenne pepper

Preheat oven to 375°. In a skillet saute the onion and green pepper in the
butter until soft. Add the reserved pineapple juice and cook until liquid evapo-
rates. Add the pineapple and ham and heat. Sprinkle the Jack cheese on the
bottom of the pie shell. Spread the ham mixture over the cheese. Combine the
last 5 ingredients and pour into the pie shell. Sprinkle with the Cheddar cheese
and bake for 40 minutes or until mixture is set. Serves 6.

Crustless Ham Quiche

1   onion, chopped
1   small green pepper, chopped
1/4 pound fresh mushrooms, thinly sliced
1   small zucchini, grated coarsely
1/2 stick butter
1   cup cooked ham, cut in julienne slices
1   package frozen chopped spinach, thawed and squeezed dry
1   pound cottage cheese, drained
1   cup grated Mozzarella cheese
1   cup grated Swiss cheese
3   large eggs, lightly beaten
2   tablespoons oil
2   teaspoons dill weed

Preheat oven to 350°. In a large heavy skillet saute the first 4 ingredients in the
butter until soft. Add the ham and saute for 5 minutes. Pour off excess liquid
and add the spinach. Remove from the heat. Combine the remaining ingre-

dients and mix with the ham mixture. Pour into a greased 10″ pie pan and bake for 45 minutes or until set. Cool slightly and cut into wedges to serve. Serves 6–8.

Garlic Leg of Lamb

6   pound leg of lamb, seasoned with salt and pepper
1   onion, sliced in slivers
4   garlic cloves, sliced lengthwise
1   bottle Worcestershire sauce
12 new potatoes
6   carrots, sliced

Preheat oven to 350°. Cut small gashes into meat and insert the garlic and onion. Place lamb in a roasting pan and bake, uncovered, for 1 hour. Cover with the Worcestershire and continue cooking for another 1½ hours or to desired doneness. During last hour of cooking, surround meat with the potatoes and carrots.

Marinated Leg of Lamb

½   cup oil
2   teaspoons salt
1   teaspoon pepper
    Juice of 2 lemons
1   garlic clove, crushed
½   teaspoon thyme
½   teaspoon oregano
½   teaspoon Italian seasoning
¼   teaspoon basil
1   teaspoon dry onion flakes
2   cups dry red wine
6   pound leg of lamb

Combine all the ingredients, except the lamb, and mix well. Place the lamb in a Pyrex baking dish and cover with the wine sauce. Marinate, covered, in the refrigerator for 24 hours, turning occasionally. Preheat oven to 300°. Remove the lamb from the marinade and bake, basting frequently with the marinade, until the desired doneness.

Leg of Lamb with Chutney

6   pound leg of lamb, boned
1   garlic clove, sliced
1   large can (1 pound—13 ounces) peach halves, including syrup
1   cup chutney, chopped
2   teaspoons curry powder
1/4 cup sweet vermouth
4   bananas

Trim lamb of excess fat. Make small incisions in the lamb and insert garlic. Season with salt and pepper and place on a rack in a shallow roasting pan. In a saucepan heat the chutney and curry powder. Add the peach juice and vermouth. Place lamb in a preheated 325° oven and roast for 1 hour or longer, basting frequently with the chutney mixture. (For rare, meat thermometer reads 130°, for pink 140°, for well done 170°.) Ten minutes before lamb is finished cooking add the bananas and peaches and pour the remaining chutney mixture over all. Remove lamb from oven. Carve lamb in thin slices and serve surrounded by fruit. Serves 8.

Curried Lamb Shanks

4   lamb shanks, seasoned with salt and pepper
1   garlic clove, minced
1/4 teaspoon oregano
1/4 teaspoon Italian seasoning
1/4 teaspoon thyme
1/4 teaspoon savory
1/2 teaspoon curry powder
1   bay leaf, crumbled
4   onions, thinly sliced
2   tablespoons soy sauce
1/4 cup dry white wine
1/4 cup water

Preheat oven to 400°. Place shanks in a roasting pan. Combine the next 7 ingredients and sprinkle over the meat. Top with the onions and sprinkle with the soy sauce. Roast, uncovered, for 15 minutes. Reduce heat to 300° and roast for 2 hours. Pour off fat and add wine and water. Roast, covered, for 1 hour longer. Serves 4.

Lamb Shanks with Artichoke Hearts

4   lamb shanks, seasoned with salt and pepper
1/2 cup lemon juice
1/4 cup olive oil
1   garlic clove, crushed
1/2 teaspoon oregano
1/2 teaspoon basil
1   onion, sliced
2   cups beef stock
1/4 cup dry red wine
1   package frozen artichoke hearts, thawed

Preheat oven to 300°. Rub the shanks with 1/4 cup lemon juice and in a skillet brown in the olive oil until well browned on all sides. Transfer to a roasting pan and sprinkle with the remaining lemon juice. Combine the next 3 ingredients and sprinkle over the meat. Cover with the onions and bake for 2 1/2 hours. Add the remaining ingredients and bake for 1 hour longer. Serves 4.

Baked Herb Lamb Shanks

4   lamb shanks
1   teaspoon dill weed
1/2 teaspoon oregano
1/4 teaspoon thyme
1/4 teaspoon basil
1/4 teaspoon rosemary
1   garlic clove, minced
2   large onions, thinly sliced
8   ounce can stewed tomatoes
1/4 cup brown sugar
1   cup white wine
1   tablespoon soy sauce
1   teaspoon salt
1/4 teaspoon pepper

Preheat oven to 300°. Place shanks in a roasting pan. Combine all the ingredients and pour over the meat. Bake, covered, for 3 hours. Bake, uncovered, for 30 minutes longer. Remove lamb to a serving platter and keep warm. Pour pan juices into saucepan and cook over high heat until sauce is reduced by half. Pour over meat and serve. Serves 4.

Broiled Lamb Chops

8   loin lamb chops, 3/4" thick (remove fat)
1   tablespoon oil
1   tablespoon butter
1   garlic clove, minced
1/4 cup dry white wine
1/2 stick butter
1   tablespoon Worcestershire sauce
2   tablespoons fresh parsley, finely chopped

In a skillet heat the oil and butter and sauté the garlic. Add the chops and sear, turning often, over medium high heat. Remove, season with salt and pepper, and keep warm. Pour off cooking fat and add the wine. De-glaze by scraping the brown bits from the bottom and sides of the pan. Add the remaining ingredients and stir until well blended. Pour over the chops and serve.

Parmesan Lamb Chops

8   lamb chops, seasoned with onion salt and freshly
    ground pepper
1/4 cup grated Parmesan cheese
1/2 teaspoon garlic powder
1/4 teaspoon oregano

Place lamb chops on a rack in the oven and broil for 8 minutes on each side. Combine the remaining ingredients and sprinkle over the chops. Cook 2 minutes longer or to desired doneness.

In a Hurry Baked Leg of Lamb—Season a 6 pound leg of lamb with salt and pepper and cut slits in the meat. Insert 4 sliced garlic cloves in the slits. Spread 1/2 cup prepared mustard over the meat and bake, in a roasting pan, for 2 1/2 hours in a preheated 350° oven. In a saucepan heat 1 jar red currant jelly with 1 stick butter and 2 tablespoons Worcestershire sauce. Slice the lamb and serve with the jelly sauce.

Chutney Lamb Chops

1 cup finely chopped chutney
1 stick butter
2 teaspoons lemon juice
1 teaspoon curry powder
1/4 teaspoon ground ginger
8 shoulder lamb chops

In a saucepan combine the first 5 ingredients and simmer, stirring occasionally, for 10 minutes. Grill the chops for 10 minutes, brushing with the sauce, on each side or until the desired doneness. Serve with the extra sauce.

Lamb Chops Dijon

2 tablespoons olive oil
1 teaspoon lemon juice
1 tablespoon soy sauce
2 garlic cloves, crushed
1 teaspoon rosemary
1/4 teaspoon powdered ginger
1/4 cup Dijon mustard
8 lamb chops

Combine all the ingredients and spread over the chops. Chill, covered, in the refrigerator overnight. Bring to room temperature and preheat oven to BROIL. Place chops on a rack in a baking pan and broil 10 minutes on each side, brushing with the sauce, or until the desired doneness.

Lamb Khorma

8   garlic cloves
2   ounces fresh ginger root, cut into small pieces
$\frac{1}{2}$ cup milk
2   ounces raw cashew nuts
2   teaspoons poppyseed
$\frac{1}{2}$ cup oil
4   onions, chopped
2   pounds lean lamb, cut into 1" cubes
$\frac{1}{2}$ cup white wine
1   pound can Italian tomatoes
2   fresh tomatoes, peeled and chopped
2   teaspoons coriander (cilantro)
$1\frac{1}{2}$ teaspoons curry powder
1   teaspoon cumin
$\frac{1}{2}$ teaspoon cayenne pepper
$\frac{1}{2}$ teaspoon tumeric
$\frac{1}{4}$ teaspoon cardamon
$\frac{1}{4}$ teaspoon cinnamon
$\frac{1}{2}$ cup sour cream or plain yogurt, at room temperature

In a blender or food processor puree the first 2 ingredients. Add the next 3 ingredients and blend until smooth. Set aside. In a large heavy skillet saute the onions and the meat in the oil until browned on all sides. Reduce heat and cook 10 minutes or until glazed. Add the wine and de-glaze the pan scraping up the browned bits from the bottom and sides of the pan. Add the next 9 ingredients and the garlic mixture and simmer, covered, for 1 hour or until meat is tender. Add the sour cream or yogurt the last 10 minutes. Serve over brown rice with the condiments of your choice. Serves 4–6.

SUGGESTED CONDIMENTS: Crumbled crisp bacon, chopped green onions, chopped peanuts, shredded coconut and chutney.

VEGETABLES

Artichoke and Cheese Ring

2   14-ounce cans artichoke hearts, drained
2   ounce jar whole mushrooms, drained
1   onion, chopped
1   can Cheddar cheese soup
4   eggs
1/4 cup mayonnaise
1/4 teaspoon Worcestershire sauce
    Dash Tabasco
    Salt and pepper, to taste

Place artichokes and mushrooms in a buttered ring mold. Combine the remaining ingredients and pour over the artichokes. Bake at 350° for 30 minutes or until firm. Unmold and serve with your favorite Hollandaise sauce. Serves 6–8.

Stuffed Artichoke Bottoms

1   can artichoke bottoms, drained
1   bottle Wishbone Italian Dressing
1   package Stouffer's Spinach Souffle, thawed
1/4 cup bread crumbs, mixed with 1/4 cup melted butter

Marinate artichokes overnight in the salad dressing. Drain. In a shallow baking dish place artichokes side by side. Fill with the spinach and top with the bread crumbs. Bake, uncovered, at 400° for 20 minutes. Serves 6–8.

Artichoke and Olive Casserole

2   14-ounce cans artichoke hearts
6   hard-cooked eggs, sliced
1   cup stuffed olives, sliced
1/2 cup water chestnuts, sliced
2   cans cream of mushroom soup, diluted with 1/2 cup milk
1/2 cup Cheddar cheese, grated
1/2 cup Monterey Jack cheese, grated
1   cup bread crumbs, mixed with 1/2 cup melted butter

In a baking dish place the artichokes. Add a layer of eggs, olives and chestnuts. Cover with the soup, cheeses, and bread crumbs. Bake at 350° for 30 minutes. Serves 8.

Fresh Asparagus Casserole

1½ pounds fresh asparagus spears, cooked (save the asparagus
     stock)
2   tablespoons butter
1   tablespoon flour
½   cup evaporated milk, mixed with 1 cup asparagus stock
½   cup corn flake crumbs
2   hard-cooked eggs, chopped
1   cup Cheddar cheese, grated

In a saucepan melt the butter, stir in the flour, and add the milk mixture,
stirring constantly, until smooth. Salt and pepper, to taste. In a greased, shallow baking dish place the asparagus. Add the crumbs, eggs and cream sauce.
Sprinkle with the cheese and bake at 350° for 30 minutes. Serves 4–6.

Asparagus Dijon

1½ cups mayonnaise
3   tablespoons lemon juice
¼   cup Dijon mustard
1   cup heavy cream, whipped
2   pounds fresh asparagus, cooked until tender but still crisp

Combine the first 3 ingredients and mix well. Fold in the cream. Just before
serving place asparagus in an ovenproof serving dish, top with the mustard
sauce and place under the broiler until browned. Serves 8.

Asparagus Pecan Bake

2   15-ounce cans asparagus spears (reserve liquid)
1   can cream of celery soup, mixed with ⅓ cup of the asparagus
     liquid
5   ounce can water chestnuts, sliced
½   cup pecans, chopped
2   cups Velveeta cheese, grated
     Salt and pepper, to taste

In a baking dish layer half the asparagus, half the soup, half the water chestnuts, half the pecans and half the cheese. Repeat. Bake at 350° for 20 minutes.
Serves 6–8.

Asparagus Cheese Bake

15 ounce can cut asparagus spears (reserve liquid)
1   can cream of asparagus soup, mixed with the asparagus liquid
2   cups cracker crumbs
2   cups Monterey Jack cheese, grated
3   hard-cooked eggs, chopped
1/2 cup pecans, chopped
1   stick butter, melted
    Salt and pepper, to taste

Mix the cheese and bread crumbs and place 1/2 cup in the bottom of a baking dish. Layer the asparagus, eggs and pecans and cover with the soup mixture. Add the remaining crumb mixture and pour in the butter. Bake at 350° for 20 minutes. Serves 6–8.

Baked Pork and Beans

4   slices bacon, diced and fried crisp (reserve drippings)
2   onions, chopped
4   ribs celery, chopped
1   green pepper, chopped
2   garlic cloves, crushed
2   31-ounce cans pork and beans
1   can Ro-tel tomatoes
1   tablespoon mustard
1   teaspoon chili powder
1   teaspoon Worcestershire sauce

In a skillet sauté the first 4 ingredients in the bacon drippings until soft. Add the remaining ingredients, salt and pepper to taste and transfer to a Dutch oven. Bake at 300° for 1½ hours.

In a Hurry Broccoli Rice Bake—Combine 2 cups cooked rice, 1 package frozen chopped broccoli, cooked, 2 beaten eggs, 1/2 cup oil, 1 cup milk, 1 chopped onion, 1 teaspoon salt, 1 teaspoon garlic powder and 2 cups grated Velveeta cheese. Pour into a baking dish and bake at 350° for 1 hour.

Black Beans

1   package dried black beans
1   onion, chopped
1   can pineapple chunks, drained
    Beer
    Chili powder, cilantro, garlic salt and pepper

Soak beans overnight in water and drain. Add beer, to cover, and the onion and pineapple. Simmer for several hours. Add the spices, to taste.

Quick Pecan Broccoli

3   packages frozen chopped broccoli, cooked and drained
1   package dried onion soup mix
1/2 cup water
1   cup pecans, chopped
5   ounce can water chestnuts, drained and sliced
2   cups Rice Krispies, mashed
1   stick butter, cut into cubes

Combine all ingredients, except Rice Krispies and butter, and place in a baking dish. Top with Rice Krispies and butter cubes and bake at 350° for 30 minutes. Serves 8-10.

Italian Broccoli

1   package frozen broccoli spears or flowerets, cooked and drained
1   package frozen sliced squash, cooked and drained
8   ounce can Italian plum tomatoes, drained
2   eggs
1   can Cheddar cheese soup
1/2 teaspoon oregano
1/2 teaspoon Italian seasoning
1/4 cup grated Parmesan cheese

Preheat oven to 325°. Place the first 3 ingredients in the bottom of a baking dish. Combine the next 4 ingredients and season with salt and pepper. Pour over the vegetables and top with the cheese. Bake for 30 minutes or until bubbly. Serves 8.

Little Mushroom Broccoli Pudding

2 packages frozen chopped broccoli
4 green onions, tops and bottoms, chopped
3 ribs celery, chopped
1/2 green pepper, chopped
1/2 yellow onion, chopped
1/2 stick butter
1 can cream of mushroom soup
1/2 cup seasoned bread crumbs
1/2 cup Cheddar cheese, grated

Cook broccoli according to the directions on the package. Drain. In a saucepan sauté the onions, celery and green peppers in the butter until soft. Add the remaining ingredients, except the cheese, and mix well. Salt and pepper, to taste. Transfer to a baking dish, top with the cheese, and bake at 350° for 20 minutes. Serves 8.

Broccoli Bacon Quiche

9″ partially baked pie shell (bake in pre-heated 400° oven for 10 minutes)
2 packages frozen chopped broccoli, cooked and drained
1 small onion, chopped
6 slices bacon cooked crisp, drained and crumbled
1/2 cup grated Monterey Jack cheese
1/2 cup grated sharp Cheddar cheese
2 eggs, lightly beaten
2/3 cup sour cream
1 teaspoon thyme
1/2 teaspoon Worcestershire sauce

Combine the first 5 ingredients and season with salt and pepper. Place in the bottom of the pie shell. Combine the next 4 ingredients and pour over the broccoli mixture. Bake, uncovered, for 40 minutes or until set. Cool slightly and cut into wedges.

Artichoke and Broccoli Bake

2   6-ounce jars marinated artichoke hearts, drained
2   packages frozen chopped broccoli, thawed and squeezed dry
8   ounce package cream cheese, softened
2   tablespoons butter, softened
1/4 cup milk
1/2 cup grated Parmesan cheese

Preheat oven to 350°. Place the artichoke hearts in the bottom of a baking dish. Arrange the broccoli on top. Combine the cream cheese, butter and milk and beat until smooth. Spread on top of the broccoli and top with the cheese. Bake, covered, for 30 minutes. Bake, uncovered, for 10 minutes longer. Serves 8.

Little Mushroom Broccoli and Rice

2   packages frozen chopped broccoli
1/2 stick butter
1/2 onion, chopped
3   ribs celery, chopped
1   cup rice, cooked
1/2 cup pecans
1   can cream of chicken soup
1/4 teaspoon chicken soup base
    Dash Tabasco
1   cup Cheddar cheese, grated
    Salt and pepper, to taste

Cook broccoli according to the directions on the package. Drain in a saucepan. Sauté the onion and celery in butter until soft. Mix with the broccoli. Mix together soup, soup base, and Tabasco. In a casserole layer broccoli, rice, pecans, soup mixture and cheese. Continue layering ending with the cheese. Bake at 350° for 30 minutes or until hot. Serves 8–10.

GOURMET HELPER—To ripen tomatoes, put them in a brown paper bag in a dark pantry and they will ripen overnight.

Broccoli with Pasta

1   small bunch fresh broccoli, trimmed into flowerets and cooked
     in salted water until slightly under-done and drained
1   pound vermicelli, cooked according to package directions
2   garlic cloves, minced
1   tablespoon olive oil
16   cherry tomatoes, halved
2/3 cup pesto sauce (see recipe below)
1/2 cup grated Parmesan cheese

PESTO SAUCE

2   cups fresh basil leaves
3   garlic cloves
1/4 cup pine nuts
1/2 cup olive oil
1/2 teaspoon salt
1/2 cup grated Parmesan cheese

Make sauce first. Put 1 cup of the basil leaves in a blender or food processor along with the next 4 ingredients and puree. Add the remaining basil and puree. Add more oil if needed. Stir in the cheese.

In a large skillet saute the garlic and broccoli in the oil until heated through. Add the tomatoes, remove from heat and cover. Season with salt and pepper. Toss with the pasta. Pour the pesto sauce over the vegetable-pasta mixture and top with the cheese. Serves 6-8.

Little Mushroom Broccoli Supreme

2   packages frozen, chopped broccoli
1/4 cup almonds, sliced
3   ounce can mushrooms, pieces and stems
2   cups milk
2   tablespoons cornstarch
1   teaspoon chicken soup base
1/4 cup sherry
1/2 cup Monterey Jack cheese, grated

Cook broccoli according to the directions on the package. Drain. Add the almonds and mushrooms. In a saucepan heat the milk. Add the cornstarch and soup base stirring constantly with a wire whisk until mixture thickens. Add the cheese and simmer until cheese is melted. Add the sherry and mix the sauce with the broccoli. Salt and pepper, to taste. Transfer to a baking dish and bake, uncovered, for 15 minutes. Serves 8.

Quick Broccoli Casserole

2   packages frozen chopped broccoli, cooked and drained
8   ounce package Velveeta cheese, grated
1/2   stick butter, cut in cubes
1/4   pound box Ritz crackers, crushed
1/2   stick butter, melted

Place broccoli in a shallow 2 quart baking dish. Sprinkle with cheese, butter cubes and cover with the cracker crumbs. Pour melted butter over the crumbs and bake at 350° for 30 minutes. Serves 6–8.

Broccoli and Roquefort Cheese Bake

1/2   stick butter
1/4   cup flour
1   can cream of celery soup
1/4   cup Roquefort cheese, crumbled
1/2   teaspoon marjoram
1/2   cup Parmesan cheese, freshly grated
2   packages frozen, chopped broccoli, cooked
1   cup sour cream
1/4   cup buttered bread crumbs

In a saucepan melt the butter, stir in the flour, and slowly add the soup, cheese, marjoram, half the Parmesan cheese and broccoli. Heat to a boil, remove, and cool slightly. Stir in the sour cream and salt and pepper, to taste. Transfer to a 2 quart baking dish and top with the remaining cheese and bread crumbs. Bake at 350° for 20 minutes. Serves 6–8.

Fried Red Cabbage

4   slices bacon cooked crisp, drained and crumbled
2   tablespoons bacon drippings
4   cups shredded red cabbage
2   cups chopped apples
1/4 cup packed brown sugar
1/4 cup tarragon vinegar
1/4 cup water
1 1/4 teaspoons salt

In a large heavy skillet heat the bacon drippings. Add all the ingredients and cook, covered, over a low heat, stirring occasionally. For crisp cabbage cook 15 minutes. For tender cabbage cook 30 minutes. Serves 6–8.

Pineapple Glazed Carrots

6   medium carrots, sliced
1   cup pineapple juice
2   tablespoons butter
2   chicken bouillon cubes
1   teaspoon brown sugar
1/4 teaspoon ginger

In a saucepan combine all the ingredients, except the carrots, and bring the mixture to a boil. Lower the heat, add the carrots and simmer until the liquid is absorbed. Season with salt and pepper. Cook for several minutes more, shaking the pan, until the slices are glazed.

Baked Carrots Casserole

12 carrots, cook, slice and reserve 1/2 cup liquid
1   onion, chopped
4   tablespoons horseradish
1   cup Hellmann's mayonnaise
    Salt and pepper, to taste
    Dash lemon juice
1/2 cup seasoned bread crumbs
2   tablespoons butter

Place the carrots in a casserole. Combine all other ingredients, except the bread crumbs and the butter, and pour over the carrots. Sprinkle with bread crumbs and butter. Bake at 375° 20 minutes.

Carrots Bombay

2   cups shredded carrots
1   stick butter
2   tablespoons butter
2   tablespoons flour
2   cups milk
1   tablespoon sugar
1/2 teaspoon cardamon
2   cinnamon sticks, finely crushed
1/2 cup raisins
1/2 cup slivered almonds

In a large heavy skillet saute the carrots in the butter until lightly browned. In a saucepan melt the butter and stir in the flour. Stir in the milk and heat, stirring with a wire whisk, until the mixture is smooth and slightly thickened. Add the cream sauce and the remaining ingredients to the carrots and cook, slowly, until heated through. Serves 8.

Carrots Grand Marnier

6   cups finely shredded carrots
1   bunch green onions, tops and bottoms, chopped
1   cup chicken stock
1/2 stick butter
1/2 teaspoon chervil
1/2 teaspoon fennel
2   tablespoons Grand Marnier

In a large saucepan cook the carrots and onions in the stock for 4 minutes or until liquid has evaporated. Add the next 3 ingredients and season with salt and pepper. Just before serving, sprinkle with the Grand Marnier.

Carrots L' Orange

³/₄   cup orange juice
¹/₂   cup maple syrup
¹/₄   cup orange marmalade
2   16-ounce cans whole baby carrots, drained

In a saucepan combine the first 3 ingredients and bring to a boil, stirring constantly. Reduce heat, add carrots and heat through. Serves 8.

Carrot Ring

³/₄   cup butter
¹/₂   cup brown sugar
1¹/₄ cups flour, sifted
1   teaspoon baking powder
2   teaspoons soda
¹/₄   teaspoon nutmeg
¹/₄   teaspoon cinnamon
1   teaspoon salt
1   egg
4   tablespoons lemon juice or sherry
1¹/₂ cups grated carrots

In a bowl cream the butter and sugar and set aside. Combine the next 6 ingredients. Fold in the egg and lemon juice and mix with the sugar mixture. Mix in the carrots. Pour into an oiled ring mold and bake at 350° for 1 hour.

Carrot Loaf

2   cups cooked rice
3   cups shredded carrots
1   cup smooth peanut butter
1   onion, grated
1   teaspoon salt
2   teaspoons garlic powder
1   tablespoon sage
2   eggs, beaten
2   cups milk
¹/₄   stick butter, melted

Preheat oven to 350°. Combine all the ingredients and place in a loaf pan. Bake for 40 minutes or until a knife inserted in the center comes out clean. Serves 8.

Cauliflower Soufflé

1   small head cauliflower, cut into flowerets
1   egg, lightly beaten
¹/₂   cup Cheddar cheese, grated
4   soda crackers, crumbled
¹/₂   teaspoon Worcestershire sauce
¹/₂   teaspoon dry mustard
     Dash cayenne pepper
     Dash nutmeg
¹/₂   cup milk

In a saucepan steam the cauliflower in salted water, covered, for 15 minutes. Drain, reserving ¹/₂ cup liquid. Place the cauliflower and the liquid in a blender until coarsely chopped. In a bowl combine the next 7 ingredients. Add the cauliflower, milk and salt and pepper, to taste. Transfer to a greased 1 quart baking dish and bake at 350° for 45 minutes. Serves 4–6.

Comely Cauliflower

2   heads cauliflower, cut into flowerets, cooked and drained
1   cup grated Swiss cheese
¹/₂   cup mayonnaise
¹/₂   cup sour cream
4   green onions, tops and bottoms, chopped
1   package Garlic Cheese Salad Dressing Mix
¹/₂   cup bacon bits or 8 slices bacon cooked crisp, drained and crumbled
¹/₂   cup Italian style bread crumbs

Preheat oven to 350°. In the top of a double boiler melt the cheese and mayonnaise. Add the next 3 ingredients. Place the cauliflower in a baking dish and top with the sauce. Sprinkle the bacon and bread crumbs on top and bake for 30 minutes. Serves 8.

Monterey Corn Bake

1/2   cup sugar
1/3   cup cornstarch
2   16-ounce cans cream-style corn
4   ounce can diced green chilies, drained
2   ounce jar chopped pimentos, drained
4   eggs, lightly beaten
2   13-ounce cans evaporated milk
1   teaspoon salt
1/4   stick butter, melted

Preheat oven to 350°. Combine the first 2 ingredients. Add the remaining ingredients except the butter and mix well. Transfer to a lightly greased baking dish, top with the butter, and bake for 1 hour or until set. Serves 8.

Mexican Corn

2   16-ounce cans cream-style corn
1   cup milk
2   tablespoons flour
2   tablespoons sugar
1/2   stick butter
1   onion, grated
1/2   teaspoon salt
2   ounce jar pimentos, chopped
1   can tamales
2   cups Monterey Jack cheese, grated

In a saucepan combine the first 8 ingredients and cook until mixture begins to thicken. In a greased baking dish place half the corn mixture, a layer of tamales, 1 cup cheese and the remaining corn mixture. Sprinkle with remaining cheese and bake at 350° for 30 minutes.

In a Hurry Corn Quiche—Fill an unbaked pie shell with 1 pound fresh sliced mushrooms, 1 package thawed Stouffer's Corn Souffle (spread to cover) and 1 cup sharp Cheddar cheese. Bake in a preheated 350° oven for 45 minutes or until set. Slice into wedges to serve.

Baked Corn with Cheese

12   ounce can LeSueur Shoe Peg White Corn
2   tablespoons butter, melted
1/3 cup Cheddar cheese, grated
1   tablespoon Parmesan cheese, freshly grated
1/2 4-ounce can green chilies, drained and chopped
1/3 cup evaporated milk
1/2 cup cracker crumbs

TOPPING

1/4 cup Cheddar cheese, grated
1/4 cup cracker crumbs
1   tablespoon Parmesan cheese, freshly grated

Combine all ingredients and place in a greased baking dish. Sprinkle with the topping ingredients and bake at 375° for 30 minutes.

Jalapeno Corn Pudding

1 1/2 cups white cream-style corn
1   cup yellow cornmeal
2   sticks butter, melted
3/4 cup buttermilk
1   onion, chopped
4   green onions, tops and bottoms, chopped
2   eggs, beaten
1   teaspoon salt
1/2 teaspoon baking soda
1   cup grated sharp Cheddar cheese
1   cup grated Monterey Jack cheese
4   ounce can chopped jalapeno peppers, drained

Preheat oven to 350°. Combine the first 9 ingredients and mix well. Pour half the mixture into a greased 9″ square baking pan. Layer half the cheese, the peppers, the remaining cheese, and top with the remaining corn mixture. Bake for 1 hour. Cool slightly and cut in squares.

Corn Souffle

¼ stick butter
1 onion, chopped
2 packages frozen corn, thawed
⅓ cup masa harina (Mexican corn flour)
8 eggs, lightly beaten
2 tablespoons sugar
1½ teaspoons salt
1 package Creamy Italian Salad Mix
2 cups sour cream
1½ cups evaporated milk
   Dash Tabasco
8 strips bacon cooked crisp, drained and crumbled

Preheat oven to 350°. In a small skillet saute the onion in the butter until soft. Combine all the ingredients, except the bacon, and pour into a lightly greased baking dish. Top with the bacon and bake for 50 minutes or until puffy. Serves 8-10.

Corn and Olive Casserole

2 pound can cream-style corn, drained
2 pound can whole kernel corn, drained
1 onion, chopped
1 green pepper, chopped
2 ounce jar pimento, drained
1 small can ripe olives, sliced
⅔ cup milk
1 egg, well beaten
2 tablespoons sugar
1 cup cracker crumbs
1 cup Cheddar cheese, grated
½ stick butter, melted

In a large bowl combine all the ingredients in the order that they are listed. Transfer to a baking dish and bake at 350° for 1 hour.

Corn and Green Chilies

2	16-ounce cans cream-style corn
6	eggs, lightly beaten
2	sticks butter, melted
1	cup yellow cornmeal
8	green onions, tops and bottoms, chopped
2	cups sour cream
1	cup evaporated milk
2	cups grated Monterey Jack cheese
1	cup grated sharp Cheddar cheese
8	ounces chopped green chilies
1	teaspoon salt
1	teaspoon Worcestershire sauce

Preheat oven to 350°. Combine all the ingredients and pour into a greased baking dish. Bake for 1 hour or until the filling is set. Let cool slightly before serving.

Corn and Broccoli Bake

16	ounce can cream-style corn
1	package frozen chopped broccoli, cooked and drained
1	egg, beaten
½	cup Pepperidge Farm croutons with chives, crushed
¼	stick butter
1	teaspoon salt
½	teaspoon onion salt
½	teaspoon garlic powder
	Dash cayenne pepper

Preheat oven to 350°. Combine all the ingredients and place in a baking dish. Bake for 30 minutes. Serves 6.

In a Hurry Broccoli Rice Casserole—Cook 1 package frozen chopped broccoli and drain. Mix with 1 cup cooked rice, 1 can cream of mushroom soup, 1 can cream of celery soup, and 1 small jar Cheez Whiz. Put in a baking dish and bake at 350° for 30 minutes.

Corn Onion Casserole

1/2	stick butter
3/4	cup green pepper, chopped
1	garlic clove, crushed
1/4	cup flour
2/3	cup milk
3/4	teaspoon salt
1/8	teaspoon pepper
1/4	teaspoon oregano
1/4	teaspoon basil
1/4	teaspoon sugar
1	cup Cheddar cheese, grated
1	cup tomatoes, drained
2	packages frozen corn, thawed
16	ounce can whole onions, drained

In a saucepan saute the green pepper and garlic in the butter until soft. Add the flour and milk, stirring until mixture thickens. Add the spices and 1/2 cup of the cheese. (Mixture should be *very* thick.) Add the tomatoes and simmer until mixture thickens. Transfer to a baking dish and add the corn and onions. Top with the remaining cheese and bake at 350° about 45 minutes. Serves 6–8.

Corn Pudding

2	16-ounce cans cream-style corn
1	stick butter, melted
1	tablespoon flour
2	tablespoons sugar
1/2	teaspoon salt
2	tablespoons pimentos, chopped
6	eggs

In a large bowl combine all the ingredients. Transfer to a lightly greased baking dish and bake at 350° for 45 minutes or until set.

Herb Baked Corn on the Cob

2 sticks butter, softened
2 garlic cloves, crushed
2 teaspoons oregano
2 teaspoons basil
1/2 teaspoon salt
8 ears of corn
1 cup grated Parmesan cheese

Preheat oven to 350°. Combine the first 5 ingredients and spread on the corn. Wrap each ear tightly with foil and bake for 20 minutes or until corn is tender. Unwrap corn and roll in the cheese.

Elegant Eggplant

1 onion, chopped
1 small green pepper, chopped
4 celery ribs, chopped
1/2 stick butter
2 medium eggplant, peeled, diced and cooked
1 cup breadcrumbs
1/2 cup evaporated milk
1/4 cup milk
2 eggs, lightly beaten
1/2 cup catsup
1 tablespoon chopped pimento
1/2 teaspoon Italian seasoning
1/2 teaspoon thyme
2 teaspoons salt
1/2 teaspoon pepper
2 cups grated Old English cheese

Preheat oven to 350°. In a large heavy skillet saute the first 3 ingredients in the butter until soft. Remove from the heat and stir in the remaining ingredients, except the cheese. Transfer to a baking dish and bake for 45 minutes. Top with the cheese and bake until the cheese melts. Serves 8.

Little Mushroom Ratatouille

2   tablespoons olive oil
2/3 cup onion, chopped
2/3 cup green pepper, chopped
1/2 cup zucchini, chopped
1/2 cup fresh tomato, seeded and chopped
1   cup eggplant, peeled and chopped
5   eggs
3   cups half and half cream
1/2 teaspoon salt
1/2 cup bread, de-crusted and diced
1   cup Cheddar cheese, grated
8   ounce package cream cheese, diced

In a skillet saute the first 5 ingredients in the oil, stirring, until vegetables are tender. Beat the eggs, cream and salt and pepper. Stir in the vegetables, bread and cheeses. Transfer to a greased 9″ square pan and bake at 350° about 30 minutes or until firm. Cut into wedges, to serve. Serves 8.

Ratatouille II

1   eggplant, peeled and cubed
2   zucchini, thinly sliced
1   onion, chopped
2   green peppers, chopped
1/4 cup oil
16   ounce can Italian tomatoes
4   garlic cloves, minced
1   cup chopped ripe olives
1   cup finely chopped parsley
1   bay leaf, crumbled
1/2 teaspoon thyme
1/2 teaspoon marjoram
1/4 teaspoon savory
1   teaspoon garlic salt
1/4 teaspoon pepper
2   cups grated Monterey Jack cheese
1   cup grated Parmesan cheese

Preheat oven to 400°. In a skillet saute the first 4 ingredients in the oil until soft. Add the next 10 ingredients and simmer, covered, for 30 minutes. Season with salt and pepper. Drain off any excess liquid. In the bottom of a baking dish sprinkle 1 cup Jack cheese. Cover with the vegetable mixture and top with the remaining Jack cheese and the Parmesan cheese. Bake for 30 minutes or until bubbly. Serves 6-8.

Baked Eggplant Monterey

1   large eggplant, peeled, boiled and mashed
2   eggs, beaten
2   cups corn flakes
1   cup grated Monterey Jack cheese
2   tablespoons Worcestershire sauce
1/8 teaspoon Tabasco
1   teaspoon salt
1/4 teaspoon pepper
1 1/4 cups evaporated milk
1/2 cup seasoned bread crumbs

Preheat oven to 325°. Combine the first 8 ingredients and mix well. Transfer to a baking dish and cover with the milk. Top with the bread crumbs and bake for 45 minutes. Serves 6.

Quick Eggplant Casserole

1   large eggplant, peeled and diced
2   pounds zucchini, peeled and sliced
8   ounce package cream cheese, softened
3   ounce package cream cheese, softened
1   egg, well beaten
4   ounce can green chilies, drained and chopped
1   cup bread crumbs, mixed with 1/2 cup melted butter

Cook eggplant and zucchini, separately, in boiling salted water until tender. Drain. Combine the two vegetables with all the ingredients, except the bread crumbs, and mix until cheese is dissolved in the hot mixture. Salt and pepper, to taste. Transfer to a baking dish and top with the crumbs. Bake at 350° for 30 minutes. Serves 8.

Little Mushroom Eggplant Supreme

1   large eggplant, peeled and diced
1/2 stick butter
4   green onions, tops and bottoms, chopped
1   small yellow onion, chopped
3   ribs celery, chopped
1   green pepper, chopped
2   eggs, well beaten
1/4 teaspoon sage
1/4 teaspoon poultry seasoning
1   teaspoon chicken soup base
1   cup Monterey Jack cheese, grated
1 1/2 cups seasoned bread crumbs

In a saucepan boil the eggplant until tender. Drain. In a skillet sauté the onions, celery and green pepper until soft. Combine the eggplant, onion mixture and the remaining ingredients, except the bread crumbs. Salt and pepper, to taste. Transfer to a baking dish and top with the bread crumbs. Bake at 350° for 30 minutes. Serves 8.

Little Mushroom Italian Eggplant

1   large eggplant, peeled
4   slices bacon, diced and fried crisp (reserve drippings)
4   green onions, tops and bottoms, chopped
1   can cream of chicken soup
16 ounce can tomatoes, drained and chopped
2   eggs, well beaten
1/4 teaspoon tarragon
1/2 teaspoon oregano
1 1/2 cups seasoned bread crumbs
1   cup Parmesan cheese, freshly grated

In a saucepan boil the eggplant until tender. In a skillet sauté the onions in the bacon drippings. Combine all the ingredients, except the cheese, and transfer to a baking dish. Top with the cheese and bake at 350° for 30 minutes. Serves 8.

Eggplant Parmesan

1   large eggplant, peeled and sliced ¹/₄″ thick
2   eggs, beaten with ¹/₂ teaspoon oregano, ¹/₂ teaspoon Italian
     seasoning, ¹/₄ teaspoon basil, ¹/₄ teaspoon garlic salt, 1
     teaspoon salt and ¹/₄ teaspoon pepper
1   cup dried bread crumbs
¹/₄   cup olive oil
1   onion, chopped
¹/₂   pound fresh mushrooms, thinly sliced
3   cups tomato sauce
1   pound Mozzarella cheese, thinly sliced
¹/₂   cup grated Parmesan cheese

Preheat oven to 350°. Dip eggplant in egg and then into the bread crumbs. In a large heavy skillet saute the eggplant in the oil until browned on both sides. Arrange in a shallow baking dish. In the same skillet saute the onions and mushrooms adding more oil if necessary. Layer half the onion mixture over the eggplant, half the tomato sauce and half the cheeses. Repeat. Bake for 45 minutes of until bubbly. Serves 6–8.

Little Mushroom Green Beans with Cheese

2   16-ounce cans Blue Lake whole green beans, drained
6   slices bacon, diced and cooked crisp (reserve drippings)
2   tablespoons pimentos
¹/₂   teaspoon sweet basil
2   cups milk
2   tablespoons cornstarch
1   teaspoon chicken soup base
1   cup Monterey Jack cheese

In a saucepan bring milk to a slow boil. Add the cornstarch and the soup base stirring constantly with a wire whisk until the mixture thickens. Add the cheese and simmer until the cheese has melted. Pour half of the bacon drippings over the beans. Add the remaining ingredients, including the cheese sauce. Salt and pepper to taste and simmer until heated through. Serves 8.

Little Mushroom Dilly Green Beans

2   packages frozen French-style green beans
3   ribs celery, chopped
2   tablespoons butter
2   tablespoons pimentos, chopped
4   ounce can mushrooms, sliced
1   can cream of mushroom soup
1/4 cup almonds, sliced
1   package Green Onion Dip Mix
1/2 teaspoon dill seed

In a saucepan cook the beans, leaving a little crisp, and drain. In a skillet sauté the celery until soft. Add the remaining ingredients and simmer for 4 minutes. Pour over the beans and toss with a fork until heated through. Serves 8.

Spanish Green Beans

6   slices bacon cooked crisp, drained and crumbled
1/2 onion, chopped
1   small green pepper, chopped
2   ribs celery, chopped
1   garlic clove, minced
2   shallots, chopped
1/4 pound fresh mushrooms, thinly sliced
28 ounce can Italian tomatoes
4   ounce can diced green chilies, drained
1/4 cup chopped ripe olives
1/2 teaspoon chicken soup base
1/4 teaspoon chili powder
1/4 teaspoon cumin
1/4 teaspoon oregano
2   16-ounce cans green beans, drained
1   tablespoon cornstarch

In a large heavy skillet saute the first 6 ingredients in the bacon drippings until soft. Add the next 7 ingredients and simmer, covered, for 30 minutes. Add the green beans, season with salt and pepper and simmer until heated through. Remove 1 cup of the tomato mixture and mix with the cornstarch. Return to pan and stir until mixture begins to thicken. Serves 8-10.

Green Beans Provencale

16 ounce can cut green beans, drained
$^1/_2$ cup julienne-sliced celery
$^1/_2$ cup julienne-sliced carrots
1 onion, thinly sliced
1 small green pepper, julienne-sliced
2 tomatoes, quartered
$^1/_2$ pound fresh mushrooms, thinly sliced
$^1/_2$ stick butter, melted
1 tablespoon sugar
2 teaspoons salt
1 teaspoon Italian seasoning
1 teaspoon oregano
$^1/_4$ teaspoon basil
3 tablespoons tapioca

Preheat oven to 325°. Combine all the ingredients and place in a baking dish. Bake for 1$^1/_2$ hours. Serves 8–10.

Green Beans Mexicana

2 16-ounce cans Blue Lake whole green beans, drained
2 cups milk
2 tablespoons cornstarch
1 teaspoon chicken soup base
2 ounce jar pimentos, drained
1$^1/_2$ teaspoons Mexican hot sauce
3 ounce package cream cheese with chives
1 cup Velveeta cheese, grated

In a saucepan heat the milk. Add the cornstarch and soup base stirring constantly with a wire whisk until the mixture thickens. Add the remaining ingredients, except the beans, and simmer until the cheeses have melted. Salt and pepper, to taste. Place the beans in a baking dish and pour in the sauce. Bake at 350° for 30 minutes. Serves 8.

Baked Green Beans Dijon

$1/2$ cup mayonnaise
$1/2$ cup sour cream
3   tablespoons Dijon mustard
1   teaspoon garlic salt
1   teaspoon minced dried garlic
1   tablespoon Worcestershire sauce
    Dash Tabasco
2   16-ounce cans green beans, drained, or 2 pounds cooked fresh green beans
$1/2$ cup ground pecans

Preheat oven to 350°. Combine the first 7 ingredients and mix well. Place the beans in a baking dish and cover with sauce. Bake for 15 minutes. Top with the pecans and bake for 10 minutes more. Serves 8.

Garlic Cheese Green Beans

1   stick butter, melted
2   cups Pepperidge Farm Cheddar Romano croutons, crushed
1   tablespoon butter
1   onion, chopped
2   16-ounce cans green beans, drained or 2 pounds cooked fresh green beans
1   cup evaporated milk
1   cup sour cream
6   ounce package Kraft's Garlic Cheese Roll, softened
$1/4$ teaspoon Worcestershire sauce
$1/4$ teaspoon garlic powder

Preheat oven to 350°. Combine the butter and croutons and spread half the mixture on the bottom of a shallow baking dish. Saute the onion in the butter until soft. Combine with the remaining ingredients and spread mixture over the crumbs. Top with the remaining crumbs and bake for 30 minutes or until bubbly. Serves 8.

Little Mushroom Green Beans Supreme

2   16-ounce cans Blue Lake whole green beans, drain and reserve
    liquid
1   green pepper, chopped
4   green onions, tops and bottoms, chopped
1/2 stick butter
1   can cream of mushroom soup
2   tablespoons pimentos, chopped
1   tablespoon cornstarch
1/4 teaspoon oregano
    Salt and pepper, to taste

In a saucepan sauté the onions and green pepper in the butter until soft. Pour liquid from green beans into a saucepan and heat. Add all other ingredients, except beans, and simmer until mixture thickens. Place green beans in a casserole. Pour mixture on top. Cover and bake at 350° for 10 minutes. Serves 8.

Baked Mexican Green Beans

1/2 stick butter
1   onion, chopped
4   green onions, tops and bottoms, chopped
2   tablespoons flour
2   cups heavy cream
1/2 package Taco Seasoning Mix
1/2 teaspoon chicken soup base
4   ounce can diced green chilies, drained
2   16-ounce cans green beans, or 2 pounds cooked fresh green
    beans
1   cup grated Monterey Jack cheese
1   cup grated sharp Cheddar cheese

Preheat oven to 350°. In a large heavy skillet saute the onions in the butter until soft. Add the flour and stir to a thick paste. Add the next 4 ingredients, stirring, until sauce begins to thicken. Season with salt and pepper. Place the beans in a baking dish and pour the sauce over them. Top with the cheeses and bake for 20 minutes or until bubbly.

East Indian Lima Beans

1   onion, chopped
1   small green pepper, chopped
2   shallots, chopped
1   garlic clove, minced
1   green apple, chopped
1   stick butter
16 ounce can tomatoes, drained
$^{1}/_{2}$ cup brown sugar
1   teaspoon curry powder
1   teaspoon salt
1   teaspoon tarragon vinegar
$^{1}/_{4}$ teaspoon tumeric
$^{1}/_{4}$ teaspoon coriander (cilantro)
2   packages frozen lima beans, cooked and drained
1   cup grated Gruyere cheese (or other white cheese)

Preheat oven to 350°. In a large heavy skillet saute the first 5 ingredients in the butter until soft. Add the remaining ingredients, except the cheese, and mix well. Transfer to a baking dish and bake for 25 minutes. Sprinkle with the cheese and bake 5 minutes longer. Serves 8.

Mushrooms Stroganoff

2   onions, finely chopped
3   tablespoons butter
1   pound fresh mushrooms, sliced
$^{2}/_{3}$ cup burgundy
2   tablespoons Worcestershire sauce
$^{1}/_{4}$ teaspoon sugar
$^{1}/_{8}$ teaspoon nutmeg
$^{1}/_{8}$ teaspoon cinnamon
2   cups sour cream

In a skillet sauté the onions in the butter until soft. Add the mushrooms and sauté for 5 minutes. Add the remaining ingredients, except the sour cream, and cook until liquid is reduced by half. Add the sour cream and simmer until mixture is heated through. Do not let boil. Add salt and pepper, to taste. Serve over rice.

Baked Mushrooms in Sour Cream

1   pound large, fresh mushrooms, remove the stems and slice the
     mushrooms into thick slices
2   tablespoons butter
1   cup sour cream
2   tablespoons flour
1/2 cup Cheddar cheese, grated
1/2 cup Monterey Jack cheese, grated
     Dash cayenne pepper

In a skillet sauté the mushrooms in the butter until they are barely tender.
Transfer them to a well buttered baking dish, arranging them in neat overlapping rows. In a saucepan combine the sour cream, flour and salt and pepper, to
taste. Simmer until heated, but do not let boil. Spoon the sauce over the mushrooms and top with the cheeses and cayenne. Bake for 15 minutes. Serves 4.

Quick English Peas

1   can cream of mushroom soup
1   roll Kraft Garlic Cheese
2   17-ounce cans small English peas, drained
1/8 teaspoon cayenne pepper

In a saucepan heat the soup and the cheese stirring until the cheese is melted.
Add the pepper and salt, to taste. Add the peas and serve. Serves 8.

Herbed Peas

4   slices bacon, diced and fried crisp (reserve the drippings)
4   green onions, tops and bottoms, chopped
2   16-ounce cans LeSueur peas
1/4 cup heavy cream
1   tablespoon cumin

In a skill sauté the onions in the bacon drippings. Pour off excess fat. Add the
bacon and peas to the onion mixture and heat. Add the cream, cumin and salt
and pepper, to taste. Remove from heat and serve. Serves 8.

Jalapeño Cheese Potatoes

4   potatoes, cooked, peeled and sliced
2   tablespoons butter
4   green onions, tops and bottoms, chopped
1   green pepper, chopped
1/2 stick butter
1   tablespoon flour
1   cup milk
2   ounce jar pimentos, drained and chopped
1/2 Kraft Jalapeño Cheese roll
1/2 Kraft Garlic Cheese roll

In a skillet sauté the onions and pepper until soft. In a saucepan melt the butter, add the flour and then the milk, stirring, until mixture thickens. Add the onion mixture, pimentos and the cheese and simmer until cheeses have melted. In a lightly greased baking dish place the potatoes. Pour in the sauce and bake at 350° for 45 minutes. Serves 6–8.

Potato and Sour Cream Bake

8   to 10 potatoes, peeled
8   ounce cream cheese, softened
1/2 cup sour cream
6   green onions, tops and bottoms, chopped
1/2 stick butter, melted

Cook potatoes in boiling, salted water until tender. Drain. Beat cream cheese, sour cream and onions with a mixer until well blended. Stir in the hot potatoes and butter and beat until fluffy. Salt and pepper, to taste. Transfer to a 2 quart buttered baking dish and bake at 350° for 30 minutes. Serves 8.

Potatoes Au Gratin

6   to 8 baking potatoes, baked in oven with the skins on
1   pound Velveeta cheese, cut in chunks
1   cup mayonnaise
1   onion, chopped
    Salt and pepper, to taste
6   strips bacon, chopped, and sautéed until half cooked
1/4 cup pimento-stuffed olives, sliced

Remove skin from cooked potatoes and cut into large dice. Toss with the next 4 ingredients. Pour into greased casserole. Sprinkle with bacon and olives. Bake at 325° for 1 hour. Serves 8–10.

Scalloped Potatoes

2   pounds potatoes, peeled
2   cups milk
1¹/₂ cup heavy cream
2   garlic cloves, finely chopped
³/₄   teaspoon salt
¹/₂   teaspoon white pepper
¹/₂   cup Swiss cheese, grated

Slice the potatoes ¹/₈″ thick and place them in a large saucepan. Add the next 5 ingredients and bring to a boil, stirring to prevent scorching. Remove the pan from the heat and transfer to a buttered shallow baking dish. Sprinkle the cheese over the mixture and bake at 375° for 1 hour. Serves 8.

Quick Cheese Potatoes

4   cups new potatoes, peeled and cooked
2   onions, thinly sliced
1   can Cheddar cheese soup
¹/₂   cup milk
¹/₂   teaspoon garlic salt
¹/₈   teaspoon cayenne pepper
¹/₄   Worcestershire sauce

Combine all ingredients and place in a well buttered 2 quart baking dish. Bake, covered, at 375° for 1 hour. Remove cover and bake 15 minutes longer.

In a Hurry Au Gratin Potatoes—Combine a 2-pound package frozen hash browns, thawed; ¹/₄ teaspoon prepared mustard; ¹/₂ cup melted butter; 1 teaspoon salt; ¹/₂ teaspoon pepper; 2 tablespoons dried minced onion; 1 can cream of chicken soup; and 2 cups grated sharp Cheddar cheese. Place in a 9″ x 13″ baking dish and pour ¹/₄ cup melted butter on top. Sprinkle 2 cups crushed corn flakes on top and bake for 45 minutes at 350°.

Parslied Rice

2   cups raw white rice
4   cups milk
1/3 cup oil
1   tablespoon salt
1   cup finely minced parsley
1   garlic clove, crushed
2   cups grated Monterey Jack cheese
2   green peppers, finely chopped
2   onions, finely chopped
2   eggs, well beaten

Preheat oven to 350°. Combine all the ingredients and place in a greased baking dish. Bake uncovered, for 45 minutes. Serves 8.

Spiced Rice

1/2 cup raisins, soaked for 10 minutes in boiling water
3   cups water
2   cups brown rice
3/4 teaspoon cinnamon
3/4 teaspoon nutmeg
1   teaspoon salt
1/2 stick butter, melted
2   garlic cloves, crushed

In a saucepan combine the first 6 ingredients and bring to a boil. Reduce heat and simmer, covered, for 45 minutes or until rice is cooked. Just before serving add the butter and garlic. Serves 6–8.

In a Hurry Green Chili Potatoes—Combine 2 pounds frozen, thawed hash brown potatoes; 1 stick melted butter; 1 chopped onion; 1 cup milk; 1 pint sour cream; 4 ounce can diced green chilies, drained; and 2 teaspoons garlic salt. Place in a shallow baking dish, top with 2 cups grated Monterey Jack cheese and bake at 350° for 45 minutes. Serves 8.

Wild Rice Casserole

1/2 pound Owen's Hot Sausage
1 pound fresh mushrooms, thinly sliced
1 onion, chopped
1 cup wild rice, cooked
1 cup Uncle Ben's Long Grain Wild Rice Blend, cooked
1/2 stick butter
1/4 cup flour
1/2 cup heavy cream
2 1/2 cups chicken broth
   Dash Tabasco
   Dash thyme, marjoram and oregano
   Salt and pepper, to taste

In a skillet sauté the sausage until browned. Remove with a slotted spoon. Sauté the onion and mushrooms in the sausage drippings until soft. Remove and mix with the sausage. In a saucepan melt the butter and mix in the flour. Slowly add the cream, stirring constantly until smooth. Add the broth and stir with a wire whisk until mixture thickens to a cream sauce consistency. Add the spices and taste for seasonings. Combine the rice, sausage mixture and cream sauce and transfer to a lightly greased casserole. Bake at 350° about 30 minutes.

Italian Rice

2 1/2 cups rice, cooked
1/2 cup oil
1/2 cup instant minced onions
1/2 teaspoon pure granulated garlic
2 chicken bouillon cubes, dissolved in 1 cup hot water
1 cup dry white wine
1 cup evaporated milk
1/4 cup butter
1/2 teaspoon basil
1/2 teaspoon oregano
2 teaspoons salt
1/2 teaspoon pepper
1 cup sliced almonds, toasted

In a large bowl combine all the ingredients. Transfer to a lightly greased baking dish and bake at 350° for 1 hour. Serves 10-12.

Risotto Rice

2¹/₂ cups Italian Rice (available at any Italian food store)
2 tablespoons butter
2 tablespoons olive oil
5 cups Swanson's Chicken Broth
1¹/₃ cups heavy cream
6 ounces Gorgonzola cheese, diced
¹/₂ stick butter
¹/₂ cup Parmesan cheese, freshly grated

Sauté rice in butter and olive oil, over moderatly high heat, until golden. Add chicken broth, reduce heat to low, and simmer until liquid is absorbed. In a double boiler, combine cream and cheese and heat mixture over a low heat until cheese is melted. Pour the sauce over the rice and simmer until rice is tender. Remove pan from heat, and toss with ¹/₂ stick butter and ¹/₂ cup freshly grated Parmesan cheese. Serves 6–8.

Rice and Artichoke Bake

1 package Uncle Ben's chicken-flavored rice, cooked according to the directions on the package.
2 jars marinated artichokes
¹/₂ cup of marinade from artichokes
¹/₂ cup of Hellmann's mayonnaise
6 green onions, diced
¹/₂ cup green olives, diced

Mix artichoke marinade and mayonnaise. Combine with other ingredients and transfer to a baking dish. Bake at 350° for 30 minutes.

Garlic Rice

2 cups uncooked white rice
1 bunch green onions, tops and bottoms, chopped
4 ounce can diced green chilies, drained
1 tablespoon pimentos
1 tablespoon granulated garlic
1 teaspoon chicken soup base
¹/₂ cup oil
3 cups water
¹/₂ cup blanched almonds

Preheat oven to 350°. Combine all the ingredients and mix well. Place in a baking dish and bake for 30 minutes or until rice is done. Serves 8.

Green Rice

3   cups rice, cooked
1   bunch green onions, tops and bottoms
1½   cups large curd cottage cheese
1   garlic clove, crushed
1   cup sour cream
¼   cup milk
     Dash Tabasco
½   teaspoon salt
½   cup Parmesan cheese, freshly grated

In a mixing bowl combine the rice and green onions. Combine the remaining ingredients, except the cheese, and mix with the rice mixture. Transfer to a lightly greased 1½ quart casserole and sprinkle with the cheese. Bake at 350° for 30 minutes. Serves 6.

Rice and Sausage Bake

½   pound smoked link sausage, cut into ½″ slices
1   onion, chopped
4   green onions, tops and bottoms, chopped
2   ribs celery, chopped
1   small green pepper, chopped
1   cup beef bouillon
1   cup water
1   cup rice
     Salt and pepper, to taste

In a saucepan sauté the sausage until lightly browned. Drain on paper towels. In the sausage drippings sauté the onions, celery and green pepper until soft. Add the water and bouillon and bring to a boil. Add the sausage and rice and transfer to a lightly greased baking dish. Cover and bake at 375° for 30 minutes. Serves 6–8.

Mushroom Rice Casserole

1 cup rice, uncooked
1 can cream of mushroom soup
1 can beef consommé
3 ounce can mushrooms, sliced
2 tablespoons butter
1 onion, chopped
¼ teaspoon mace
¼ teaspoon curry powder
¼ teaspoon tumeric
 Salt and pepper, to taste

In a saucepan sauté the onion in the butter. Add the spices. Combine all the ingredients and transfer to a lightly greased baking dish. Bake, covered, at 350° for 1 hour. Do not stir. Serves 6-8.

Coconut Rice

3 cups water
1½ cups rice
1 teaspoon curry powder
1 teaspoon salt
½ cup canned coconut milk
½ cup toasted coconut
¼ cup chopped green onion
¼ cup raisins
2 tablespoons butter

Combine the first 4 ingredients in a saucepan and bring to a boil. Reduce heat and simmer, covered, for 25 minutes or until rice is tender. Add remaining ingredients and heat through. Serves 6-8.

In a Hurry Yummy Cauliflower—Boil whole cauliflower in half milk, half water and salt until tender. Drain and place in a baking dish. Spread with mayonnaise and top with grated sharp Cheddar cheese. Sprinkle with paprika and bacon bits and BROIL for 10 minutes or until browned. Serves 4.

Little Mushroom Jalapeno Rice

3   cups rice, cooked
1/2 stick butter
2   bunches green onions, tops and bottoms, chopped
1/2 small onion, chopped
2   tablespoons pimentos, chopped
4   ounce can green chilies
1   teaspoon chicken soup base
2   cups sour cream
2   cups Monterey Jack cheese, grated

In a saucepan sauté the onions in the butter until soft. Combine the onions with all the other ingredients, reserving 1 cup of cheese for the topping. Transfer to a lightly greased baking dish, top with the cheese, and bake at 350° for 30 minutes. Serves 8.

Rice and Cheese Bake

2 1/2 cups water
1   package dry chicken-noodle soup mix
1   cup uncooked long grain rice
1   can cream of chicken soup
1   cup Cheddar cheese, grated
6   ounce can evaporated milk
1/4 cup pimento, chopped

In a saucepan combine the water, soup mix and rice. Bring to a boil, cover, and simmer 20 minutes. Combine the rice and the remaining ingredients and transfer to a lightly greased baking dish. Bake at 350° for 30 minutes. Serves 6.

In a Hurry Zucchini with Bacon and Chives—Boil whole zucchini in salted water for 5 minutes. Cool and cut lengthwise. Rake with a fork and let a lot of butter soak in. Add salt and pepper and chopped chives. Sprinkle with bread crumbs and top each zucchini with a bacon slice. Bake at 325° until bacon is browned.

Tomato Rice Bake

1/3	cup bacon drippings
3/4	cup uncooked long grain rice
1	onion, chopped
1/4	cup green pepper, chopped
1	garlic clove, crushed
1	pound-13-ounce can Italian plum tomatoes
1	small jalapeño pepper, seeded and chopped
1/2	cup Monterey Jack cheese, grated
1/2	cup Cheddar cheese, grated

In a heavy skillet sauté the rice in the bacon drippings, stirring, until rice turns yellow. Add the onion and continue to sauté until rice starts to brown. Add the remaining ingredients, except the cheeses, and simmer, covered, about 20 minutes or until rice is tender. Transfer to a lightly greased baking dish and sprinkle with the cheeses. Bake at 400° until the cheese is heated. Serves 4.

Quick Spinach Bake

2	packages frozen chopped spinach, cooked and drained
1	package dry onion soup mix
1	cup sour cream
1/2	cup Monterey Jack cheese, grated

Combine all ingredients, except the cheese, and place in a lightly buttered 2 quart baking dish. Sprinkle with the cheese and bake at 350° for 20 minutes. Serves 6–8.

Spanish Spinach

2	packages frozen chopped spinach, cooked and drained or 2 bags fresh spinach, cooked and chopped
1/2	stick butter
1	onion, chopped
4	green onions, tops and bottoms, chopped
4	ounce can diced green chilies, drained
1	teaspoon coriander (cilantro)
1	teaspoon sugar
6	ounce package Jalapeno Pepper Cheese Roll, softened

Preheat oven to 350°. In a skillet saute the onions in the butter until soft. Add the remaining ingredients and stir until well mixed. Season with salt and pepper and place in a shallow baking dish. Bake for 30 minutes or until bubbly. Serves 8.

Spinach and Raisin Bake

2   packages frozen chopped spinach, cooked and drained
    or 2 bags fresh spinach, cooked and chopped
1   cup raisins, pre-soaked in cold water for 15 minutes
2   cups cooked rice
4   eggs
2/3 cup evaporated milk
1   small onion, grated
8   ounce package cream cheese, softened
2   cups grated Old English cheese
1/2 stick butter, melted
2   teaspoons Worcestershire sauce
1/2 teaspoon rosemary
1/2 teaspoon thyme
1 1/2 teaspoons salt

Preheat oven to 350°. Combine all the ingredients and turn into a baking dish. Bake for 30 minutes or until set. Serves 8–10.

Little Mushroom Spinach Supreme

2   packages frozen chopped spinach
4   green onions, chopped
1   small yellow onion, chopped
3   slices bacon, fried crisp (reserve the drippings)
1/4 cup seasoned bread crumbs
1   3-ounce can mushrooms, pieces and stems
    Salt and pepper, to taste

Cook spinach according to the directions on the package. Drain well. In a saucepan sauté the onions in the bacon drippings until they are soft. Combine all the ingredients and mix well. Check for seasonings. Place in a casserole and bake at 350° for 20 minutes. Serves 8.

Splendid Spinach

2   packages frozen chopped spinach, cooked and drained
2   packages frozen artichoke hearts, cooked and drained
1   stick butter, softened
4   green onions, tops and bottoms, chopped
8   ounce package cream cheese, softened
1/2 package Kraft's Garlic Cheese Roll, softened
1   jalapeno pepper, seeded and chopped

Preheat oven to 350°. Combine all the ingredients, season with salt and pepper, and place in a baking dish. Bake for 30 minutes or until bubbly. Serves 8.

Spanakopita

1/2 pound feta cheese, drained
8   ounce package cream cheese, softened
3   eggs
1/2 teaspoon nutmeg
1   teaspoon basil
2   garlic cloves, crushed
     Dash Tabasco
2   packages frozen chopped spinach, thawed and squeezed dry
1/2 cup pine nuts (or other nut of your choice)
1/2 cup chopped onion, sauteed in 2 tablespoons butter
2   sticks butter, melted
1/2–3/4 pound phyllo pastry

Preheat oven to 350°. In a blender or food processor blend the first 7 ingredients. Mix with the next 3 ingredients. Brush a 10" pie or quiche pan with melted butter and line with 5 sheets of dough, brushing each with butter. Let ends fall over the sides of the pan. Add the filling and place 3 more sheets of dough on top. Fold overhanging edges toward the middle. Brush with butter and bake for 45 minutes or until brown. Serves 8.

GOURMET HELPER—When boiling corn add sugar to the water instead of salt. Salt will toughen the corn.

Spinach Olé

1/2 stick butter
4 green onions, tops and bottoms, chopped
1 onion, chopped
3 ribs celery, chopped
3 cups tomato puree
1/4 cup lemon juice
2 garlic cloves, crushed
2 tablespoons chili powder
1 teaspoon cumin
1 teaspoon salt
1/4 teaspoon pepper
2 packages frozen chopped spinach, cooked and drained
1 cup Monterey Jack cheese, grated

In a saucepan sauté the onions and celery in the butter until soft. Add the next 7 ingredients and simmer for 5 minutes. Mix with the spinach and transfer to a buttered baking dish. Top with the cheese and bake at 350° for 20 minutes. Serves 8.

No-Crust Spinach Quiche

1 bunch green onions, tops and bottoms, chopped
1 small green pepper, chopped
2 small zucchini, thinly sliced
1/2 pound fresh mushrooms, thinly sliced
2 teaspoons dill weed
1/2 stick butter
2 packages frozen chopped spinach, thawed and squeezed dry
1 pound Ricotta cheese
1/2 teaspoon chicken soup base
4 eggs, lightly beaten
Dash Tabasco
1/2 cup grated Mozzarella cheese
1/2 cup grated sharp Cheddar cheese

Preheat oven to 350°. In a large heavy skillet saute the first 5 ingredients in the butter until soft. Combine the next 7 ingredients and mix with the first mixture. Season with salt and pepper. Spoon into a 9" spring-form pan and bake for 1 hour or until set. Serves 8.

Busy Day Spinach Bake

2   packages frozen chopped spinach, cooked and drained
14 ounce can artichoke hearts, drained
1   teaspoon onion salt
1   teaspoon celery seed
1   cup sour cream
1   cup grated Parmesan cheese

Preheat oven to 350°. Combine all the ingredients and place in a baking dish. Bake for 30 minutes or until bubbly. Serves 8.

Spinach Provancale

1   onion, chopped
1/4 pound fresh mushrooms, thinly sliced
1/2 stick butter
2   packages frozen chopped spinach, cooked and drained
    or 2 bags fresh spinach, cooked and chopped
1   tablespoon lemon juice
1   teaspoon Dijon mustard
1/2 teaspoon salt
1/4 cup sour cream
2   large ripe tomatoes, sliced 1/4" thick
1   cup grated sharp Cheddar cheese
1   cup grated Mozzarella cheese

Preheat oven to 375°. In a large heavy skillet saute the first 2 ingredients in the butter until soft. Add the next 5 ingredients and remove from the heat. Place the spinach mixture in the bottom of a shallow baking dish. Layer half the tomatoes, salt and pepper to taste and half the cheeses. Repeat. Bake for 30 minutes or until bubbly. Serves 8.

In a Hurry Garlic Cheese Potatoes—Place 3 pounds frozen hash browns in a 9" x 13" baking dish. In a saucepan melt 2 sticks butter, 2 rolls Kraft's Garlic Cheese Roll and 1 cup grated Cheddar cheese. Stir in 1 pint half and half and pour over the potatoes. Let stand at room temperature for 1 hour. Bake at 350° for 1 hour. Serves 12.

Quick Spinach and Cream Cheese

2 packages frozen, chopped spinach, cooked and drained
1/2 stick butter
2 hard-cooked eggs, chopped
8 ounce package cream cheese, softened

In a saucepan combine the butter and salt and pepper, to taste, with the hot spinach. Stir in the egg and add the cheese, stirring until well blended. Simmer over very low heat until mixture is hot. Serves 8.

Quick Spinach Potato Bake

2 packages frozen, chopped spinach
1 can cream of potato soup
1 cup Parmesan cheese, grated
1 cup Pepperidge Farm Herb Seasoned Stuffing

Thaw the spinach; do not drain. Place in the bottom of a casserole. Cover with the soup. Combine the cheese and the stuffing mix. Sprinkle over the top and bake at 350° for 40 to 50 minutes. Serves 8.

Little Mushroom Spinach and Cheese Bake

2 packages frozen, chopped spinach
3 green onions, tops and bottoms, chopped
2 tablespoons butter
1 cup cream of mushroom soup
2 tablespoons mustard
1/2 cup Mozzarella cheese

Cook spinach according to the directions on the package. Drain. Sauté the onions in the butter. Add all other ingredients and transfer to a casserole. Bake at 350° for 30 minutes. Serves 8.

Spinach Stroganoff

1/2   stick butter
4   green onions, tops and bottoms, chopped
1/2   pound fresh mushrooms, thinly sliced
1   can cream of mushroom soup
8   ounce carton sour cream
1   teaspoon Worcestershire sauce
1/2   teaspoon pure granulated garlic
2   packages frozen chopped spinach, cooked and drained
1   cup Parmesan cheese, freshly grated (topping)

In a skillet sauté the onions and mushrooms in the butter until soft. Add the remaining ingredients and simmer until heated through. Do not let boil. Combine with spinach and salt and pepper, to taste. Transfer to a buttered baking dish, top with cheese, and bake at 350° for 30 minutes. Serves 6-8.

Little Mushroom Spinach Imperial

2   packages frozen, chopped spinach
1/2   stick butter
1   can cream of mushroom soup
1/4   cup seasoned bread crumbs
1/4   cup pimentos, chopped
1   package Green Onion Dip Mix
1/2   cup Cheddar cheese, grated

Cook spinach according to the directions on the package. Drain. Combine all the other ingredients and transfer to a buttered casserole. Bake at 350° for 20 minutes. Serves 8.

In a Hurry Rotel Potatoes—Slice 8 small potatoes and place in the bottom of a baking dish. Pour 1 can Rotel tomatoes with green chilies, 1 can Cheddar cheese soup, 1 tablespoon dried onion flakes, 1 teaspoon salt, and 1/2 stick butter over the potatoes. Bake at 350° for 1 hour. Serves 8.

Soused Squash

4   acorn squash, halved and seeded
1   tablespoon lemon juice
½   cup raisins
3   cups applesauce
½   cup packed brown sugar
1   teaspoon cinnamon
¼   teaspoon allspice
½   cup rum
½   cup chopped walnuts
½   stick butter

Preheat oven to 400°. Place squash in a baking dish cut side up. Sprinkle with salt and pepper. Combine the remaining ingredients, except the butter, and spoon in the squash cavities. Pat with butter. Pour ½″ hot water into the bottom of the baking dish. Cover and bake for 30 minutes. Remove cover and bake for 30 minutes more. Serves 8.

Sexy Squash

1   onion, chopped
4   green onions, tops and bottoms, chopped
2   shallots, finely chopped
½   green pepper, chopped
½   stick butter
8   yellow squash, sliced, cooked and drained
½   cup evaporated milk
2   ounce jar chopped pimentos, drained
1   teaspoon Worcestershire sauce
½   package Kraft's Garlic Cheese Roll
2   teaspoons brown sugar
1   teaspoon salt
1   cup seasoned bread crumbs mixed with 2 tablespoons
    melted butter

Preheat oven to 350°. In a large heavy skillet saute the first 4 ingredients in the butter until soft. Add the remaining ingredients, except the bread crumbs, and mix well. Place in a baking dish and top with the crumbs. Bake for 30 minutes or until bubbly. Serves 8.

Baked Squash with Green Chilies

2   pounds yellow squash, diced
1   onion, chopped
1   small green pepper, chopped
1/2 stick butter
1   cup grated Monterey Jack cheese
2   eggs
1   cup mayonnaise
2   teaspoons sugar
1   teaspoon salt
1/4 teaspoon pepper
4   ounce can diced green chilies, drained
2   ounce jar chopped pimentos, drained

Preheat oven to 350°. In a sauce pan simmer the first 3 ingredients, in water to cover, until the squash is tender. Drain well and add the butter, stirring until the butter melts. Cool slightly and add the remaining ingredients. Transfer to a baking dish and bake for 30 minutes or until bubbly. Serves 8.

Baked Gingered Squash

2   pounds yellow squash, diced
1/2 stick butter
1/2 teaspoon basil
1   cup heavy cream
1/4 teaspoon ginger
1/2 cup brown sugar
1   cup finely sliced almonds

Preheat oven to 350°. In a large heavy skillet saute the squash in the butter until lightly browned. Sprinkle with salt, pepper and basil. Transfer to a baking dish and add the remaining ingredients. Bake for 20 minutes or until bubbly. Serves 8.

GOURMET HELPER—To keep cauliflower white while cooking—add a little milk to the water.

Little Mushroom Baked Squash Supreme

8   medium yellow squash, sliced
1/2 stick butter
4   green onions, tops and bottoms, chopped
1/2 yellow onion, chopped
3   ribs celery, chopped
1   small green pepper, chopped
1   can cream of mushroom soup
3   ounce can mushrooms, pieces and stems
1/4 teaspoon sugar

Cook the squash in boiling, salted water until tender. Drain. In a saucepan sauté the onions, celery and green pepper in the butter until soft. Mix with the squash and add the remaining ingredients. Salt and pepper, to taste and transfer to a lightly buttered baking dish and bake at 350° for 30 minutes. Serves 8.

Little Mushroom Baked Squash with Cheese

8   medium yellow squash, sliced
1/2 stick butter
4   green onions, tops and bottoms, chopped
1/2 yellow onion, chopped
3   ribs celery, chopped
2   cans cream of chicken soup
1   package Green Onion Dip Mix
2   cups Swiss cheese, grated

Cook the squash in boiling, salted water until tender. Drain. In a saucepan sauté the onions, and celery in the butter until soft. Mix with the squash and add remaining ingredients, except 1 cup cheese for topping, and toss until well blended. Salt and pepper, to taste and transfer to a lightly buttered baking dish and top with remaining cheese. Bake at 350° for 30 minutes. Serves 8.

In a Hurry Artichoke Cheese Bake—Combine a 14-ounce can drained artichoke hearts, 3 ounce package softened cream cheese with chives, 1 cup bottled blue cheese dressing, 1/4 cup dry vermouth and 1/2 teaspoon lemon juice. Transfer to a baking dish and bake for 40 minutes. Top with 1 cup grated Parmesan cheese and bake for 5 minutes longer. Serves 4.

Squash and Applesauce Bake

1 package frozen yellow squash, cooked and drained
3/4 cup applesauce, drained
1/4 cup brown sugar
1/4 cup butter, melted
1/4 teaspoon nutmeg
1/4 teaspoon salt
1/4 cup evaporated milk
2 slices bread, de-crusted, and cubed
2 tablespoons butter

In a skillet sauté the bread crumbs in butter until golden. Drain. Combine all other ingredients and transfer to a buttered baking dish. Sprinkle the crumbs on top and bake, covered, at 350° for 45 minutes. Serves 8.

Little Mushroom Baked Squash with Tomatoes

8 medium yellow squash, sliced
4 slices bacon, diced and fried crisp (reserve drippings)
4 green onions, tops and bottoms, chopped
1 cup tomatoes, drained and chopped
1/4 cup sour cream
1/4 cup seasoned bread crumbs
1/2 teaspoon tarragon
1 cup Parmesan cheese, freshly grated

Cook the squash in boiling, salted water until tender. Drain. In a saucepan sauté the onions in the bacon drippings until soft. Mix with the squash and add the remaining ingredients, except the cheese. Salt and pepper, to taste and transfer to a buttered baking dish. Top with the cheese and bake at 350° for 30 minutes. Serves 8.

In a Hurry New Potatoes—Fill a 13″ x 9″ baking dish with sliced new potatoes. Cover with 1 cup sliced onions. Pour 1/2 pint whipping cream on top and sprinkle with 1 cup grated Parmesan cheese. Bake at 350° for 30 minutes or until potatoes are tender.

Sweet Potato Cranberry Bake

$^1/_2$	cup flour
$^1/_2$	cup packed brown sugar
$^1/_2$	cup uncooked minute oats
1	teaspoon cinnamon
$^1/_3$	cup butter
2	17-ounce cans yams, drained
2	16-ounce cans cranberries

Combine the first 4 ingredients. Cut in the butter making coarse crumbs.
Combine 1 cup of the crumb mixture with the remaining ingredients. Place in
a baking dish, top with the remaining crumbs, and bake for 30 minutes.
Serves 8.

Orange Sweet Potato Bake

30	ounce can yams, drained and mashed
$^3/_4$	stick butter, melted
$^1/_2$	teaspoon cinnamon
$^1/_2$	teaspoon nutmeg
2	cups miniature marshmallows
$^1/_2$	cup orange marmalade
$^1/_4$	cup chopped walnuts

Preheat oven to 350°. Combine all the ingredients and place in a baking dish.
Bake for 25 minutes. Serves 8.

Yankee Yams

30	ounce can yams, drained (reserve syrup)
2	tablespoons lemon juice
$^1/_4$	stick butter, melted
1	cup packed brown sugar
12	gingersnaps, crushed
1	teaspoon baking powder
$^1/_2$	teaspoon salt

Preheat oven to 350°. Place yams in a baking dish and add the next three
ingredients. Mix the gingersnaps with the reserved syrup. Add the remaining
ingredients and mix well. Pour over the yams and bake, covered, for 30 minutes. Serves 6–8.

Sweet Potatoes with Grand Marnier

1½ sticks butter
½   cup sugar
½   cup orange juice
3   ounces Grand Marnier
1   cup apples, sliced
2   cups sweet potatoes, cooked and sliced
1   cup peaches, sliced
2   bananas, sliced
¼   cup almonds, browned in butter

In a saucepan melt the butter and sugar and simmer over low heat. Add the orange juice and bring to a boil. Remove from heat and stir in the Grand Marnier. Spread the sauce on the bottom of a buttered baking dish and layer with the apples, potatoes, peaches and bananas. Sprinkle with almonds and bake at 350° for 25 minutes. Serves 6.

Sweet Potatoes with Sherry

6   sweet potatoes, boiled, peeled and mashed
1   stick butter, melted
2   eggs, well beaten
½   cup brown sugar
½   cup dry sherry
¼   teaspoon salt
½   cup walnuts, chopped

In a mixing bowl beat the hot potatoes with all the ingredients until smooth. Transfer to a buttered baking dish and bake at 350° 30 minutes. Serves 6.

Curried Tomatoes

1   onion, chopped
¼   stick butter
1   teaspoon curry powder
½   cup orange marmalade
½   cup chutney
1   teaspoon cinnamon
8   tomatoes, sliced 1" thick

Preheat oven to 400°. In a skillet saute the onion in the butter until soft. Add the next 4 ingredients and mix well. Place the tomatoes in the bottom of a shallow baking dish. Spoon the sauce over each slice. Bake for 10 minutes or until bubbly. Remove with a slotted spoon and serve. Serves 8.

Zucchini Mushroom Bake

1	pound zucchini, sliced and cooked (reserve 1½ cups cooking liquid)
½	pound fresh mushrooms, thinly sliced
1	garlic clove, minced
3	tablespoons butter
2	tablespoons flour
1	cup sour cream
1	teaspoon dill weed
1	teaspoon salt
1	cup seasoned bread crumbs

Preheat oven to 350°. In a large skillet saute the mushrooms and garlic in the butter until soft. Add the flour and cook to a thick paste. Add the reserved liquid and the remaining ingredients, except for the bread crumbs, and remove from the heat. Transfer to a baking dish and top with the bread crumbs. Bake for 30 minutes or until bubbly. Serves 4–6.

Zany Zucchini

4	cups sliced zucchini
1	onion, chopped
1	stick butter
¼	cup finely chopped parsley
¼	teaspoon garlic powder
¼	teaspoon Italian seasoning
¼	teaspoon oregano
1	teaspoon salt
2	eggs, lightly beaten
2	cups grated Monterey Jack cheese
8	ounce can refrigerated crescent rolls
2	tablespoons Dijon mustard

Preheat oven to 375°. In a large heavy skillet saute the first 2 ingredients in the butter until soft. Add the next 5 ingredients and mix well. Combine the eggs and the cheese and mix with the zucchini mixture. Separate the dough into 8 triangles and press over the bottom and sides of a 10″ pie or quiche pan. Spread the bottom with mustard. Pour the zucchini mixture into the pastry shell and bake for 20 minutes or until set. Serves 6–8.

Zucchini Frittata

4   eggs, beaten
1/2   cup buttermilk
4   ounce can diced green chilies, drained
1/4   cup finely chopped parsley
2   cups grated Jarlsberg or Monterey Jack cheese
1   garlic clove, crushed
1 1/2   teaspoons salt
2   teaspoons baking powder
1/2   teaspoon thyme
1/2   teaspoon tarragon
8   medium zucchini, chopped, cooked and drained
1   cup Pepperidge Farm onion and garlic croutons, crushed
1/4   stick butter, melted

Preheat oven to 350°. Combine the first 10 ingredients and mix well. Fold in the zucchini and transfer to an 8″ square baking pan which has been dusted with 1/2 the crushed croutons. Sprinkle with the remaining croutons and dot with the butter. Bake for 45 minutes or until set. Serves 8.

Poppyseed Zucchini

1/2   stick butter
4   cups zucchini, sliced
1   onion, chopped
1/2   cup sour cream
1   teaspoon salt
2   teaspoons poppy seeds

In a large skillet simmer the first 3 ingredients, covered, until the zucchini is tender. Add the remaining ingredients and heat through. Serves 4.

Little Mushroom Zucchini Supreme

8 medium zucchini, sliced
1/2 stick butter
4 green onions, tops and bottoms, chopped
1 small yellow onion, chopped
1 small green pepper, chopped
1/4 teaspoon tarragon
1/4 teaspoon Italian Herb Seasoning
1 teaspoon sugar
2 tablespoons pimento, chopped
1/2 cup Old English cheese, grated
1 cup bread crumbs (mixed with 1/2 cup melted butter)

Cook the zucchini in boiling, salted water until tender. Drain. In a saucepan sauté the onions and green pepper in the butter until soft. Combine with all the other ingredients, except the bread crumbs. Salt and pepper, to taste and transfer to a lightly buttered baking dish. Top with bread crumbs and bake at 350° for 30 minutes. Serves 8.

Zucchini and Tomato Casserole

8 medium zucchini, sliced
Flour (seasoned with salt and pepper)
1/2 cup olive oil
1 large onion, thinly sliced
2 large tomatoes, peeled and sliced
2 cups Mozzarella cheese, grated
1/3 cup Parmesan cheese, freshly grated (topping)

Dredge the zucchini in the flour and in a large skillet sauté them in the oil until browned. (Add more oil if needed.) Transfer to paper towels to drain. In a buttered baking dish arrange third of the zucchini, half the onion slices, half the tomato slices, salt and pepper and half the cheese. Repeat, ending with the zucchini. Top with Parmesan cheese and bake, covered, at 350° for 1 hour. Uncover and bake 10 minutes more. Serves 8.

Little Mushroom Italian Zucchini

8   medium zucchini, sliced
14 ounce can tomatoes, drained
4   green onions, tops and bottoms, chopped
1/2 yellow onion, chopped
3   ribs celery, chopped
1/2 stick butter
3   ounce can mushrooms, stems and pieces
1/4 teaspoon sweet basil
1   cup Monterey Jack cheese, grated.

Cook the zucchini in boiling, salted water until tender. Drain. In a saucepan sauté the onions and celery in butter until soft. Combine all the ingredients and mix well. Salt and pepper, to taste. Transfer to a lightly buttered casserole and bake at 350° for 30 minutes. Serves 8.

Little Mushroom Zucchini with Green Chilies

8   medium zucchini, sliced
4   green onions, tops and bottoms, chopped
1/2 yellow onion, chopped
1/2 green pepper, chopped
1/2 stick butter
2   tablespoons green chilies, chopped
1/2 teaspoon dill seed
1/2 roll Kraft Jalapeño Pepper cheese spread

Cook the zucchini in boiling, salted water until tender. Drain. In a saucepan, sauté the onions and green pepper in butter until soft. Combine all the ingredients and mix well. Taste for seasonings. Transfer to a lightly buttered casserole and bake at 350° for 30 minutes or until bubbly. Serves 8.

In a Hurry Summer Squash with Dill—Cook yellow squash in boiling, salted water until tender and drain. Chop coarsely and add buttermilk, some dill weed and salt and pepper, to taste.

Vegetable Lasagne

This recipe makes two 9" x 11" x 2" pans of Lasagne.

2   large onions, chopped
5   garlic cloves, minced
¹/₂ stick butter
1   large green pepper, diced
1   large eggplant, peeled and diced
4   zucchini, diced
1   pound fresh mushrooms, thinly sliced
2   15-ounce cans tomato sauce with tomato bits
6   ounce can tomato paste
6   ounce can water
3   tablespoons spaghetti sauce seasoning
1¹/₂ teaspoons salt
1   teaspoon sugar
1   teaspoon beef soup base

FILLING

2   16-ounce cartons Ricotta cheese
16 ounce carton cottage cheese (small curd)
2   packages frozen chopped spinach, cooked and squeezed dry
1   egg
1   pound grated Mozzarella cheese
2   cups grated Parmesan cheese
1   pound lasagne noodles, cooked according to package
    directions

Preheat oven to 350°. In a large heavy skillet saute the first 2 ingredients in the butter until soft. Add the next 4 ingredients and saute for 5 minutes. Add the remaining ingredients and simmer, covered, for 30 minutes. Blend the Ricotta cheese, cottage cheese, spinach and egg and season with salt and pepper. Lightly grease 2 9" x 11" x 2" pans and layer fourth of the noodles in the bottom of each pan. Layer fourth of the cheese filling, fourth vegetable sauce, fourth Mozzarella cheese and ¹/₂ cup Parmesan. Repeat. Bake for 40 minutes or until bubbly. (You may bake one for now and freeze the other one.)

Curried Vegetables

1	onion, chopped
1	small green pepper, chopped
1	cup raw potatoes, peeled and thinly sliced
1	stick butter
1	tablespoon tarragon vinegar
1	garlic clove, minced
2	teaspoons curry powder
1	tablespoon coriander (cilantro)
2	teaspoons salt
1	teaspoon tumeric
¹/₂	teaspoon dry mustard
¹/₄	teaspoon ginger
1	stick cinnamon
2	bay leaves, crumbled
¹/₈	teaspoon cayenne pepper
1	cup cauliflowerets
1	cup julienne sliced carrots
1	cup cut fresh green beans
1	cup chicken stock
4	slightly green bananas, sliced
2	cups cooked rice
2	cups sour cream

In a large heavy skillet saute the first 3 ingredients in the butter for 10 minutes. Add the next 15 ingredients and simmer, covered, for 30 minutes. Add the bananas and rice and cook for 5 minutes. Fold in the sour cream and cook slowly until heated through. Serves 10.

Vegetable Potpourri

1	package frozen broccoli flowerets, drained
1	package frozen cauliflower flowerets, drained
1	green pepper, cut in julienne slices
1	cup evaporated milk
1	cup mayonnaise
1	cup grated Parmesan cheese

Preheat oven to 300°. Combine the first 3 ingredients and season with salt and pepper. Layer on the bottom of a baking dish. Combine the next 2 ingredients and spoon over the vegetables. Top with the cheese and bake for 30 minutes. Serves 8.

Vegetable Garden Bake

1   cup cooked brown rice
1   cup fresh broccoli, cut into flowerets
1   cup carrots, cut into julienne strips
1   cup zucchini, thinly sliced
1   cup fresh green beans, cut French-style
1/2 stick butter, melted
1   cup grated sharp Cheddar cheese
1   cup grated Monterey Jack cheese

Preheat oven to 350°. Place rice in the bottom of a shallow baking dish. In a saucepan cook the vegetables in boiling salted water for 5 minutes or until undercooked and crispy. Spoon vegetables over the rice. Drizzle butter over the mixture and top with the cheeses. Bake for 10 minutes. Serves 8.

In a Hurry Scalloped Potatoes—In a buttered baking dish layer 2 peeled, sliced, potatoes, 1 thinly sliced onion and 1 thinly sliced green pepper. Sprinkle each layer with salt and pepper. Pour in 1 can cream of celery soup mixed with 1/3 cup milk. Bake, covered at 300° for 1 hour. Remove cover the last 15 minutes.

BREADS

Apple Muffins

3½ cups flour
3   cups peeled, finely minced apples
2   cups sugar
1   teaspoon salt
1   teaspoon baking soda
1   teaspoon cinnamon
1½ cups oil
½   cup chopped, toasted pecans
1   teaspoon vanilla

Preheat oven to 350°. Grease and lightly sprinkle with flour 12 muffin tins. In a bowl combine the first 6 ingredients and mix well. Fold in the remaining ingredients and pour into the muffin tins filling two-thirds full. Bake for 30 minutes or until the top springs back when gently touched in the center. Makes 24 muffins.

Applesauce Muffins

2   cups biscuit mix
¼   cup sugar
½   cup applesauce
¼   cup milk
1   egg
2   tablespoons oil

TOPPING

½   stick butter
½   cup sugar
2   teaspoons cinnamon

Preheat oven to 400°. Grease 12 muffin tins. In a large bowl combine all the ingredients and beat for 30 seconds. Fill the muffin tins two-thirds full and bake for 12 minutes. Combine the topping ingredients and brush over the tops of each muffin.

Banana Muffins

1³/₄ cups flour
2   teaspoons baking powder
¹/₄ teaspoon baking soda
¹/₄ teaspoon salt
¹/₃ cup sugar
3   tablespoons melted butter
1   egg, lightly beaten
1   cup mashed ripe bananas

In a bowl sift together the first 5 ingredients. Combine the shortening, egg and bananas and stir into the dry ingredients until just moistened. Fill greased muffin tins two-thirds full. Bake in a preheated 400° oven for about 20 minutes. Makes about 18 muffins.

Bourbon Muffins

1   box yellow cake mix
3   ounce package instant vanilla pudding mix
4   eggs
¹/₂ cup oil
¹/₂ cup bourbon
¹/₂ cup milk
1   teaspoon vanilla
¹/₂ cup chopped pecans

ICING

¹/₂ stick butter
1   cup sugar
2   teaspoons water
¹/₄ cup bourbon

Preheat oven to 350°. Mix all the ingredients, except the pecans, and beat with an electric mixer at medium speed for 5 minutes. Stir in the pecans and bake in greased muffin tins for 25 minutes. Poke a few holes in each muffin and pour on a little icing. To make the icing, combine the first 3 ingredients and bring to a boil. Remove from the heat and stir in the bourbon. Pour on the muffins. Makes 36 muffins.

Oatmeal Muffins

1   cup raw oatmeal
1   cup buttermilk
1   egg
½   cup brown sugar
½   cup melted butter
1   cup flour
1   tablespoon baking powder
½   teaspoon baking soda
½   teaspoon salt

Preheat oven to 400°. Grease 12 muffin tins. Combine the first 2 ingredients and soak for 1 hour. Add the next 3 ingredients and mix well. Combine the remaining ingredients and sift into the oatmeal mixture. Fill the muffin tins two-thirds full and bake for 30 minutes or until done. Makes 12 muffins.

Carrot Muffins

½   cup oil
2   cups brown sugar, firmly packed
4   eggs
2   cups flour
2   teaspoons baking powder
2   teaspoons lemon juice
2   teaspoons vanilla extract
1   teaspoon salt
2   cups carrots, grated

In a bowl combine first 3 ingredients and mix well. Blend in remaining ingredients, except carrots, and mix until well blended. Add carrots and mix well. Spoon batter into lightly greased muffin tins. Bake at 375° for 30 minutes. Makes 24 muffins.

GOURMET HELPER—To test bread dough to see if it has risen enough, press 2 fingers into the dough about ½" deep. If the impression remains, the dough is ready.

Lemon Muffins

2   cups butter
2   cups sugar
8   egg yolks, well beaten
1/2   cup lemon juice
1/4   cup milk
4   cups flour
4   teaspoons baking powder
2   teaspoons salt
8   egg whites, stiffly beaten
1   tablespoon grated lemon peel

Preheat oven to 375°. Cream the butter and the sugar until smooth. Add the egg yolks and beat until light. Combine the lemon juice and milk. Sift the next 3 ingredients together and add the lemon juice mixture alternately with the flour mixture to the egg mixture. (DO NOT OVERMIX). Fold in the egg whites and the lemon peel and fill greased muffin tins two-thirds full. Bake for 20 minutes or until the top springs back when gently touched in the center.

Double Corn Muffins

1   cup sifted flour
2   tablespoons sugar
2   teaspoons baking powder
3/4   teaspoon salt
1   cup yellow cornmeal
1   egg, beaten
1   cup cream-style corn
3/4   cup milk
2   tablespoons oil

Preheat oven to 425°. Grease 20 muffin tins. In a large bowl sift together the first 4 ingredients. Stir in the corn meal. Combine the remaining ingredients and add to the corn meal mixture. Stir until moistened (do not beat). Fill the muffin tins two-thirds full and bake for 30 minutes or until golden brown. Makes 20 muffins.

Cheese Corn Muffins

3/4 cup flour
2¹/2 teaspoons baking powder
3/4 teaspoon salt
1 tablespoon sugar
¹/2 cup yellow cornmeal
1 cup Cheddar cheese, grated
1 egg, beaten
3/4 cup milk
2 tablespoons butter, melted

In a bowl combine flour, baking powder, salt and sugar; stir in cornmeal and cheese. Make a well in the center of the dry ingredients. Add the egg, milk and butter. Stir just to moisten dry ingredients. Grease muffin tins and pour in batter two-thirds full. Bake at 400° for about 20 to 25 minutes or until golden brown. Makes 12 muffins.

Orange Pecan Muffins

¹/2 cup sugar
¹/2 cup orange juice
1 egg, lightly beaten
2 tablespoons oil
2 cups biscuit mix
¹/2 cup orange marmalade
¹/2 cup chopped pecans

TOPPING
¹/4 cup sugar
1¹/2 tablespoons flour
¹/2 teaspoon cinnamon
¹/2 teaspoon nutmeg
1 tablespoon butter

Preheat oven to 400°. Grease 12 muffin tins. In a bowl combine the first 4 ingredients and mix well. Add the biscuit mix and beat vigorously for 30 seconds. Stir in the next 2 ingredients and turn into the muffin tin, filling each cup two-thirds full. In a bowl combine the first 4 topping ingredients and mix well. Cut in the butter until the mixture is crumbly. Sprinkle over the batter and bake for 25 minutes or until the top springs back when gently touched in the center. Makes 12 muffins.

Ice Cream Muffins

2   cups self-rising flour, sifted
2   cups vanilla ice cream, softened
1   teaspoon vanilla flavoring

Preheat oven to 400°. Grease 12 muffin tins. In a large bowl combine all the ingredients and mix gently with a wooden spoon (do not use a mixer). Fill the muffin tins two-thirds full and bake for 15–20 minutes or until just barely done.

Little Mushroom Blueberry Muffins

3   sticks butter, softened
2¼   cups sugar
4   eggs, well beaten
4   cups flour
4   teaspoons baking powder
2½   cups milk
2   cups canned blueberries, drained

In a mixing bowl cream butter and sugar together until light. Add the eggs and beat until well mixed. Add the flour and baking powder and gradually add the milk beating until mixture is smooth. Fold in the blueberries. Pour into oiled muffin tins, fill about half full and bake in a preheated 400° oven for 20 to 30 minutes. Make about 2 dozen muffins.

Honey Crumb Muffins

2¼   cups flour, sifted
4   teaspoons baking powder
½   teaspoon salt
½   cup corn flake crumbs
1   egg, lightly beaten
1   cup milk
¼   cup honey
¼   cup melted shortening

In a mixing bowl sift together the flour, baking powder and salt. Mix in corn flake crumbs. In a bowl combine egg, milk and honey. Add egg mixture to dry ingredients. Add shortening and stir only until combined. Fill greased muffin cups two-thirds full. Bake in a preheated 425° oven for about 20 minutes. Makes 1 dozen muffins.

Brown Sugar Muffins

1¹/₂ cups flour
¹/₄   cup sugar
¹/₄   teaspoon salt
¹/₄   teaspoon cinnamon
3¹/₂ teaspoons baking powder
¹/₄   cup light brown sugar
1   egg, lightly beaten
¹/₂   cup oil
¹/₂   cup milk

In a mixing bowl sift together the first 5 ingredients. Blend in the brown sugar. Combine the egg, oil and milk and stir into the dry ingredients until just moistened. Fill oiled muffin tins two-thirds full and bake at 350° for about 20 minutes or until done. Makes about 18 muffins.

Little Mushroom Creole Muffins

2   eggs, well beaten
1¹/₂ cups milk
³/₄   cup butter, melted
2   tablespoons green pepper, chopped
2   tablespoons onion, chopped
2   tablespoons pimento, chopped
³/₄   cup Cheddar cheese, grated
2¹/₂ cups flour
1   teaspoon salt
2   tablespoons baking powder
5   tablespoons sugar
5   tablespoons yellow cornmeal

In a mixing bowl beat the eggs, milk and butter. Add the next 4 ingredients to all the dry ingredients. Add the egg mixture and stir lightly. Pour into oiled muffin tins and bake at 400° for about 30 minutes.

Sour Cream Peach Muffins

1   cup fresh chopped peaches
1   cup sour cream
1   egg
1/2 stick butter, melted and cooled
2   cups flour
1   tablespoon baking powder
1/4 teaspoon baking soda
1/4 teaspoon salt
1/2 teaspoon cinnamon
1/4 teaspoon nutmeg
1/4 cup sugar (if peaches are not sweet add 1/4 cup more sugar)

Preheat oven to 375°. Grease 12 muffin tins. In a bowl combine the first 3 ingredients and mix well. Stir in the butter and set mixture aside. In a large mixing bowl combine the remaining ingredients. Pour the sour cream mixture over the flour mixture and stir only to blend. (The mixture should be thick). Fill the muffin tins two-thirds full and bake for 35 minutes or until the top springs back when gently touched in the center. Makes 12 muffins.

Zucchini Muffins

2 1/2 cups flour
2   eggs
1 1/4 cups sugar
3/4   cup + 1 tablespoon oil
2 1/2 cups grated zucchini
2   teaspoons vanilla
1   teaspoon salt
1   teaspoon baking soda
1   teaspoon baking powder
1   teaspoon cinnamon
1/4   teaspoon nutmeg
1   cup buttermilk

Preheat oven to 350°. Grease 24 muffin tins. In a large bowl combine all the ingredients and mix well. Pour into the muffin tins filling two-thirds full. Bake for 25 minutes or until the top springs back when gently touched in the center. Makes 24 muffins.

Mexican Cornbread

1	stick butter, softened
1	cup sugar
16	ounce can cream-style corn
4	ounce can green chilies, diced
1/2	cup Monterey Jack cheese, grated
1/2	cup Cheddar cheese, grated
1	cup flour
1	cup cornmeal
4	teaspoons baking powder
1/2	teaspoon salt
4	eggs, well beaten

In a bowl mix butter and sugar. Add corn, chilies and cheeses. Mix together flour, cornmeal, baking powder and salt. Stir into corn mixture. Add eggs and mix well. Pour into 2 loaf pans and bake at 375° for 40 minutes.

Mexican Cornbread II

2	cups cornmeal
3/4	cup flour
3	eggs
2/3	cup oil
1	cup sour cream
16	ounce can cream-style corn
1	tablespoon baking powder
1	teaspoon sugar
1	teaspoon salt
3	jalapeno peppers, seeded and chopped
1	cup grated sharp Cheddar cheese

Preheat oven to 450°. Combine all the ingredients, except the cheese, and mix well. Pour half the batter into a greased baking pan. Sprinkle with half the cheese. Pour remaining batter on top and sprinkle with the remaining cheese. Bake for 30 minutes or until done.

Fluffy Cornbread

1   stick butter, softened
1/2 cup sugar
1 1/2 cups unbleached flour
1 1/2 cups yellow cornmeal
2   tablespoons baking powder
1   teaspoon salt
3   eggs
1 1/2 cups milk

Preheat oven to 425°. In a bowl beat the butter with an electric mixer until light and fluffy. Add the sugar and mix for 10 minutes. In another bowl combine the next 4 ingredients. Add the eggs to the butter mixture one at a time, beating well each time. Stir in the flour mixture alternately with the milk and beat for 5 minutes. Pour into a greased 9″ square pan and bake for 40 minutes or until done.

Onion-Cheddar Cornbread

3/4 stick butter
2   onions, finely chopped
2   eggs
2   tablespoons buttermilk
2   17-ounce cans cream-style corn
1   pound package corn muffin mix
1   cup sour cream
2   cups grated sharp Cheddar cheese

Preheat oven to 425°. In a skillet saute the onion in the butter until soft. Set aside. In a large bowl combine the eggs and buttermilk and mix until smooth. Stir in the next 2 ingredients and mix well. Pour into a greased 9″ x 13″ baking pan. Spoon onion over the batter, spread the sour cream over the onion and sprinkle with the cheese. Bake for 30 minutes. Let cool for 10 minutes before cutting.

Busy Day Biscuits

2   cups flour
3½ teaspoons baking powder
1   teaspoon salt
⅓ cup oil
⅔ cup milk

Preheat oven to 400°. Combine all the ingredients and roll out to desired thickness. Cut and arrange on a greased baking sheet. Bake for 12 minutes.

Buttermilk Biscuits

2   cups flour
1   tablespoon double acting baking powder
1   teaspoon salt
½ teaspoon soda
½ cup shortening
1   cup buttermilk

Preheat oven to 500°. In a mixing bowl combine the first 4 ingredients. Add the shortening. Using a pastry blender cut shortening into dry ingredients until mixture resembles rough meal. Blend in buttermilk with a fork until combined. Put dough on floured board. DO NOT OVERHANDLE. Roll out with floured rolling pin. Cut out biscuits and place on ungreased pan. Put in top part of oven, immediately reduce heat to 450° and bake until done.

Sour Cream Biscuits

2   cups flour
½ teaspoon salt
½ teaspoon baking soda
1   tablespoon baking powder
1   cup sour cream

Preheat oven to 450°. Combine all the ingredients and turn out on a floured surface. Roll out to desired thickness and cut with a biscuit cutter. Place on a greased baking sheet and bake for 10–12 minutes.

Herbed Biscuits

2   cups flour
4   teaspoons baking powder
1   teaspoon salt
1   teaspoon caraway seeds
1   teaspoon sage
6   tablespoons Crisco
1/2 cup milk

Preheat oven to 450°. Combine all the ingredients and roll out to desired thickness. Cut and arrange on a greased baking pan. Bake for 10 minutes.

7-Up Biscuits

2   cups flour
4   teaspoons baking powder
1   teaspoon salt
2   teaspoons sugar
1/2 cup Crisco
3/4 cup 7-Up

Preheat oven to 450°. Sift together the first 4 ingredients. Cut in the Crisco until mixture resembles coarse crumbs. Add the 7-Up and stir with a fork until dry ingredients are moistened. Place on a floured surface and knead 8 or 10 times. Roll out to 1/2″ thickness. Cut and arrange on a baking sheet. Bake for 10–12 minutes.

In a Hurry Herb Baked Biscuits—Pour 1 stick melted butter into an 8″ square pan. Sprinkle with 2 tablespoons chervil, 2 tablespoons parsley flakes, 2 tablespoons grated Parmesan cheese, 1 tablespoon dill weed and 1 tablespoon onion salt. Place an 8-ounce package refrigerated biscuits on top and bake in a preheated 400° oven for 12-15 minutes. Invert on a platter and serve.

Biscuit Mix Bread

5   cups biscuit mix
1/4 cup sugar
1/2 teaspoon salt
2   envelopes active dry yeast
2   cups warm milk
4   eggs, well beaten
1/4 teaspoon cream of tartar

In a large bowl sift the biscuit mix, sugar and salt. In a separate bowl dissolve the yeast in the warm milk. Beat the eggs with cream of tartar and combine with the yeast mixture. Add to the dry ingredients stirring until the dough is well mixed. The dough should be sticky. Cover and let rise in a warm place until it doubles in bulk. Stir the dough thoroughly and pour into 2 oiled 8½" x 4½" x 2½" pans. Let the dough rise to the top of the pans. Bake at 350° for 30 minutes or until done.

Apple Bread

1   cup oil
2   cups sugar
3   eggs
2   cups chopped apples
2   teaspoons vanilla
3   cups flour
1   teaspoon soda
1/2 teaspoon salt
1   cup chopped pecans

In a mixing bowl beat the oil, sugar and eggs. Stir in the apples, vanilla and the combined dry ingredients. Mix in the nuts and pour into 2 ungreased 8¼" x 4½" x 2¾" loaf pans. Bake in a preheated 350° oven for about 1 hour. Cool 10 minutes and remove from pan and cool on wire rack.

In a Hurry Beer Biscuits—Blend 4 cups biscuit mix with 1 tablespoon sugar. Add 1 can cold beer and let mixture rest for 15 minutes. Fill greased muffin tins two-thirds full and bake in a pre-heated 400° oven for 15 minutes or until brown.

Batter Bread

2   1-pound coffee cans or 1 2-pound coffee can
1   package dry yeast
$1/2$ cup warm water
$1/8$ teaspoon ginger
3   tablespoons sugar
13   ounce can evaporated milk
$1^1/2$ teaspoons salt
2   tablespoons salad oil
4   to $4^1/2$ cups flour
     Butter, melted

Dissolve yeast in water in a large mixing bowl. Blend in ginger and 1 table-spoon of the sugar. Let stand in a warm place until mixture is bubbly, about 15 minutes. Stir in remaining 2 tablespoons sugar, milk, salt and salad oil. With mixer on low speed, beat in flour 1 cup at a time, beating well after each addition. Beat in last cup of flour with a heavy spoon. Add flour until dough is very heavy but too sticky to knead. Place dough in a well-greased 2-pound coffee can or two 1-pound coffee cans. Cover with well-greased coffee plastic lids from original cans. Let covered cans stand in a warm place until dough rises and pops off lids. This will take approximately 45 to 60 minutes for 1-pound cans or $1^1/2$ hours for 2-pound can. Discard lids and bake at 350° for 45 minutes for 1-pound loaf or 60 minutes for 2-pound loaf. Brush top lightly with melted butter. You may freeze after placing the dough in coffee cans before the dough has risen.

VARIATION: LIGHT WHEAT BREAD
$1^1/2$ cups wheat flour and 3 cups white Honey rather than sugar

In a Hurry Orange Bread—Prepare 1 package orange muffin mix according to package directions. Add $3/4$ cup whole cranberry sauce and 1 cup chopped nuts. Pack dough into 6 6-ounce orange juice cans and bake in a preheated 375° oven for 35 minutes. Cool for 5 minutes. Cut end from can and push out the bread.

Amaretto Almond Bread

8   eggs, separated
3   cups sugar
4   sticks butter, softened
3   cups sifted flour
1/2 cup Amaretto
1   tablespoon black walnut flavoring
1   cup blanched almonds

Preheat oven to 350°. In a large bowl beat the egg whites until soft peaks form. Add 1 cup of the sugar and beat until stiff peaks form. Set aside. In a large bowl cream butter with the remaining sugar. Add the egg yolks and beat well. Add the flour alternately with the Amaretto and mix well. Stir in the flavoring and the almonds. Gently fold in the egg whites. Pour into 3 well greased 8" x 4" loaf pans. Bake for 45 minutes or until done.

Banana Strawberry Bread

1³/₄ cups sifted flour
2¹/₂ teaspoons baking powder
³/₄ teaspoon salt
1   cup Crisco
²/₃ cup sugar
2   eggs, beaten
1   tablespoon grated lemon peel
1   cup mashed bananas
1/2 cup pureed strawberries
1/2 cup rolled oats
1/2 cup chopped pecans

Preheat oven to 350°. Sift together the first 3 ingredients. In a large bowl cream the Crisco with the sugar. Add the eggs and mix well. Add the remaining ingredients and turn into a greased loaf pan. Bake for 1 hour or until done.

Strawberry Liqueur Bread

1   package frozen strawberries packed in syrup, thawed and
    pureed in a blender or food processor
2   eggs
3/4 cup oil
1 1/2 cups flour
1   cup sugar
1/2 teaspoon baking soda
1   teaspoon cinnamon
1   tablespoon strawberry liqueur

Preheat oven to 325°. Combine the eggs and oil and mix well. Sift the next 4
ingredients into a large bowl. Make a well in the center and pour in the egg
mixture, the puree and the liqueur. With a wooden spoon mix well and pour
into a 9" x 5" loaf pan and bake for 1 hour and 10 minutes. Let cool before
serving.

Orange Peanut Butter Bread

1/2 cup smooth peanut butter
2   tablespoons oil
1 1/3 cups orange juice
1   egg
3/4 cup sugar
2   cups flour
1/2 teaspoon salt
1   tablespoon baking powder

Preheat oven to 350°. Beat the peanut butter until smooth and fluffy. Add the
next 4 ingredients and mix well. Combine the remaining ingredients and add
to the peanut butter mixture. Pour into 2 greased loaf pans and bake for 1 hour.

In a Hurry Cranberry Nut Bread—Combine 1 package Nut Bread Mix, 1
cup flour, 1 tablespoon orange peel, 1 teaspoon cinnamon, 1/2 teaspoon nutmeg, 2 eggs and a 10-ounce package frozen cranberry orange relish. Pour into
a greased pan and bake in a preheated 375° oven for 1 hour or until done. Cool
for 10 minutes before removing from pan. Cool completely before slicing.

Pumpkin Bread

3⅓　cups flour
3　　cups sugar
1　　teaspoon cinnamon
2　　teaspoons nutmeg
2　　teaspoons baking soda
1　　teaspoon salt
4　　eggs, beaten
1　　cup oil
⅓　　cup sherry
⅓　　cup water
16　ounce can pumpkin
¾　　cup chopped walnuts

Preheat oven to 325°. In a large bowl combine the first 6 ingredients and mix well. Add the next 4 ingredients and mix well. Fold in the last 2 ingredients and pour into 2 greased loaf pans and bake for 1 hour or until done.

Monkey Bread

1　　cup milk, scalded and cooled to lukewarm
1½　cakes yeast
¼　　cup sugar
1　　teaspoon salt
1　　cup melted butter
2¼　cups sifted flour

Preheat oven to 400°. Add yeast to milk and stir until dissolved. Add the sugar, salt and ½ cup butter and mix well. Stir in the flour and beat well. Cover and let rise until almost doubled in bulk, about 1 hour. Punch down and roll out on a lightly floured board to ¼″ thickness. Cut in diamond-shaped pieces about 2½″ long. Dip each piece in remaining ½ cup butter. Arrange in a 9″ ring mold filling the pan about half full. Cover and let rise until doubled in bulk. Bake for 20-25 minutes or until brown.

In a Hurry Dallas Biscuits—Combine 1 cup self-rising flour, ½ cup evaporated milk and 3 tablespoons mayonnaise. Drop into greased muffin tins and bake in a preheated 425° oven for 20 minutes. Makes 8 biscuits.

Zucchini Bread

3   eggs, beaten
2   cups sugar
1   cup oil
1   tablespoon vanilla
2   cups grated zucchini
2   cups flour
1   tablespoon cinnamon
2   teaspoons soda
1   teaspoon salt
$1/4$ teaspoon baking powder
1   cup chopped pecans

Preheat oven to 350°. In a mixing bowl beat eggs until frothy. Add the next 3 ingredients and beat until mixture is thick. Add the remaining ingredients and mix well. Pour into 2 greased loaf pans and cook for 1 hour or until done.

Grapenut Bread

1   cup grapenuts
2   cups buttermilk
2   cups sugar
2   tablespoons honey
2   eggs
$3^{1}/_{2}$ cups flour
$1/2$ teaspoon salt
1   teaspoon baking soda
2   teaspoons baking powder

Preheat oven to 350°. Soak the grapenuts in the buttermilk for 10 minutes. Cream the sugar, honey and eggs. Add the grapenut mixture. Sift the remaining ingredients and add to the grapenut mixture. Pour into 2 greased loaf pans and bake for 45 minutes or until done.

Dilly Cheese Bread

3   cups biscuit mix
1½ cups grated Monterey Jack cheese
1   tablespoon sugar
1¼ cups evaporated milk
1   egg, beaten
1   tablespoon oil
1   teaspoon dill weed
½   teaspoon dry mustard

Preheat oven to 350°. Place all the ingredients in a large bowl and beat with an electric mixer for 2 minutes. Pour into a greased 8" x 12" baking pan and bake for 45 minutes.

Chili Cheese Bread

13 ounce package hot roll mix
2   cups grated Swiss cheese
2   cups grated sharp Cheddar cheese
½   egg, lightly beaten
½   teaspoon oregano
4   green onions, tops and bottoms, chopped
4   ounce can diced green chilies, drained

Preheat oven to 350°. Prepare hot roll mix according to package directions. When dough has risen turn onto a lightly floured pastry board. Divide in half. Roll half to a 9" round and fit into the bottom of a 9" spring-form pan. Combine the next 5 ingredients and spread on the dough mixture. Top with the chilies. Roll the remaining dough to a 9" round and cut into 8 pie-shaped wedges. Place over the filling with the tips meeting in the center. Cover and let rise in a warm place until puffy, about 45 minutes. Brush top with remaining egg and bake for 50 minutes or until brown. Cool for 10 minutes and then remove rim.

In a Hurry Cream Biscuits—Combine 2½ cups biscuit mix with ½ pint heavy cream. Knead 10 times. Roll out to ½" thickness and cut. Arrange on a greased baking sheet and bake in a preheated 400° oven for 12 minutes.

Olive Cheese Bread

3   cups biscuit mix
1   cup milk
1/3 cup butter
1   tablespoon dry onion flakes
1   teaspoon Worcestershire sauce
1/8 teaspoon Tabasco
2   cups grated Monterey Jack cheese
1   cup sliced ripe olives
1   egg, lightly beaten
1   teaspoon Italian seasoning

Preheat oven to 425°. Mix the first 2 ingredients and spread in a greased 14″ pizza pan. Mix the remaining ingredients and spread over the dough. Bake for 20-25 minutes. Cut into 12 wedges to serve.

Onion Cheese Bread

1/2 cup chopped onion, sauteed in 2 tablespoons butter until soft
1   egg
1/2 cup milk
1 1/2 cups biscuit mix
1   cup grated sharp Cheddar cheese
2   tablespoons finely minced parsley
2   tablespoons melted butter

Preheat oven to 400°. Combine the egg, milk and biscuit mix. Add the onion, parsley and half the cheese. Spread in a greased round cake pan. Sprinkle with the remaining cheese and drizzle with the butter. Bake for 20 minutes.

DESSERTS

Little Mushroom Strawberry Cheese Pie

1¹/₂ pounds cream cheese, softened
1   cup sugar
1   cup pecans, chopped
2   tablespoons vanilla
9"   graham cracker crust, baked and cooled
2   cups whole fresh strawberries
1   tablespoon cornstarch
1   tablespoon milk

In a mixing bowl beat the cream cheese and sugar for about 10 minutes until smooth. Add the nuts and vanilla. Pour into the graham cracker crust and chill for several hours. In a bowl marinate the strawberries in enough sugar to cover. Let stand for about 3 hours. Drain the marinade and in a saucepan heat the marinade with the cornstarch and milk. Simmer until mixture thickens. Cool and add the strawberries. Slice the pie and top with the strawberry topping.

Little Mushroom Lemon Cheese Pie

³/₄ cup sugar
3   tablespoons cornstarch
1   cup water
1   teaspoon grated lemon peel
¹/₃ cup lemon juice
2   egg yolks, slightly beaten
3   ounce package cream cheese, softened
     Whipped cream, sweetened
9"   graham cracker crust, baked and cooled

In a saucepan combine the first 6 ingredients. Beat with electric mixer until mixture is well-blended. Cook over medium heat, stirring constantly, until thick. Remove from heat. Add cream cheese and stir until well blended. Cool. Spoon into the graham cracker crust and chill for 2 hours. Top with whipped cream.

In a Hurry Frozen Strawberry Yogurt Pie—Combine 1 8-ounce carton any flavor fruit yogurt, 1 10-ounce carton frozen strawberries, thawed, and ¹/₂ of 9-ounce carton Cool Whip. Pour into a graham cracker crust and freeze.

Frozen Chocolate Cheese Pie

8   ounces semi-sweet chocolate
8   tablespoons milk
6   ounces cream cheese, softened
1/4 cup pecans, chopped
1   cup sugar
1/4 teaspoon salt
1   teaspoon vanilla
9"   graham cracker crust

In the top of a double boiler melt chocolate with 4 tablespoons of milk. Soften cream cheese with 4 tablespoons of milk. Combine all the ingredients, pour into the crust and freeze. Remove from freezer about 20 minutes before serving. You may top with sweetened whipped cream or leave untopped.

Brownie Pie

3   egg whites
3/4 cup sugar
3/4 cup fine chocolate wafer crumbs
1/2 cup chopped pecans or walnuts
1/2 teaspoon vanilla
     Whipped cream, sweetened

In a mixing bowl beat the egg whites with a dash of salt until soft peaks form. Gradually add sugar, beating until stiff peaks form. Fold in crumbs, nuts and vanilla and spread evenly in a lightly buttered 9" pie plate. Bake at 325° for about 35 minutes. Cool thoroughly. Spread top with sweetened whipped cream. Chill for 3 to 4 hours. Trim with curls of shaved unsweetened chocolate.

In a Hurry Chocolate Pie—In the top of a double boiler melt 1 can sweetened condensed milk with 2 squares of semi-sweet chocolate. Cook stirring until thick. In another saucepan cook 1 package of chocolate pudding as directed. Mix the two chocolates together and let cool in a baked pie shell. Top with whipped cream and grated chocolate curls.

Little Mushroom French Chocolate Pie

2   8 ounce packages semi-sweet chocolate
$1/2$ cup water
$1/2$ cup brandy
1   pint heavy cream, whipped
9″   graham cracker crust, baked and cooled

In the top of a double boiler melt the chocolate in the water. Add the brandy and cool. Fold in the whipped cream and pour into the graham cracker crust. Chill. Top with sweetened whipped cream and shaved chocolate.

Chocolate Marshmallow Pie

15   marshmallows
6   small Almond Hershey Bars
$1/2$ cup milk
1   pint heavy cream, whippped
1   tablespoon vanilla
9″   graham cracker crust, baked and cooled

In the top of a double boiler melt the marshmallows, chocolate and milk. Fold in the whipped cream and pour into the pie shell. Refrigerate several hours before serving.

Little Mushroom Hershey Bar Pie

10   small Hershey Bars with Almonds
$1/2$ cup brandy
$1/2$ cup water
1   cup heavy cream, whipped
9″   graham cracker crust, baked and cooled

In the top of a double boiler melt the chocolate in the brandy and water. Remove from fire and let cool. Fold in the whipped cream and pour into the graham cracker crust. Chill for several hours. Top with sweetened whipped cream and shaved chocolate.

Mystery Pie

3   egg whites
1   cup sugar
¹/₂ teaspoon baking powder
1   teaspoon vanilla extract
24 saltine crackers, crushed
1   cup chopped walnuts
2   14-ounce cans condensed milk
1   cup heavy cream, whipped

Preheat oven to 300°. In a bowl beat the egg whites until stiff. Gradually beat in sugar, baking powder and vanilla. Fold in the next 2 ingredients and spread in a well-greased 9″ pie plate. Bake for 25-30 minutes. Remove labels from the milk and place, unopened, in a pan of water. Bring to a boil. Cover pan with a lid and simmer for 2 hours. Cool cans under cold water. Open both ends and push out caramelized filling into the cooled pie shell. Spread evenly and chill before serving. Top with the whipped cream.

Limeade Pie

CRUST

1   cup flour
1   stick butter, softened
¹/₄ cup powdered sugar
¹/₄ cup chopped pecans

FILLING

6   ounce can frozen limeade, thawed
14 ounce can condensed milk
15 ounce container Cool Whip

Preheat oven to 400°. Mix all the crust ingredients with your hands until pliable. Press evenly against the sides and bottom of a 9″ pie plate. With a fork, prick the bottom of the pie shell and bake for 12 minutes or until lightly browned. Cool before filling. Add the first 2 ingredients and mix well. Fold in the Cool Whip and spread in the shell. Chill before serving.

Little Mushroom Key Lime Pie

CRUST

1½ cups graham cracker crumbs
6 tablespoons melted butter
¼ cup confectioner's sugar
1 teaspoon cinnamon

FILLING

4 egg yolks, well beaten
1 can sweetened condensed milk
1 cup fresh lime juice
Whipped cream, sweetened
Grated lime

Mix the crust ingredients and line the bottom and sides of a 9″ pie pan. Bake at 375° for 15 minutes. Cool.

In a bowl gradually add the milk to the well beaten eggs and mix well. Add the lime juice. Pour the mixture into the pie shell and freeze. Remove 10 minutes before serving. Top with whipped cream and garnish with the grated lime.

Butterscotch Pecan Pie

8 ounce package butterscotch morsels
¾ cup light corn syrup
3 eggs
½ teaspoon salt
¾ cup chopped pecans
8″ unbaked pie shell

In the top of a double boiler melt the butterscotch morsels. Remove from heat. In a bowl combine syrup, eggs and salt and beat well. Add the butterscotch mixture slowly, stirring rapidly, to egg mixture. Add the pecans and pour into the pie shell. Bake at 350° for 45 minutes.

In a Hurry Pecan Pie—Combine 3 beaten eggs, ½ cup sugar, 1 cup dark Karo syrup, ¼ teaspoon salt and 1 cup pecan halves. Pour into a 9″ unbaked pie shell and bake for 1 hour at 375°.

Little Mushroom Pecan Rum Pie

6   eggs, well beaten
1   cup butter, creamed
1/3   cup sugar
1½   cups light corn syrup
2   cups chopped pecans
½   cup light rum
2   teaspoons vanilla
9″   unbaked pie shell

In a bowl combine the butter and eggs and mix well. Add the remaining ingredients and pour into the pie shell. Bake at 450° for 10 minutes. Lower oven to 300° and bake 30 minutes more.

Peach Praline Pie

½   cup flour, sifted
¼   cup brown sugar
½   cup chopped pecans
½   stick butter
4   cups fresh peaches, sliced
½   cup sugar
2   tablespoons quick cooking tapioca
1   teaspoon lemon juice

In a mixing bowl combine the first 4 ingredients. Place a third of the mixture in an unbaked pie shell. Combine the next 4 ingredients and pour over the crumb mixture in the pie shell. Top with the remaining crumb mixture and bake at 450° for 10 minutes. Turn to 350° and bake for 20 minutes. Top with whipped cream.

In a Hurry Peach Cream Pie—Layer 3 cups peaches in a 9″ unbaked pie shell. Combine 2 beaten eggs, 1 cup sugar, ¼ cup flour and a dash salt. Stir in 1 cup heavy cream and 1 teaspoon vanilla. Pour over the peaches and bake for 1 hour.

Sour Cream Raisin Pie

2   cups raisins, soaked in boiling water for 15 minutes
3/4 cup sugar
1/4 teaspoon salt
1   teaspoon cinnamon
1/2 teaspoon nutmeg
1/4 teaspoon ground cloves
2   eggs, lightly beaten
1   cup sour cream
9" unbaked pie shell

Preheat oven to 350°. Combine all the ingredients and pour into the pie shell. Bake for 45 minutes.

Lemon Custard Ice Cream Pie

6   tablespoons butter, softened
1   cup flour
1/4 cup confectioner's sugar
2   eggs, beaten
3/4 cup sugar
2   tablespoons flour
3   tablespoons lemon juice
1   teaspoon grated lemon peel
1   quart lemon custard ice cream
1   cup heavy cream, whipped
8   thin slices of lemon

Make a shortbread crust by blending butter, flour and confectioner's sugar. Press mixture into the bottom and sides of a 9" greased pie pan. Bake at 350° for 5 minutes. Mix eggs, sugar, flour, lemon juice and lemon peel. Pour over hot crust and bake 20 minutes more. Let cool completely. Fill crust with slightly softened ice cream. Freeze. Top with whipped cream and garnish with twisted lemon slices. Freeze for 3 hours. Remove from freezer about 10 minutes before serving. Serves 8.

In a Hurry Lemonade Pie—Thaw 6 ounces of frozen pink lemonade. Mix with 1 can sweetened condensed milk and 15 ounces Cool Whip. Pour into 9" baked graham cracker crust. Refrigerate for at least 1 hour.

Toffee Ice Cream Pie

CRUST

18 vanilla wafers, crushed
2 tablespoons melted butter

FILLING

2 pints vanilla ice cream, softened
1¼ cups crushed Heath bars

SAUCE

1½ cups sugar
1 cup evaporated milk
½ stick butter
¼ cup light corn syrup
Dash salt

Combine the crushed wafers and the butter and press on the bottom of a 9″ pie pan. Spread half the ice cream on the crust and sprinkle with half the candy. Add the remaining ice cream and freeze while making the sauce. Combine all the sauce ingredients and boil over a low heat for 1 minute. Add the remaining candy and cool. Pour over the pie just before serving.

Frozen Daiquiri Pie

6 ounce can frozen Daiquiri Mix, thawed
½ cup mayonnaise
4 ounce package egg custard mix
8 ounce package cream cheese, softened
1 jigger rum
1 cup crushed pineapple, drained
½ cup chopped nuts
1 envelope Dream Whip

In a blender place the first 6 ingredients and blend for 2 to 3 minutes. Prepare the Dream Whip according to the directions on the package. Fold in the nuts and fold into the cheese mixture. Place in a wax paper lined Pyrex dish and freeze for 3 hours. Serves 9.

Frozen Chocolate Pecan Pie

CRUST

2   cups finely chopped, toasted pecans
5   tablespoons + 1 teaspoon firmly packed brown sugar
5   tablespoons chilled butter, cut into small pieces
2   teaspoons rum

CHOCOLATE FILLING

6   ounces semi-sweet chocolate
1/2 teaspoon instant coffee powder
4   eggs
1   tablespoon dark rum
1   teaspoon vanilla
1   cup heavy cream, whipped

Blend all the crust ingredients until mixture holds together. Press into the bottom and sides of a 9″ pie plate. Freeze for at least 1 hour. In the top of a double boiler melt the chocolate with the coffee. Remove from the heat and whisk in the next 3 ingredients mixing until smooth. Let cool for 5 minutes. Gently fold the whipped cream into the chocolate mixture, mixing well. Pour into the crust and freeze. Transfer the pie to the refrigerator 1 hour before serving and top with whipped cream and chocolate shavings.

Chocolate Mint Pie

1   stick butter, softened
1   cup powdered sugar, sifted
2   ounces unsweetened chocolate, melted and cooled
2   eggs, lightly beaten
3   drops peppermint extract
1/2 cup heavy cream
2   tablespoons powdered sugar
1/2 teaspoon vanilla
1/4 cup chopped walnuts
9″ vanilla wafer crust

In a bowl cream together the first 2 ingredients until the mixture is light. Beat in the next 2 ingredients until the mixture is fluffy. Stir in the peppermint and spread mixture into the crust. Chill, loosely covered, for 24 hours. Beat the cream until stiff. Fold in the remaining ingredients and spread on top the chocolate mixture.

Sour Cream Apple Pie

3¹/₄ cups canned apple slices
1 cup sour cream
1 egg, lightly beaten
2 teaspoons lemon juice
1¹/₂ teaspoons flour
¹/₂ cup sugar
¹/₄ cup flour
³/₄ teaspoon cinnamon
1 stick butter, softened
9" unbaked pie crust

Preheat oven to 375°. Combine the first 5 ingredients and mix well. Spoon into the pie shell. Sift together the next 4 ingredients and with your fingers work in the butter until mixture is crumbly. Sprinkle over the apple mixture and bake for 1 hour or until top is golden brown. Top with a little sour cream.

Chocolate Chess Pie

4 tablespoons (heaping) cocoa
1¹/₂ cups sugar
2 eggs
¹/₂ cup chopped pecans
¹/₂ stick butter, softened
¹/₂ cup evaporated milk
¹/₂ cup coconut
9" unbaked pie shell

Preheat oven to 400°. Combine all the ingredients and pour into the pie shell. Bake for 30 minutes or until set. Top with whipped cream.

In a Hurry Almond Hershey Pie—Melt 1 giant Almond Hershey Bar in 2 tablespoons hot water in the top of a double boiler. Cool and fold in ¹/₂ pint of heavy cream, whipped. Pour into a 9" baked pie shell. Chill.

Busy Day Chocolate Pecan Pie

3   6-ounce packages semi-sweet chocolate morsels
3   eggs
1/8   teaspoon salt
1/2   cup firmly packed brown sugar
1   cup chopped pecans
9″   unbaked pie shell

Preheat oven to 375°. In the top of a double boiler melt 2 packages chocolate morsels. Remove from the heat and cool for 5 minutes. In a mixing bowl combine the eggs and salt and beat until very thick and lemon colored. Gradually beat in the brown sugar. Add the melted chocolate, the pecans and the remaining package of chocolate morsels. Pour into the pie shell and bake for 20-25 minutes. Top with whipped cream.

Caramel Peach Pie

28   caramels
1/2   stick butter
1   cup chopped walnuts
3/4   cup sugar
1/4   teaspoon salt
1   teaspoon rum flavoring
2   eggs, lightly beaten
29   ounce can cling peaches, sliced and drained
9″   unbaked pie shell

Preheat oven to 350°. In the top of a double boiler melt the first 2 ingredients, stirring until smooth. Add the nuts. In a large bowl combine the next 4 ingredients and mix well. Mix in the caramel mixture. Arrange the peaches in the bottom of the pie shell and cover with the caramel mixture. Bake for 45 minutes.

In a Hurry Peanut Butter Pie—Combine 1/2 cup crunchy peanut butter and a 9-ounce carton Cool Whip and pour into a graham cracker crust. Chill before serving.

Buttermilk Pie

2 cups sugar
3 tablespoons flour (heaping)
3 eggs, beaten
1 cup buttermilk
1 teaspoon vanilla
1/4 cup melted butter
   Dash nutmeg
9" unbaked pie shell

Preheat oven to 350°. Combine the sugar and flour. Add the next 4 ingredients and pour into pie shell. Sprinkle with the nutmeg and bake for 45-50 minutes.

Peach Cream Cheese Pie

8 ounce package cream cheese, softened
1 cup grated sharp Cheddar cheese
1/4 cup sugar
1 egg
2 cups fresh peeled, sliced peaches
1/2 cup chopped walnuts
2 tablespoons dark brown sugar
1 tablespoon flour
9" unbaked pie shell

Preheat oven to 350°. Combine the first 4 ingredients and mix well. Pour into the pie shell and bake for 25 minutes or until the filling is set. Arrange the peaches over the filling. Combine the remaining ingredients and sprinkle over the top. Bake 10 minutes longer.

In a Hurry Peanut Butter-Cream Cheese Pie—Combine 1/2 cup chunky peanut butter, 1 8-ounce package cream cheese, softened, 1/2 cup milk and 1 cup powdered sugar. Fold in 1 4-ounce container Cool Whip and pour into a 9" graham cracker crust.

Chocolate Pecan Rum Pie

2   squares unsweetened chocolate
3   tablespoons butter
3/4 cup light corn syrup
3/4 cup sugar
1/2 teaspoon salt
3   eggs, lightly beaten
1/4 cup rum
1   teaspoon rum flavoring
1   cup chopped pecans
9″   unbaked pie shell

Preheat oven to 375°. In the top of a double boiler melt the chocolate and the butter together. In a saucepan combine the syrup and the sugar and simmer for 2 minutes. Add the chocolate mixture and cool. Combine the salt and eggs and slowly add the syrup mixture, stirring constantly. Fold in the rum, rum flavoring and the nuts. Pour into the pie shell and bake for 35 minutes or until set.

Apple Walnut Pie

2   tablespoons flour
1/2 cup sugar
3/4 teaspoon cinnamon
1/4 teaspoon salt
1   egg, lightly beaten
1   teaspoon almond extract
1/2 cup chopped walnuts
1   cup sour cream
6   apples, peeled, cored and sliced
9″   unbaked pie shell

TOPPING

1/3 cup sugar
1/3 cup flour
3/4 teaspoon cinnamon
1/4 cup butter

Preheat oven to 400°. Combine the first 8 ingredients and mix well. Fold in the apples. Pour into the pie shell and bake for 15 minutes. Reduce heat to 350° and bake for 30 minutes longer. Combine the topping ingredients and crumble over the warm pie. Bake 10 minutes longer.

Peanut Butter Cheese Pie

2   3-ounce packages cream cheese, softened
1   cup powdered sugar
$^1/_2$ cup smooth peanut butter
$^3/_4$ cup milk
$^3/_4$ cup heavy cream, whipped
1   teaspoon vanilla
1   cup chopped peanuts
9″   graham cracker crust

In a mixing bowl beat the first 3 ingredients until smooth. Add the milk beating until well mixed. Fold in the cream and vanilla and pour into the crust. Freeze for several hours. Top with the peanuts and serve.

Mud Pie

$1^1/_2$ cups chocolate wafer crumbs (about 30 wafers)
$^3/_4$ stick butter, melted
1   teaspoon cinnamon
1   quart coffee ice cream, softened
12   ounce can chocolate topping
$^1/_2$ cup chopped walnuts
1   cup heavy cream, whipped

Preheat oven to 300°. Combine the first 3 ingredients and pat into a 9″ pie plate. Bake for 15 minutes and cool. Spread the ice cream in the cooled crust. Cover with plastic wrap and freeze. When frozen solid, add the chocolate topping and the walnuts. Re-freeze. When ready to serve top with the whipped cream.

Bourbon Walnut Pie

7 apples, peeled, cored and sliced
1 cup chopped walnuts
3/4 cup raisins
1/2 cup firmly packed brown sugar
1/4 cup corn syrup
2 tablespoons flour
2 tablespoons bourbon
1 1/2 tablespoons butter, softened
1/2 teaspoon allspice
3/4 teaspoon cinnamon
1/2 teaspoon ginger
   Juice of 1 lemon
9" unbaked pie shell

Preheat oven to 350°. In a large mixing bowl combine all the ingredients and mix well. Pour into the pie shell and bake for 45 minutes.

Pecan Bourbon Pie

4 eggs
2 cups dark corn syrup
2 tablespoons melted butter
2 tablespoons bourbon
1 1/2 cups chopped pecans
9" unbaked pie shell

Preheat oven to 400°. In a large mixing bowl beat the eggs for 30 seconds. Slowly add the syrup, beating until well mixed. Add the next 2 ingredients and fold in the pecans. Pour into the pie shell and bake for 35 minutes or until the filling is firm.

Grand Marnier Fudge Pie

3 1.5-ounce Hershey Bars with Almonds
2 squares Baker's semi-sweet chocolate
1/2 cup sliced almonds
9 ounce container Cool Whip
1/4 cup Grand Marnier
9" graham cracker crust

In the top of a double boiler melt the first 2 ingredients. Cool slightly and add the next 3 ingredients. Fold until well mixed and pour into the pie crust. Freeze for several hours before serving.

Chocolate Walnut Pie

3 eggs, lightly beaten
1½ cups sugar
¾ stick butter, melted and cooled
2 teaspoons vanilla
½ cup flour
1½ cups semi-sweet chocolate chips
1½ cups chopped walnuts
9″ unbaked pie shell

Preheat oven to 350°. Combine the first 4 ingredients and beat until mixed well. Stir in the remaining ingredients and pour into the pie shell. Bake for 1 hour. Top with whipped cream or vanilla ice cream.

Double Nut Pie

3 eggs, separated
¾ cup packed brown sugar
1 tablespoon flour
1 tablespoon cinnamon
¼ teaspoon salt
¾ stick butter, melted
1 teaspoon vanilla
1¼ cups dark corn syrup
¾ cup chopped pecans
¾ cup chopped walnuts
9″ unbaked pie shell

Preheat oven to 350°. In a mixing bowl beat the egg yolks until lemon colored. Add the next 7 ingredients and mix well. Beat the egg whites until stiff and fold in the egg yolk mixture. Fold in the nuts and pour in the pie shell. Bake for 50 minutes.

Little Mushroom Cheesecake

CRUST
1½ cups graham cracker crumbs
½   cup butter
2   tablespoons sugar

FILLING
3   8-ounce packages cream cheese, softened
1½ cups sugar
5   eggs
2   tablespoons vanilla

Combine the graham cracker crumbs, butter and sugar. Press into the bottom of a 9″ spring-form pan.

In a mixing bowl combine the cream cheese and the sugar and beat for about 10 minutes until smooth. Add the eggs and vanilla and beat until well blended. Pour into the pan and bake at 350° for 1 hour or until set. Cool and top with strawberry topping *or* sour cream topping.

STRAWBERRY TOPPING
2   cups whole fresh strawberries
2   cups sugar
1   tablespoon cornstarch
1   tablespoon milk

In a bowl marinate the strawberries in the sugar. Let stand for about 3 hours. Drain the marinade and in a saucepan heat the marinade with the cornstarch and milk. Simmer until mixture thickens. Cool and add the strawberries. You may top the cheese cake whole or slice and serve topping on each slice.

SOUR CREAM TOPPING
1   pint sour cream
4   tablespoons sugar
1   tablespoon vanilla

Combine the sour cream, sugar and vanilla and mix until well blended. Spread on top of cooled cheese cake and bake at 350° for about 15 minutes.

Banana Cheesecake

1½ pounds cream cheese, softened
¾ cup sugar
3   eggs
3   cups mashed bananas
2   teaspoons vanilla
10″ springform pan covered with a graham cracker crust

Preheat oven to 300°. In a mixing bowl cream the cream cheese and sugar until light and fluffy. Add the eggs, one at a time, beating well after each addition. Add the remaining ingredients and pour into the crust. Bake for 1 hour. Let cool in the oven for 1 more hour (DO NOT OPEN OVEN DOOR). Chill before serving

Chocolate Cheesecake

CRUST

8   ounce package chocolate wafers, crushed fine
⅓ cup butter, melted
2   tablespoons sugar
¼ teaspoon nutmeg

FILLING

3   eggs
1   cup sugar
3   8-ounce packages cream cheese, softened
2   6-ounce packages semi-sweet chocolate pieces, melted
2   teaspoons vanilla
⅛ teaspoon salt
1   cup sour cream

Combine crust ingredients and press on the bottom of a 9″ spring-form pan. Refrigerate. In a large mixing bowl beat the eggs and sugar at high speed until light. Beat in cream cheese until well mixed. Add the remaining ingredients and beat until smooth. Pour into the crust and bake for about 1 hour or until firm. Cool in the pan. Refrigerate for several hours before serving.

Chocolate Cheesecake II

CRUST

½   cup shortbread cookies, crushed
1   tablespoon dark brown sugar
1   tablespoon cinnamon
¼   teaspoon nutmeg
¾   stick butter, melted

FILLING

1   pound cream cheese, softened
2   cups Ricotta cheese
4   large eggs
⅓   cup unsweetened cocoa powder
2   tablespoons Kahlua
1   teaspoon vanilla
1   cup sugar
3   tablespoons instant coffee powder
2   tablespoons cinnamon
¼   teaspoon nutmeg
1   teaspoon mace

TOPPING

1   cup sour cream
½   cup sugar
1   tablespoon unsweetened cocoa powder
1   teaspoon cinnamon

Preheat oven to 350°. Combine all the crust ingredients and press on the bottom of a 9″ spring-form pan. Combine the first 6 ingredients of the filling and with a mixer beat until well mixed. Combine the remaining ingredients and add to the cream cheese mixture. Beat on high speed for 15 minutes. Pour into the crust and bake for 35 minutes (the center should not be set). Let cool for 45 minutes. Raise oven temperature to 400°. Combine all the topping ingredients and spread over the cheesecake. Bake for 15 minutes. Cool before serving.

Cream Cheesecake

1   stick butter, melted
1   package yellow cake mix
2   eggs, lightly beaten
8   ounce package cream cheese, softened
1   pound powdered sugar
1   teaspoon vanilla

Preheat oven to 350°. Pour butter into a 9" x 13" baking dish. With a fork blend the cake mix with the eggs. Add to the butter and pat firmly in the bottom of the baking dish. Combine the remaining ingredients and blend until smooth. Pour over the cake mix and bake for 25 minutes.

Praline Cheesecake

CRUST

1¼ cups crushed graham cracker crumbs
¼   cup sugar
¼   cup finely chopped pecans

FILLING

24   ounces cream cheese, softened
1   cup firmly packed brown sugar
5   ounce can evaporated milk
½   cup chopped pecans
2   tablespoons flour
2   teaspoons vanilla
3   eggs

SAUCE

1   cup dark corn syrup
¼   cup cornstarch
2   tablespoons brown sugar
1   teaspoon vanilla

Preheat oven to 350°. Combine the crust ingredients and press over the bottom and halfway up the sides of a 9" spring-form pan. Bake for 10 minutes. For the filling beat together all the ingredients, except the eggs, until well mixed. Add the eggs and pour into the baked crust. Bake for 50 minutes or until set. Cool for 30 minutes. Loosen sides and remove rim from the pan. Cool. In a sauce-pan combine the first 3 ingredients and cook, stirring, until thick. Remove from the heat, add the vanilla, and spoon over the cake.

Chocolate Chip Cheesecake

CRUST

2¹/₂ cups graham cracker crumbs
¹/₄   cup sugar
¹/₂   teaspoon cinnamon
1   stick butter, melted

FILLING

2¹/₂ pounds cream cheese, softened
1³/₄ cups sugar
¹/₄   cup flour
1   teaspoon vanilla
6   eggs
¹/₄   cup half and half
8   ounces chocolate chips, chopped

Preheat oven to 300°. Combine the first 3 ingredients. Add the butter and mix well. Press on the bottom of a 9¹/₂ " spring-form pan. In a large mixing bowl beat the cream cheese until smooth. Add the next 3 ingredients and beat until well mixed. Add the eggs, one at a time, beating well after each addition. Add the half and half and beat until well mixed. Fold in the chocolate chips and transfer to the spring-form pan. Bake for 2 hours or until set. Chill before serving.

Pumpkin Cheesecake

CRUST

1¹/₂ cups vanilla wafer crumbs
1   cup finely chopped pecans
¹/₄   cup powdered sugar
³/₄   stick butter, softened

FILLING

16   ounce carton small curd cottage cheese
4   eggs
1¹/₂ pounds cream cheese, softened
1   cup sugar
16   ounce can pumpkin puree
¹/₄   cup rum
3   tablespoons flour
¹/₂   teaspoon salt
¹/₂   teaspoon cinnamon
¹/₄   teaspoon nutmeg

Preheat oven to 350°. Combine all the crust ingredients and press on the bottom and 1½" up the sides of a 10" spring-form pan. Bake 10 minutes and cool. Lower heat to 300°. In a blender or food processor blend the cottage cheese and 2 of the eggs until smooth. Remove to a large bowl and blend in the cream cheese. Add the remaining ingredients and stir until well mixed. Pour into the crust and bake for 1½ hours or until set.

Almond Cheesecake

CRUST

3/4   cup graham cracker crumbs
1/2   cup ground blanched almonds
3/4   stick butter, melted
3   tablespoons sugar

FILLING

24   ounces cream cheese, softened
2/3   cup sugar
4   eggs
1/2   cup ground, blanched almonds
1½ teaspoons almond extract

TOPPING

1   pint sour cream
3   tablespoons sugar
1   teaspoon vanilla
1   teaspoon almond extract

Preheat oven to 350°. Combine all the crust ingredients and press on the bottom and half-way up the sides of a buttered 9" spring-form pan. Chill. In a mixing bowl beat the cream cheese for 20 minutes until it is light and fluffy. Beat in the sugar and the eggs, one at a time, beating well after each addition. Add the remaining ingredients and pour into the crust. Bake for 45 minutes. Let cool in the pan for 20 minutes. In a bowl combine all the topping ingredients and spread on the cake. Bake in a pre-heated 400° oven for 5 minutes. Let the cake cool in the pan for 2 hours.

Lemon Creamcheese Pound Cake

2¼ cups cake flour
2   teaspoons baking powder
¼   teaspoon salt
8   ounce package cream cheese, softened
2   sticks butter, softened
1½ cups sugar
4   eggs
2   tablespoons lemon juice
1   teaspoon grated lemon rind
1   teaspoon vanilla

Preheat oven to 325°. In a large bowl sift together the first 3 ingredients. In another large bowl cream the next 2 ingredients until smooth. Add the sugar, a little at a time, beating well after each addition. Add the remaining ingredients, beating well. Gradually add the flour mixture. Pour the batter into a buttered tube pan and bake for 1 hour or until set.

Sour Cream Pound Cake

2   sticks butter
3   cups sugar
1   cup sour cream
6   eggs
1   teaspoon vanilla
1   teaspoon lemon flavoring
3   cups flour
¼   teaspoon salt
¼   teaspoon baking soda

Preheat oven to 325°. Combine the first 3 ingredients and beat until well mixed. Add the eggs one at a time, beating after each addition. Add the remaining ingredients and pour into a tube pan. Bake for 1½ hours.

In a Hurry 7-Up Cake—Combine 1 package lemon cake mix, 1 package instant vanilla pudding. Beat in ¾ cup oil, 10 ounce bottle of 7-Up, and 4 eggs, one at a time. Beat well and pour into a greased 13" x 9" x 2" baking pan. Bake at 350° about 45 minutes.

Milk Chocolate Pound Cake

2   sticks butter, softened
1½   cups sugar
4   eggs
9   ounces Milky Way candy, melted
1   cup buttermilk
2½   cups flour
¼   teaspoon baking soda
1   cup chopped pecans
5   ounces Hershey's chocolate syrup
2   teaspoons vanilla

Preheat oven to 325°. Cream the butter and sugar until light and fluffy. Add the eggs, one at a time, beating well after each addition. Add the next 2 ingredients and mix well. Combine the next 2 ingredients and add to the chocolate mixture. Add the remaining ingredients and pour into a greased and floured 10" tube pan and bake for 1 hour or until done.

Lemon Pound Cake

2½   cups flour
1½   cups sugar
1   tablespoon baking powder
½   teaspoon salt
¾   cup apricot nectar
¾   cup oil
1   teaspoon vanilla
2   teaspoons lemon extract
4   eggs

Preheat oven to 325°. Combine all the ingredients and beat for 3 minutes. Pour into a greased 10" tube pan and bake for 45 minutes.

In a Hurry Apple-Nut Cake—Beat 1 egg with ½ cup sugar. Sift in 2 tablespoons flour, 1½ teaspoons baking powder, ½ teaspoon salt. Add ½ cup nuts, 1 tablespoon vanilla and 1 cup peeled, diced apples. Pour into a baking pan and bake at 350° for 30 minutes. Top with whipped cream or your favorite flavor of ice cream.

Marsala Pound Cake

3/4 cup chopped walnuts
1   box yellow layer cake mix
3   ounce package vanilla instant pudding mix
1   cup Marsala wine
1/2 cup oil
4   eggs
1/2 teaspoon cinnamon
1/2 teaspoon ground cloves
1/4 teaspoon nutmeg
1/4 teaspoon salt

GLAZE
1/4 cup Marsala wine
1/2 cup sugar

Preheat oven to 300°. Grease and lightly flour a Bundt pan. Sprinkle the nuts on the bottom of the pan. In a large mixing bowl combine the remaining ingredients and beat for 2 minutes scraping the sides of the bowl. Pour into the pan and bake for 1 hour. Cool in pan. Invert and cover with the glaze. For glaze combine the 2 ingredients and heat until the sugar dissolves, stirring constantly. Do not let boil.

French Coffeecake

1 1/2 sticks butter
2   cups sugar
4   cups flour
4   teaspoons baking powder
3   eggs
1   can evaporated milk
2   teaspoons vanilla
1   teaspoon almond flavoring
1/2   cup pecans, chopped
       Cinnamon and sugar mix

In a mixing bowl cream the butter and sugar together. Mix in the flour and baking powder. Add the eggs, one at a time. Mix alternately the milk, flour mixture, flavorings and pecans. Put half the batter in a buttered angel food cake pan, sprinkle with cinnamon and sugar mix. Repeat. Bake at 350° for about 1 hour and 10 minutes.

Blueberry Coffeecake

2 cups flour, sifted
4 teaspoons baking powder
1/2 teaspoon salt
1 1/2 tablespoons butter
3/4 cup sugar
1 egg, lightly beaten
3/4 cup milk
1 cup blueberries
3 tablespoons sugar
1 teaspoon cinnamon

In a bowl sift the sifted flour, baking powder and salt. Blend in the butter and sugar and mix well. Beat in the egg and the milk. Stir in the blueberries and pour in a buttered 8″ square baking pan, spreading it evenly. In a small bowl combine the sugar and cinnamon and sprinkle over the batter. Bake at 350° for 40 minutes or until cake pulls away from the sides of the pan.

Crunchy Sour Cream Coffeecake

3 cups flour
1 1/2 teaspoons baking powder
1 1/2 teaspoons baking soda
1/4 teaspoon salt
3 sticks butter
1 1/2 cups sugar
3 eggs
1 1/2 cups sour cream
1 1/2 teaspoons vanilla
3/4 cup firmly packed brown sugar
3/4 cup chopped walnuts
1 1/2 teaspoons cinnamon
2 tablespoons vanilla mixed with 2 tablespoons water

Preheat oven to 325°. Sift together the first 4 ingredients and set aside. In a large mixing bowl combine the next 2 ingredients and beat until fluffy. Add the eggs, one at a time, beating well after each addition. Blend in the next 2 ingredients. Gradually add the sifted ingredients and beat well. In a small bowl combine the next 3 ingredients. Turn a third of the batter into a greased 10″ tube pan and sprinkle with half the nut mixture. Repeat. Add remaining batter and spoon diluted vanilla over the top. Bake for 1 hour or until done. Cool for 10 minutes before removing from the pan.

Sticky Coffeecake

1½ cups granola
¾ cup firmly packed brown sugar
1½ teaspoons cinnamon
2 8-ounce packages refrigerated biscuit dough
1 stick butter, melted

Preheat oven to 350°. Combine the first 3 ingredients and mix well. Separate dough and cut each biscuit in half. Dip in melted butter, then roll in cereal mixture coating generously and pressing into dough. Layer in a 10" greased bundt pan. Sprinkle with remaining cereal mixture and drizzle with the remaining butter. Bake for 30 minutes and turn out immediately onto a plate. Serve warm.

Little Mushroom Milky Way Cake

10 small bars Milky Way
1 stick butter
2 cups sugar
1 stick butter, softened
½ teaspoon butter flavoring
4 eggs
2½ cups flour
¼ teaspoon soda
¼ teaspoon salt
1 cup buttermilk
1 cup pecans, chopped

In the top of a double boiler melt the Milky Way bars and butter. Set aside. In a mixing bowl combine the sugar, butter and flavoring. Add the eggs, one at a time, beating after each egg. Add alternately the flour, soda, salt and buttermilk. Slowly add the Milky Way mixture. Fold in the pecans. Bake in a greased tube pan for 1½ to 2 hours at 275°.

In a Hurry Sourcream Coffeecake—Combine 1 package golden butter cake mix with ½ cup sugar. Beat in ¾ cup butter-flavored oil and 4 eggs, one at a time, beating after each addition. Blend in 8-ounce carton sour cream. Pour half the batter in a greased and floured tube pan. Sprinkle 2 teaspoons cinnamon and ½ cup chopped nuts over batter. Pour in remaining batter and bake at 350° for 1 hour.

Hershey Bar Cake

2 cups sugar
2 sticks butter
4 eggs
10 small Hershey Bars, melted
1½ cups Hershey syrup
2½ cups flour
¼ teaspoon soda
1 teaspoon vanilla
1 cup buttermilk
½ cup chopped pecans

In a mixing bowl cream the sugar and butter. Add the eggs, one at a time, and beat well. Add melted chocolate bars and syrup. Sift the flour, soda and a pinch of salt. Add alternately with buttermilk to the egg mixture. Add vanilla and pecans. Pour in a greased and floured tube pan and bake at 300° for 1½ hours.

Chocolate Chip Cake

1 package Devils Food Cake Mix
4 ounce package Instant Chocolate Pudding Mix
4 eggs
½ cup oil
¾ cup water
1 cup sour cream
6 ounce package chocolate chips

In a mixing bowl beat the first 6 ingredients together until mixture is smooth. Fold in the chocolate chips and pour into a greased and floured tube pan. Bake at 350° for 45 minutes or until done.

In a Hurry Coffeecake—Cream 1 stick butter with 2 eggs and 1 cup sugar. Gradually add 2 cups flour, 2 teaspoons baking powder, 1 cup milk, and 1 tablespoon vanilla. Top with ½ cup chopped nuts, ¼ cup cinnamon, ¼ cup sugar and pour into a greased 9" x 13" baking pan and bake at 350° for 35 minutes.

Little Mushroom Baked Fudge Cake

4   eggs
2   cups sugar
1/2 cup flour
1/2 cup cocoa
1   cup melted butter, cooled
1   cup pecans, chopped
1/2 pint heavy cream
     Confectioners sugar

In a mixing bowl combine the eggs, sugar, flour and cocoa. Beat at medium speed until well blended. Add the butter and nuts and continue to beat for about 1 minute. Transfer to a lightly greased 8″ square pan and bake in a preheated 350° oven for 1/2 hour. Cool. Cut into squares. Whip cream adding confectioner's sugar, to taste. Top each square with the whipped cream.

Chocolate Mint Pistachio Cake

1   package yellow cake mix
1/3 cup oil
1/2 cup water
1/2 cup cream de menthe
1   package instant pistachio pudding mix
4   eggs
5   ounce can Hershey syrup

In a bowl combine the first 6 ingredients and mix well. Pour three-fourths of the batter into a bundt pan. Blend the remaining batter with the syrup. Add to batter cutting through to marble. Bake at 350° for 40 minutes.

In a Hurry Chocolate Cherry Cake—Combine 1 package Duncan Hines Swiss Chocolate Deluxe II Cake Mix, 21-ounce can cherry pie filling, 1 teaspoon vanilla and 2 beaten eggs. Pour into a greased and floured 9″ x 13″ cake pan. Bake in a preheated 350° oven for 25–30 minutes.

Heath Bar Cake

½   stick butter, softened
2   cups flour
1   cup firmly packed brown sugar
½   cup white sugar
1   cup buttermilk
1   teaspoon baking soda
1   egg, beaten
1   teaspoon vanilla
½   teaspoon salt
3   tablespoons Kahlua
6   7-ounce Heath candy bars
¼   cup chopped pecans

Preheat oven to 350°. In a mixing bowl combine the first 4 ingredients and beat until well mixed. Reserve half the mixture for later. To half the mixture add the next 6 ingredients and mix well. Pour into a greased baking pan. In a blender or food processor crush the candy bars and the pecans. Add the remaining reserved mixture and sprinkle over the batter already in the pan. Bake for 30 minutes.

Chocolate Decadence

1½ sticks butter, softened
½   cup firmly packed brown sugar
½   cup light corn syrup
½   cup chopped pecans
1   cup sugar
1   egg, separated
2   squares unsweetened chocolate, melted and cooled
1¼ cups flour
1   teaspoon baking powder
¼   teaspoon salt
¾   cup milk
1   teaspoon vanilla

Preheat oven to 350°. Cream 1 stick butter with the brown sugar until smooth. Add the next 2 ingredients and spread evenly on the bottom of a greased 10" tube pan. In a large mixing bowl cream the remaining butter and sugar. Beat in the egg yolk and chocolate. Sift together the next 3 ingredients and beat in alternately with the milk and vanilla. Beat egg white until stiff and fold into the batter. Pour into the pan and bake for 45 minutes. Let cool for 10 minutes,

turn pan onto a plate and let stand for 10 minutes more. Remove pan. If some
of the candy mixture sticks it can be easily pressed onto the cake.

Chocolate Rum Cake

$^1/_2$ cup pecans, chopped
1   package Duncan Hines Devils Food Cake Mix
4   ounce package instant vanilla pudding mix
$^1/_2$ cup light rum
$^1/_2$ cup water
$^1/_2$ cup Mazola oil
4   eggs
$^1/_2$ cup butter
1   cup sugar
$^1/_4$ cup rum
$^1/_4$ cup water

Grease a 10″ tube pan. Put nuts in the bottom of the pan. Blend cake mix,
pudding mix, rum, water, oil and the eggs. Mix 2 minutes at medium speed.
Pour into the pan. Bake about 1 hour at 325° or until top springs back when
lightly touched. Boil butter, sugar, rum and water for 2 minutes. Shortly after
removing cake from oven, while it is still in the pan, spoon glaze over top of
cake. Cool cake 30 minutes in the pan, then turn out onto serving plate. Just
before serving, sprinkle with confectioner's sugar.

In a Hurry Walnut-Rum Cake—Combine 1 package yellow cake mix and 1
large box instant vanilla pudding. Beat in $^1/_2$ cup oil, $^1/_3$ cup sour cream, $^1/_2$
cup dark rum and 4 eggs, one at a time. Beat well. Place 1 cup walnuts on the
bottom of a greased and floured tube pan. Pour mixture over nuts and bake at
325° for 50 to 60 minutes.

Chocolate Sheath Cake

2 cups sugar
2 cups flour
2 sticks butter
4 tablespoons cocoa
1 cup water
1/2 cup buttermilk
2 eggs, lightly beaten
1 teaspoon soda
2 teaspoons vanilla

ICING

1 stick butter
4 tablespoons cocoa
6 tablespoons milk
1 box confectioner's sugar, sifted
1 teaspoon vanilla
1 cup pecans, chopped

In a large bowl sift together the sugar and the flour. In a saucepan melt the butter, cocoa and water and bring to a boil. Pour over the flour mixture and stir until well mixed. Add the buttermilk, eggs, soda and vanilla and mix well. Pour into a greased 11″ x 16″ x 1/2″ pan and bake at 400° for 20 minutes. In a double boiler melt the butter, cocoa and milk and bring to a boil. Remove from heat and add the sugar, vanilla and pecans. Beat well with a spoon and spread on cake while hot.

Vanilla Coconut Cake

2 sticks butter, softened
2 cups sugar
6 eggs
7 ounce package angel flake coconut
12 ounces vanilla wafers, crushed
1/2 cup milk
1 cup chopped pecans

In a mixing bowl cream the butter, add the sugar and beat well. Add the eggs, one at a time, and beat well after each egg. Add the wafers and milk alternately. Add the coconut and fold in the pecans. Bake in a tube pan at 275° for 1 1/2 hours. Turn oven to 300° for the last few minutes of baking.

Pumpkin Pudding Cake

1   box yellow cake mix
1   stick butter, softened
6   eggs
2   cups sugar
2   cups milk
3½ cups pumpkin
½   teaspoon salt
2   tablespoons pumpkin pie spice

In a mixing bowl beat the eggs, sugar, milk, pumpkin, salt and spice. Pour into an ungreased 9 " x 13 " x 2 " pan. Cut together the cake mix and butter until coarse. Sprinkle over the pumpkin mix and bake at 350° for 45 minutes to 1 hour. Cut in squares to serve.

Pumpkin Rum Cake

2   packages pound cake mix
16   ounce can pumpkin
1½   teaspoon pumpkin pie spice
1   cup sugar
1   cup orange juice
2   cinnamon sticks
¼   cup rum

Prepare pound cake according to directions on the package decreasing the water to a total of ⅔ cup and adding the pumpkin and spice. Pour into a well greased and floured bundt pan. Bake at 325° for 1 hour and 20 minutes. Cool in pan for 10 minutes. Remove to cooling rack and cool with pan inverted for 45 minutes more. Place on serving plate. Punch holes in top of cake with a fork at 1 " intervals. In a saucepan combine the sugar, orange juice and cinnamon sticks. Bring to a boil, remove cinnamon and pour in rum. Spoon mixture slowly over the cake allowing the cake to absorb the sauce. Chill.

In a Hurry Orange Poppyseed Cake—Combine 1 package yellow cake mix with 1 package instant vanilla pudding mix. Beat in 5 eggs, ½ cup oil, 1 cup orange juice, 2 teaspoons almond extract and beat for about 10 minutes. Add 1 tablespoon poppyseeds and pour into a greased and floured tube pan. Bake at 350° about 1 hour.

Pina Colada Cake

CAKE

1   box (2 layer) white cake mix
4   ounce package Coconut Cream Instant Pudding mix
4   eggs
1/2 cup water
1/2 cup dark rum (80 proof)
1/4 cup oil

FROSTING

8   ounce can crushed pineapple, drained
4   ounce package Coconut Cream Instant Pudding mix
1/3 cup dark rum (80 proof)
9   ounce container Cool Whip, thawed

Preheat oven to 350°. In a large mixing bowl combine all the cake ingredients and beat on medium speed for 4 minutes. Pour into 3 greased and floured 9" layer cake pans and bake into 3 greased and floured 9" layer cake pans and bake for 25–30 minutes. Cool in pans for 15 minutes. Remove and cool on racks. Combine the first 3 frosting ingredients and beat until well mixed. Fold in the Cool Whip and spread between each layer and on the top and sides of the cake.

Peach Cake

1   cup flour
1/4 cup sugar
1 1/2 teaspoons baking powder
1/2 teaspoon salt
1/2 stick butter
1/4 cup milk
1   egg, well beaten
3   peaches, peeled and sliced
1/4 cup sugar
1/2 teaspoon cinnamon
1/4 teaspoon nutmeg
3   tablespoons butter, melted
1/3 cup currant jelly

In a bowl sift together the flour, sugar, baking powder and salt. With 2 knives cut in the butter. In another bowl mix milk with egg and pour into the flour mixture. Beat the batter until smooth and pour into a buttered 8" square baking pan. Arrange the peaches in rows on top of the batter. Sprinkle with the sugar, cinnamon, nutmeg and butter. Bake in a preheated 400° oven for about 30 minutes. Mix the jelly with 1 tablespoon hot water and glaze the top of the cake. Cool on a wire rack.

Zucchini Cake

3   cups zucchini, peeled and grated
3   cups sugar
1   cup oil
4   eggs
3   cups flour
2   teaspoons baking powder
1   teaspoon soda
1½ teaspoons cinnamon
½   teaspoon salt
1   cup walnuts

In a mixing bowl beat the first 4 ingredients. Combine the remaining ingredients and mix well. Pour into a greased and floured tube pan and bake at 350° for 1 hour. Let cool in pan before removing.

Strawberry Cake

1   package yellow cake mix
3   ounce package strawberry gelatin
1   cup boiling water
1   cup strawberry soda
2   cups milk
3   ounce package vanilla instant pudding mix
4   ounce carton non-dairy whipped topping

Preheat oven to 350°. Prepare cake mix according to package directions and place in a 9″ by 13″ pan. Bake until done. Combine the gelatin and water and heat until gelatin is dissolved. Blend in the strawberry soda. Poke entire surface of cake with a toothpick. Pour gelatin over top and cool for 1 hour. Combine milk and pudding mix and blend according to package directions. Chill for 5 minutes or until set. Fold in topping and spread on cake. Chill for 1 hour.

Banana Pecan Cake

1   package yellow cake mix
3   ounce package butterscotch instant pudding mix
4   eggs
1   cup water
¼   cup oil
1   tablespoon rum
1   cup mashed very ripe bananas
½   cup chopped pecans

TOPPING
1   cup powdered sugar
1   tablespoon hot milk

Preheat oven to 350°. Combine all the ingredients and mix well. Pour into a well greased bundt pan and bake for 40–45 minutes. Combine topping ingredients and dribble over the baked cake.

Carrot Cake

1   cup brown sugar
¾   cup oil
2   eggs, beaten
1   cup sifted flour
1   teaspoon baking soda
1   teaspoon baking powder
½   teaspoon salt
½   teaspoon cinnamon
¼   teaspoon coriander
¼   teaspoon ginger
¼   cup chopped walnuts
¼   cup raisins, soaked in hot water for 30 minutes
1½   cups grated carrots

Preheat oven to 325°. Combine the first 2 ingredients and mix well. Add the eggs, one at a time, beating well after each addition. Sift all the dry ingredients and fold into the sugar mixture. Fold in the remaining ingredients and pour into a greased loaf pan and bake for 35–40 minutes.

Fudge Walnut Bake

2   squares semi-sweet chocolate
1   stick butter
1   cup sugar
¼   cup flour
2   eggs, lightly beaten
1   teaspoon vanilla
1   teaspoon almond flavoring
½   cup chopped walnuts

Preheat oven to 350°. In a saucepan melt the chocolate in the butter. Add the remaining ingredients and pour into a greased 9″ square baking dish. Bake for 20–25 minutes.

Chocolate Chip Peanut Butter Cake

2 ¼ cups flour
2   cups firmly packed brown sugar
1   cup crunchy peanut butter
1   stick butter, softened
1   tablespoon baking powder
1   cup milk
3   eggs
1   tablespoon vanilla
½   6-ounce package peanut butter chips
½   6-ounce package chocolate chips

Preheat oven to 350°. In a large bowl combine the first 4 ingredients. Blend at low speed until crumbly. Reserve 1 cup mixture for later. To remaining crumb mixture add the next 5 ingredients and mix well. Batter should be slightly lumpy. Pour into a well greased 9″ x 13″ pan and sprinkle with the reserved crumbs. Sprinkle the chocolate chips over the crumbs and bake for 40 minutes.

Chocolate Chip Bundt Cake

1   package Swiss Chocolate Cake Mix
3   ounce package chocolate pudding mix
4   eggs
1/2 cup oil
1/2 cup water
8   ounce carton sour cream
12 ounce package chocolate chips

Preheat oven to 350°. In a large bowl combine the first 6 ingredients and mix well. Fold in the chocolate chips and pour into a greased Bundt pan. Bake for 55 minutes. Cool for 15 minutes and invert.

Chewy Chocolate Bars

1   box light brown sugar
1/2 cup oil
4   eggs, well beaten
2   cups Bisquick
1   cup coconut
1   cup chopped pecans
1   cup chocolate chips
1   teaspoon vanilla

Preheat oven to 350°. Combine the first 3 ingredients and mix well. Add the remaining ingredients and pour into a greased and floured 13" x 9" baking pan. Bake for 40–45 minutes and slice into 48 square cookie bars.

Double Chocolate Brownies

1   box German chocolate cake mix
1/2 cup evaporated milk
1/2 cup melted butter
2   eggs
15 ounce package caramels
1/3 cup evaporated milk
12 ounce package chocolate chips

Preheat oven to to 350°. Combine the first 4 ingredients and mix well. Spread 1/2 the batter in a greased and floured 13" x 9" baking pan and bake for 5 minutes. Melt the caramels in the milk and spread over the first mixture. Sprinkle with the chocolate chips and spread remaining batter over top. Bake for 20 minutes more. Cool and cut into squares to serve.

Butterscotch Brownies

1   stick butter, softened
2   cups firmly packed brown sugar
2   teaspoons vanilla
2   eggs
1   cup flour, sifted
2   teaspoons baking powder
1   teaspoon salt

Preheat oven to 350°. With a mixer or in a food processor cream the butter and sugar until smooth. Beat in the vanilla and eggs. Sift together the remaining ingredients and add to the sugar mixture. Pour into a greased 9″ x 13″ baking pan and bake for 35 minutes or until done.

Kentucky Belles

1   stick butter
1   cup graham cracker crumbs
3¹/₂ ounce can flake coconut
6   ounce package chocolate bits
6   ounce package butterscotch bits
1   can condensed milk
1   cup chopped pecans

Place butter in a 13″ x 9″ x 3″ pan and melt in a preheated 350° oven. Remove from oven and sprinkle the graham cracker crumbs over the butter, packing them down. Sprinkle in the coconut. Sprinkle in the chocolate bits. Sprinkle in the butterscotch bits and pour in the milk. Sprinkle with the pecans and push down lightly. Bake at 350° for 30 to 40 minutes. Let cool and cut into bars.

Chocolate Nut Squares

1   cup graham crackers, crushed
1   stick butter, melted
1   large package chocolate chips
1   large package butterscotch chips
1   package chopped pecans
1   can coconut flakes
1   can sweetened condensed milk

Layer the ingredients in a 9″ x 13″ x 2″ Pyrex pan and dribble the milk on top. Bake at 300° for about 50 minutes.

Pecan Surprise Bars

1   package yellow cake mix
1   egg
1   stick butter

FILLING

⅔   cup reserved cake mix
½   cup brown sugar, firmly packed
1½ cups dark corn syrup
1   teaspoon vanilla
3   eggs
1   cup pecans, chopped

Grease the bottom and sides of a 9″ x 13″ baking pan. Reserve ⅔ cup cake mix for filling. In a large mixing bowl, combine remaining cake mix, butter and 1 egg. Mix until crumbly. Press in greased pan. Bake at 350° for 15 to 20 minutes until light golden brown. Meanwhile prepare filling by combining ingredients and beating at medium speed for 1 to 2 minutes. Pour filling over partially baked crust and sprinkle with pecans. Return to oven and bake for 30 to 35 minutes until filling is set. Cool and cut into bars.

In a Hurry Coconut-Pecan Cookies—Combine 1 box yellow cake mix, 1 package Coconut Pecan Frosting, 1 stick butter and 2 eggs. Drop dough by the teaspoonfuls on a cookie sheet. Bake in a preheated 350° oven for 10–12 minutes. Makes 24 large cookies.

Little Mushroom Chocolate Mousse

2   8-ounce packages semi-sweet chocolate
1   cup water
4   tablespoons instant coffee
8   eggs, separated
1/2 cup light rum

In the top of a double boiler heat the chocolate, water and instant coffee. Beat the egg yolks into the chocolate mixture. Add the rum and cool mixture slightly. In a separate bowl beat the egg whites to form soft peaks. Fold them gently into the chocolate mixture. Pour into individual soufflé dishes and refrigerate. Top with sweetened whipped cream and shaved chocolate.

Quick Chocolate Mousse

6   ounce package semi-sweet chocolate morsels
6   eggs, separated
2   teaspoons vanilla

In top of a double boiler melt the chocolate. Remove from heat. Beat yolks and gradually stir into chocolate mixture. Cool. Add vanilla. Beat egg whites until stiff peaks form. Fold into chocolate mixture. Spoon into individual soufflé dishes. Chill at least 4 hours.

Minute Mousse

8   squares Baker's semi-sweet chocolate
1/3 cup water
7   eggs, separated
1/2 cup Kahlua
1/2 cup heavy cream, whipped

In the top of a double boiler melt the chocolate in water and stir until smooth. Remove from heat. Beat the egg yolks until lemon colored and add to the chocolate mixture. Beat the egg whites until stiff and fold into the chocolate mixture. Add the Kahlua and whipped cream and turn into individual mousse dishes. Refrigerate until ready to serve.

Grand Marnier Chocolate Mousse

8   ounces semi-sweet chocolate
2   tablespoons black coffee
2   tablespoons butter
6   eggs, separated
1   teaspoon vanilla flavoring
3   tablespoons Grand Marnier
   Heavy cream, whipped
   Slivered, blanched almonds, toasted

Melt the chocolate in a heavy pan over low heat. Add coffee and mix well. Remove from heat and add butter. Beat egg yolks until light and add to chocolate mixture. Add vanilla and Grand Marnier. Beat egg whites until stiff and fold into the chocolate mixture. Pour into individual mousse dishes and refrigerate. Top with whipped cream and almonds. Serves 6.

Cream Cheese Mousse

1   pound cream cheese, softened
4   egg yolks
1/2 cup sugar
2   tablespoons dark rum
   Fresh raspberries

In a blender or food processor blend the cream cheese until creamy and smooth. In a mixing bowl beat the next 3 ingredients for 10 minutes or until thick and creamy. Mix with the cream cheese. Transfer to individual stemmed glasses and chill. Just before serving top with the raspberries.

Fabulous Fudge Nut Pudding

3   eggs
1 1/2 cups sugar
3/4 cup flour
3/4 cup butter, melted and cooled
1   cup pecans
8   squares Baker's semi-sweet chocolate, melted

Preheat oven to 350°. In a mixing bowl beat the first 3 ingredients together until fluffy. Add the next 2 ingredients and pour into a greased 8" square pan.

Pour the melted chocolate over the batter and swirl through with a knife. Bake for 20–30 minutes or until done.

Grapenut Custard

3   eggs, beaten
1/2 cup sugar
1/2 teaspoon vanilla
2   cups milk, scalded
3   tablespoons grapenuts

Preheat oven to 375°. Combine the first 3 ingredients and mix well. Add the milk and pour into individual greased custard cups. Sprinkle grapenuts on top and bake in a hot water bath for 30 minutes or until set.

Sugared Brie

8″ round of Brie, not fully ripened with the top rind removed
1   cup chopped pecans
2   cups firmly packed brown sugar

Preheat oven to BROIL. Place Brie in a pie or quiche pan and sprinkle with the pecans. Cover the top and sides with the sugar. Place on lowest rack in the oven and broil until the sugar melts (about 3 minutes). Cut into wedges to serve.

Champagne Freeze

1   pint vanilla ice cream, softened
1   split (2 cups) chilled champagne
1/2 cup fresh strawberries

Place all the ingredients in a blender and puree. Place the mixture in the freezer and freeze until mushy. Pour into stemmed glasses and serve.

In a Hurry Peach Cobbler—In a shallow baking pan place 2 packages frozen, thawed peaches. Sprinkle liberally with sugar and 3 tablespoons water. Thaw 2 frozen pie crusts, flatten and cut into strips. Place strips across peaches and sprinkle with more sugar and melted butter. Dust with cinnamon and bake at 350° for 1 hour.

Peanut Butter Ice Cream

1   quart vanilla ice cream, slightly softened
$^1/_2$ cup chunky peanut butter
$^1/_2$ cup unsalted peanuts, crushed
$1^1/_2$ tablespoons vanilla
10″ graham cracker crust

Combine the first 4 ingredients and pour into the pie crust. Freeze for several hours.

Delicious Pralines

2   cups sugar
$^1/_2$ cup dark brown sugar
    Dash salt
2   tablespoons white Karo syrup
$^2/_3$ cup evaporated milk
$^1/_3$ teaspoon soda
$^1/_4$ pound butter
2   teaspoons vanilla
1   pound pecans (or as many as the mixture will hold) toasted
    lightly, just until crisp

In a saucepan combine the first 7 ingredients and bring to a hard boil, stirring until sugar dissolves. Cook to the soft ball stage (liquid forms a soft boil when a little is dropped into cold water.) Add the pecans and vanilla and beat well. Remove from heat and drop from a teaspoon onto waxed paper. Cool.

Easy Pralines

$1^1/_2$ packages butterscotch pudding (not instant)
$1^1/_2$ cups sugar
$^3/_4$ cup brown sugar
$^3/_4$ cup evaporated milk
$1^1/_2$ tablespoons butter
$2^1/_4$ cups pecan halves

In a heavy saucepan combine the first 5 ingredients. Cook and stir, over low heat, until sugar dissolves. Add the pecans and bring to a full boil. Stir often until candy reaches the soft ball stage (234°). Remove from heat and beat until candy thickens. Drop quickly by teaspoon onto waxed paper spreading each with spoon to form patties about 2" in diameter. Cool. Makes about 32 patties.

Quick Chocolate Chip Cookies

1	cup brown sugar
1	cup sugar
1	egg
2	cups flour
1	cup shortening
1	stick butter, softened
1	teaspoon vanilla
6	ounce package chocolate chips
1	cup chopped pecans

Preheat oven to 350°. Combine the first 7 ingredients and mix well. Spread on a greased cookie sheet and bake for 25 minutes. Melt the chocolate chips and pour over the baked cookie. Sprinkle with the pecans and cut into squares while warm.

Dallas Cookies

1	pound box light brown sugar
2	cups biscuit mix
4	eggs, well beaten
2	cups chopped pecans
1	tablespoon vanilla

Preheat oven to 325°. Combine all the ingredients and mix well. Pour into a greased and floured 13" x 9" baking pan and bake for 30–35 minutes. Cool and slice into 48 square cookie bars.

Chinese Cookies

1	package chocolate chips
1	package butterscotch chips
1	can salted nuts
1	can chow mein noodles

In the top of a double boiler melt the chocolate and butterscotch chips. Pour over the nuts and noodles. Mix and drop on waxed paper on a cookie sheet. Refrigerate to harden.

Apple Walnut Dessert

1   package (8) frozen apple walnut crepes
1   stick butter, melted
2   cups sour cream
6   eggs, beaten
1/4 cup orange juice
1/4 cup sugar
2   teaspoons vanilla
2   teaspoons salt
8   ounce carton sour cream
1/2 cup fresh strawberries, sliced

Preheat oven to 350°. Place the crepes in a greased shallow baking dish and cover with the butter. Combine the next 6 ingredients and pour over the crepes. Bake for 1 hour or until puffed and browned. Top with the sour cream and berries.

Rum Peaches

4   large ripe peaches, peeled and halved
1 1/2 tablespoons rum extract
1 1/4 cups sour cream
1/4 cup light brown sugar
1/4 cup sliced almonds

Preheat oven to 350°. Arrange peaches, cut side up, in a shallow baking pan. Drizzle with the rum flavoring. Spread the sour cream over the peaches and sprinkle with the sugar and almonds. Bake for 20 minutes or until the sugar turns to caramel and the almonds have browned.

Apple Crisp

4   Golden Delicious apples, unpeeled, cored and sliced
2   tablespoons cinnamon
1/4   cup sugar
1   tablespoon lemon juice
1/4/ cup water
1   cup Cheddar cheese, grated
1/2   cup flour, sifted
3/4   cup sugar
1/4   teaspoon salt
1/2   stick butter, melted

Place apples in the bottom of a Pyrex dish. Sprinkle cinnamon sugar mixture generously over the apples. Pour lemon juice and water over the apples and mix well so that apples will not turn brown. Sift together over mixture the flour, sugar and salt. Pour melted butter and cheese on top and bake at 350° for 30 minutes. Top with your favorite ice cream. Serves 6–8.

Apple Dump Crunch

1/2   package Spice Cake Mix
2   16-ounce cans sliced apples
3/4   cup brown sugar
1   cup pecans, chopped
1   stick butter, melted

Lightly grease a 9″ pie pan. Pour in apples and sprinkle with brown sugar. Cover with cake mix. Sprinkle with pecans and pour melted butter over the top. Bake at 325° for 1 hour.

In a Hurry Apple Crunch—Spread 1 can apple pie filling in the bottom of a 9″ square baking pan. Cover with 1 box yellow cake mix, 1 cup chopped pecans and 1/3 cup melted butter. Bake in a preheated 350° oven for 40–45 minutes or until top is golden brown.

Blueberry Crunch

1   package Wild Blueberry Muffin Mix
1/4   cup sugar
1/2   teaspoon cinnamon
1/2   stick butter, melted
1/2   cup pecans, chopped
2   16-ounce cans blueberry pie filling
1/4   cup sugar
1   teaspoon cinnamon
1   teaspoon almond extract

In a bowl combine the first 3 ingredients. Pour butter on top of the mixture and stir in the nuts. Set aside. Combine the remaining ingredients and pour into a lightly greased 8" square pan. Spread the crumb mixture on top and bake at 350° for 35 minutes or until topping is golden brown.

Pecan Crunch

CRUST

3   cups flour
3/4   cup firmly packed brown sugar
1 1/2 cups butter

FILLING

3/4   cup firmly packed brown sugar
1 1/2 cups corn syrup
1   cup milk
1/3   cup melted butter
1   teaspoon vanilla
4   eggs
1 1/2 cups chopped pecans

Preheat oven to 400°. In a large bowl combine all crust ingredients and blend until crumbly. Reserve 2 cups crumbs for filling and topping. Press remaining crumbs in the bottom of an ungreased 15" x 10" jelly roll pan. Bake for 10 minutes. In a large bowl combine 1/4 cup of the reserved crumbs and all the filling ingredients and mix well. Pour over the crust and bake for 10 minutes. Reduce temperature to 350°. Sprinkle remaining reserved crumbs over the filling and bake for 20-25 minutes or until filling is set and crumbs are brown. Top with whipped cream.

Apricot Coconut Crunch

2   15-ounce cans apricots, drain and reserve juice
6   tablespoons minute tapioca
1   tablespoon lemon juice
1/2 cup dry sherry
1   package caramel cake mix
1   stick butter, softened
1   cup coconut

In a saucepan pour juice from apricots. Add the tapioca and lemon juice and cook until it begins to boil. Remove from heat and cool. Add apricots and sherry and let stand overnight. Place in a well-buttered baking dish. Crumble the cake mix and butter together, and sprinkle over fruit mixture. Top with coconut and bake at 325° for about 45 minutes.

In a Hurry Apple Crisp—Combine 2/3 cup sugar, 3/4 teaspoon cinnamon, 1/4 teaspoon nutmeg, 6 cups sliced apples, 1/4 cup raisins, and 1 1/2 teaspoons lemon juice and mix well. Place in a baking dish. Sprinkle 2/3 cup complete pancake mix and 1/4 cup brown sugar over the top and drizzle 1/3 cup melted butter over all. Bake at 350° for 45–50 minutes.

INDEX